PRAISE FOR THIS ONE WILD AND PRECIOUS LIFE

'I've encountered no other book that articulates with so much passion or clarity the unique feeling of this moment in history. *This One Wild and Precious Life* is the ideal guidebook for our long overdue journey back to nature, to each other, and to sanity in the deepest sense of the word'
Oliver Burkeman, author of *Four Thousand Weeks: Time Management for Mortals*

'This book will stay with me; I loved it so much. It gets to the roots and truth of what really matters and shakes us from the numbness that has crept in'
Fearne Cotton, broadcaster and author

'I began writing "Yes!" in margins, so well does Sarah Wilson articulate the problems of our time. Speaking as someone who has spent much of the past few years despairing about the state of the world, I believe we need more people like her'
Marianne Power, *The Times*

'*This One Wild and Precious Life* is what the UK has been waiting for; Sarah Wilson's journey is inspiring'
Rio Ferdinand, former professional footballer

'Sarah Wilson is a force of nature – quite literally. She has taken her pain and grief about our sick and troubled world and alchemised it into action, advocacy, adventure, poetry and true love. She's a great teacher and a great leader, and I admire her with all my soul'
Elizabeth Gilbert, author of *Eat Pray Love*

'This practical, actionable, spiritual guidebook proposes a path to joy even amid pandemics, climate change, social injustice, and other profound crises'
USA Today

'The inchoate sense that something is missing – something related to connection and community and meaning – nags at many of us. This book has some smart suggestions for how to move out of that purgatory, and perhaps, in the process, help build a world that works'
Bill McKibben, author of *Falter: Has the Human Game Begun to Play Itself Out?*

'Anxiety and disconnection are natural consequences of over-consumptive modern life, argues Wilson in this vibrant take on how to build a more joyful existence and sustainable world... The reading experience has the feel of an impassioned conversation with a friend'
Publishers Weekly

'Sarah Wilson is a traveller of worlds, outer and inner. And her reports from the journey are both intensely personal and germane to a sick and distracted world. In the midst of the collective malaise, she zeros in on her determination to live her life, not someone else's, and on the work to which we are all summoned if this species is to survive. Her work is, as the world is, both wild and precious'
James Hollis PhD, Jungian analyst and author of *Living Between Worlds: Finding Personal Resilience in Changing Times*

'Sarah Wilson's mission is our joyful survival. With curiosity and heart, she delves into the biggest questions facing our planet. Essential reading – I defy you not to feel deeply inspired'
Katherine May, author of *Wintering*

'Her thought-provoking call to action shines light on the personal fog and spiritual trauma experienced while living with consumerism, climate change, Covid-19, social injustice and collective anxiety... This book is inspiring'
Booklist

'Sarah's courageous book illuminates a path to preserve and cherish this Wild and Precious life'
Dr Martin Rice, The Climate Council

'Wilson explores why it's worth it to take the risk and move past the comfortable, assuring her readers that doing this is how we find meaning – and hope'
Spirituality and Health

'The timing of this book couldn't be more critical. Sarah takes us on a series of wild hikes around the world and shows us how inherently connected to nature we truly are, while also shedding light on how desperately we need to find a new path in our changing world. *Wild and Precious* speaks to my soul'
Emilie Ristevski, wilderness photographer

'Sarah Wilson's stories are fascinating and her message is universal and hopeful. Readers with wanderlust will be inspired by her journey and calls to action'
Library Journal

'One of the most beautifully messy, visceral, wise and wonder-inducing non-fiction books I've read. It's not often you see such clarity in a person: an understanding of who they are, what they are committed to and why they must be this way. It shakes you'
Rebel Book Club

ALSO BY SARAH WILSON

first, we make the beast beautiful

I Quit Sugar
I Quit Sugar for Life
I Quit Sugar Slow Cooker Cookbook
I Quit Sugar Kids' Cookbook
Simplicious Simplicious Flow

this
one
wild
and
precious
life

the path back to connection
in a fractured world

sarah wilson

Published by Eye Books
29A Barrow Street
Much Wenlock
Shropshire
TF13 6EN

www.eye-books.com

Previously published in the US by Dey St and in Australia by Pan Macmillan

Typeset in Bembo Std and Mercury

British Library Cataloguing in Publication Data
A catalogue record for this book is available from the British Library

ISBN: 9781785633843

To young people

contents

welcome

A writer's greatest hope for her book is that it will *hold*. That it will continue to serve readers through the time it takes to get the damn thing to the printers, onto bookshelves, released in different languages and finally to emerge, hopefully, as special editions, a little down the track.

Writing this book took me a long time – three years, drawn out by my choice to research it by hiking around the world in the footsteps of the thinkers and creatives I reference or interview. Another two years have now passed. Has *This One Wild and Precious Life* held? Well, a lot has certainly changed. The world has moved faster than expected to the 1.5°C threshold set out by the Paris Agreement, but it's also shifted far more rapidly than predicted to renewable energy sources. Which has, flip side, prompted the beleaguered fossil fuel industry to dial up plastic production. These kind of details were easy to update.

But what about my theses? Did they hold? From the outset, I identify the real pain point as not so much the existential threat of the climate emergency per se, but an *itch*. Which is to say an overwhelming sense that we are not living life as we are meant to. That we have lost our way and become disconnected and lonely. And what is happening to the planet is a reflection of what is happening for us at a spiritual level. This thesis has only deepened; the itch has become more profound. For example, I referred to the unprecedented declining life expectancy in the United States from 'diseases of despair' (suicide, opioid and alcohol deaths). This has now declined for another four years in a row, and the UK has just reported the same trend, which just breaks my heart.

And has the book held for me? Do I live by my own rally call and continue my fight to save our one wild and precious life by connecting back to it, to nature, to *our nature*? Hell, yes! As the crisis and itch deepens, I've had to draw on all the salves and wisdoms I reference and explore. I've donned my backpack anew to go deeper into the itch and my love of the planet and humanity, intensifying my activism. I've stripped myself of possessions and distractions once again and moved to Europe, now basing myself between Paris and London, continuing this big, bamboozling conversation via a podcast – Wild with Sarah Wilson, and a Substack newsletter community.

This One Wild and Precious Life holds because this journey back to what matters is a long and eternal one. As you hold it now, I invite you to join me in its continual unfurling.

first...

1   The customs queue at Los Angeles International Airport at 5.30am is a lonely place. Flights from Australia often land here at this fractured hour. None of us has had enough sleep. The overhead lights flicker. We smell stale and too-human and our nerves are frayed.

I have come to LA to do some research for this book. We land as the smoggy sky hues orange and in the arrivals hall I'm shunted to the long interrogation line. 'A writer, hey?' says the stocky uniformed and armed guy looking at my form when I get to the front of the line. His badge says his name is Jose. 'What do you write?'

'Books,' I say.

'What are you writing right now?' He's flicking through my passport.

'Well, the working title is *Wake the Fuck Up*.'

Jose looks up, his eyes widen. 'As in, wake up to what's

going on? Around us…the planet, what's happening to kids?'

'Yeah, that's it.'

'Boy, I'd read that,' he tells me.

'Really?' I ask, excited. At any given point in the many years it takes me to write a book, I am 98 per cent convinced I'm entirely off target. I grasp at glimpses of recognition from people like Jose. I lean in closer over the bench. 'I think it's making us so sad…the climate stuff, the leaders we've voted in, all the consuming, the inequalities, the scrolling on our phones.'

'Yes, exactly!' Jose says.

'Do you talk about it with your friends?' I ask. 'Your family?'

He winces. 'We're starting to. We're definitely starting to. But we don't really know how to talk about it.'

Jose writes down my name on a scrap of paper and hands back my passport. 'I'll be looking out for your book,' he says and nods his head to dismiss me.

2   I hear you, Jose. It's hard to talk about something so… nebulous. To talk about something that is so…everything. Something is not right. We're not living life right. To try to grasp such a pain, to find the beginning and end, is like trying to bite your own teeth.

When I started writing this book, I pointed out to my publisher Ingrid that we had a very unorthodox battle on our hands. 'You realise,' I said to her over the phone in a mild panic, 'no one even has a word for this thing I'm going to try to write about.' It's a foggy feeling, not a defined phenomenon that we can point at. It's a deep itch that we can't quite get to. 'I'll have to first convince everyone that the itch is a legit thing before I can come galloping in with some kind of fix.' Which is not how books like this tend to go.

For me, this all-encompassing, itchy feeling was in part a state of shock from the constant bludgeoning of global crises and news of the stunningly immoral behaviour of our world leaders. We now receive hourly the kind of highly charged headline that we used to get perhaps a few times a year. We once had time to digest the news, to frame it against the backdrop of the rest of life and talk about it in a measured fashion over watercoolers and dinner tables. Now it's a multi-car pileup every time we turn on social media. As I worked on this book, the 'leader of the Free World' was telling his Department of Homeland Security to nuke hurricanes and suggesting Americans inject bleach to treat a pandemic; Brits 'accidentally' voted to leave the EU; Australia's Deputy Prime Minister blamed exploding horse manure for the devastating bushfires that changed a nation; koalas and giraffes faced extinction; a revered Hollywood producer was found to have sexually assaulted more than 100 women (and we're told most of the industry knew but said zilch for decades); I first learned robots were coming for our jobs and maybe even our lives…and…and how can we possibly emotionally process it all? It's truly stunning stuff.

And so you might call this itch a form of PTSD.

This itch was also a despair that I have strayed from the values that matter to me, mixed with a bewilderment that life was meant to get better not worse. Indeed, we were being told the world was richer, there were fewer wars and less slavery, yet it felt like we'd gone backward. My itch was also a gnawing worry for young people and how they will cope with the planet we're leaving them, combined with a cringey guilt that I'm complicit, liberally sprinkled with a frustration that no one can answer a question honestly any more! All of which was polluted with a horrible, and alienating, rage that surfaced when I felt that no one was bloody doing anything! The planet is burning, refugees cry out for our help, the gap between haves and have-nots has become a cruel chasm, and we…yeah, well, we scroll.

And binge-watch.

And buy stuff.

Which makes the itch worse.

I didn't ask Jose about his stance on the climate crisis.

(Was he a denier? Did he recycle adequately?) Nor what his politics were. Because it almost doesn't matter any more. I thought about this as I stood at the baggage claim listening to Cat Power in my headphones, feeling the surreal expansiveness of arriving alone at the beginning of something. We might rage about our differences and troll and blame each other, but deep down we are all feeling the same shock and despair. The same itchy sense that we are so fundamentally off track.

Was there a word we could put to this societal shitstorm? I

had to find a better word than 'itch'. I looked around at other people's faces, downcast and scrolling as they waited for their bags, and I realised that what we're all feeling, at the most basic level, is *disconnected*. Disconnected from what matters, disconnected from life as we thought we were meant to be living it, disconnected from our care and love for it all.

Ironically, in such inverted times, it's our disconnection that actually unites – or connects – us.

3   Indeed.

Because then COVID-19 hit. The corona virus pandemic landed precisely two days before this book was due at the printer. It was almost comical. Or divine. Or something.

Suddenly, as the virus spread in an exponential curve out of Wuhan, this itch I describe was thrown into sharp relief and we were slammed up against everything I'd just spent a good part of three years writing about. The entire globe was unified in a truly surreal isolation, brought together in a disconnection from the (disconnected) lives we'd been leading. As I wrote on an Instagram post, 'It's like nature has sent us all to our rooms to have a good hard look at ourselves.'

Me, I went back to my home study, called the manuscript back from my publishers and sat with it for a few weeks, then a few more. I knew I'd have to include, or at least acknowledge, this whopping beast that had just joined us in this itch-fest. It wasn't the first time the book had been stalled. The bushfires that swept my beautiful Australia only a few months earlier, that saw rainbow lorikeets and kookaburras and slabs of black ash wash up on beaches, had called for a rewrite. Like everything around me, this book you're now holding had become a self-referring phenomenon. Things had gotten supremely meta!

But here's the thing. The world had been upended, and then inverted, nothing was as it was, but did it change this book? Nah, not really. Rather, it amplified and distilled the godawful itch and plonked it slap-bang under our noses. Which is what crises tend to do.

Then, two days before my second deadline, in Minneapolis, a white police officer named Derek Chauvin knelt on the neck of a Black man named George Floyd, setting into motion a 'waking up' to the systemic racism that has long been eating away at our world.

Again, I went back to my home study and wrote. And on it went.

With this UK edition I'm doing the same once again. I was in the UK in the Summer of 2022 when temperatures broke multiple records. I'd been hiking with my friends Rick and Brad in The Peak District and the fields were barren, the earth cracked like outback Australia. Chat GPT and AI has dialled up existential risk since the first edition such that more than half of experts think the chances of AI wiping out humanity by 2100 is at least 10 per cent. Many think the probability is much higher. The culture wars have proliferated, the transgender wars have killed kids. Oh, and Russia started an old-fashioned kind of war with Ukraine which saw *The*

Bulletin of the Atomic Scientists set its Doomsday Clock at a record 90 seconds to midnight.

There are no rules for how to manage what is ahead, including how to rewrite a book that aims to reflect and serve a world that has flipped inside out. The choice we have then, my friends, it to treat what we have before us as an opportunity – yes, an opportunity! – to reimagine a more connected, entirely-not-normal, joyous path forward. Which is more than just a bit perfect.

4 So.

I wrote a book about anxiety a few years back called *first, we make the beast beautiful.* My argument was that anxiety stemmed from a yearning for a connection to life that we felt we were missing. Edvard Munch's *The Scream* – that's it in oils, I wrote. This primordial sense of lack, this disconnect from what life is meant to be about, makes us anxious. So we frantically grasp outward, looking for instant fixes and consuming stuff that we think will fill the lack. In *The Beast* I went on a largely inward seven-year journey to understand my bipolar disorder and various other symptoms of this disconnect, and to find ways to cope.

But as I toured with the book after publication, and chatted to readers in the Q&A sessions, it occurred to me that even as we were having more heartfelt, deeper conversations about our personal anxiety, our larger and more original sense of disconnection – our itchy sense that things are not right –

SARAH WILSON

remained. In fact, it had become more pronounced. While the economy had grown in most western nations, our sense of well-being had plummeted. Happiness levels were down, anxiety and depression were up. Political and social distrust was the highest it's been. We were more politically polarised, we'd lost trust in the media, and extremist groups were on the rise.

In early 2020, the growing security threat in both the UK and Australia was neo-Nazism. According to Freedom House's assessment of global political rights and civil liberties we are experiencing the fourteenth consecutive year of worldwide democratic deterioration.

It felt like everyone around me was fighting – over Trump, Brexit, China, if it was worth recycling any more, should we go vegan, 5G conspiracy theories, who was doling out the fakest news. Where was the love? Why weren't we finding peace?

Oh, and while humanity seemed to be falling apart, the planet literally did. In the short time since I wrote *The Beast*, 11,000 scientists and almost 1,700 governments have declared a climate emergency, with many experts alerting us to a 'mass human extinction event'. We also wiped out another 20 per cent of the animal species on the WWF's Living Planet Index, the Great Barrier Reef had three major bleaching events and Australia lost more than one billion wild creatures over one summer of fires.

And all of it – the whole despairing itch – I learned, was killing us. Life expectancy in the United States declined for

I use 'climate emergency' and 'climate crisis' interchangeably. There is debate in the activist and scientific communities as to which is more accurate and motivating, which I don't feel is important to engage in.

20

the third year in a row, the reason cited being 'diseases of despair' – suicide and opioids mostly. This statistic tears my heart. The only other time in US history that this happened was in 1918, when there was a war and a major flu pandemic that killed almost 700,000 young people. And this was before corona virus struck. (Cut to the present day, and it's dropped another two years in a row post-Covid – devastatingly, largely due to the numbers of young people being killed by guns.) In the UK, the Institute for Fiscal Studies has now reported the same pattern in the UK.

I saw this mass despair in other people's faces. At book signings, on buses, at LA immigration desks. And not just in the faces of those with diagnosed anxious disorders. Very quickly, I realised this primordial lack, this despairing disconnect that I'd identified at the core of our personal anxiety, remained unaddressed and was now playing out at the collective level. Our entire world was itching.

5   Some of you might recall that I opened *The Beast* with a humble-braggish tale of the time I interviewed His Holiness the Dalai Lama and decided to ask him how best to quieten my frantic mind. He'd waved his hand dismissively and told me not to bother. 'Waste of time,' he'd said. Rather than sitting in some cave trying to perfect mindfulness, he'd suggested we practise altruism out in the world. At the time, I took from this that His Holiness was saying we could be both frantic in our minds, and have a big, great, helpful life. Not either/or.

I realise now that he was also saying we needed to steer our energy beyond our own issues to helping others and helping the planet. Out not in.

I thought about this as the collective pain weighed down on me. I couldn't let it go. I could no longer distract myself or limit my focus to the inward anxious struggle. I found myself with a visceral need to understand these larger crises we were facing and to find a way to reconnect.

You might know the parable of the monk who comes down from the mountain. He'd been up there for years, meditating alone in, yep, a cave, funnelling his energy inward to that still space within. But one day he wakes to the realisation, *What's the point if I don't share this dreamy wisdom and openness with others?* And so he sets out for the villages in the valley. I am no monk, but I knew I had to switch direction. To go out not in.

And so I did the only thing I felt I could do, which was to collect my shame, my hypocrisies, my loneliness, my guilt, my overwhelm and − anxious or otherwise − get back on the road, writing as I went so that I might be able to share what I had learned. I set out with an itch, and no idea how I was going to attend to this far vaster, original 'beast' (and clearly no idea of the unfathomable ways this collective itch was going to play out on the road ahead); just a burning question: what could we be doing better? What could we be doing differently?

Do yourself a life-affirming favour and look up the formidable spoken word artist Kae Tempest's poem 'People's Faces,' which they performed in Glastonbury in 2017 −

6 I will flag it bluntly here. The impetus for me was – and remains – the climate emergency. The pandemics (and there will be more) and bushfires, both AI and nuclear threat, conspiracy theories and all the other 'Black Swans' (wildly unpredictable and extreme global events set to increase as the world gets increasingly complicated, globalised and fragmented) in coming years are climate issues at one level or another, and they are all manifestations of the same disconnection we have been feeling in our souls. Bushfires and viruses largely peak and pass. The impact of climate change, however, is cumulative and forever, accompanied by more natural disasters and pandemics. As black climate expert Ayana Elizabeth Johnson wrote in a *Washington Post* op-ed, racism 'distracts' from the bigger issue of saving the planet. She reminds readers that Americans of colour are significantly more concerned about climate change than white people (59 per cent of black and 70 per cent of Hispanic vs 49 per cent of white Americans), in large part because they disproportionately bear climate impacts, from storms to heat waves to pollution, and fossil-fuelled power plants and refineries are disproportionately located in black neighbourhoods (68 per cent of black people live within thirty miles of a coal-fired power plant), leading to a host of health issues. The climate emergency is a social and racial justice issue and is our fundamental existential threat.

As I shared with Jose, the working title for this book was *Wake the Fuck Up.* I was trying to convey the urgent need for us to become alive to what was happening to life around us

Fuck is an overused literary — trope these days, don't you think?

(so we might have a chance of saving it and our humanity). When I shared it with people like Jose they immediately got the gist, even if 'climate emergency' were not words he'd use. The despair is real! The urgency is real! Wake up, people! We need you!

But I soon realised such aggression was alienating and unhelpful. And besides, the cascading world events rang the alarm bell more effectively than any shouty profanity could.

I also realised this book could not be a book about climate science. Nor the specifics of where corona virus started, nor politics, nor the economy or oil prices. Nor critical race theory, nor the intersectional nuances involved.

An extensive meta study has shown that polarisation over the reality of — climate change increases with more discussion of the science and politics.

For our purposes here, I believe disputing issues and focusing on differences (especially aggressively) — which is what we've been doing to date — is distracting and only splitting us further apart. As David Suzuki puts it, 'We're in a giant car heading toward a brick wall and everyone's arguing over where they're going to sit.'

Dear reader, more than anything else I do not want to antagonise or further polarise my fellow humans.

As with many Einstein quotes, there is conjecture as to whether these were his actual words, although he spoke to this effect often in relation to the threat of — nuclear war.

Climate science avoiders and even deniers, and those for whom other aspects of our collective despair are more pressing (such as unemployment, hunger, inequality or mental illness), are also craving the same compassionate reconnection. There is a more common story in our humanity, and we need to get on that page together.

As Albert Einstein infamously said, 'No problem can be solved from the same level of consciousness that created it.'

Our right vs wrong, us vs them approach won't fix things. Right now, our consciousness, or collective awareness, is that of an aggressive and fragmented society of self-flagellating economic units arguing with each other in confused despair.

We must do things differently.

Sufi poet Rumi posed the idea of a field. I was reminded of it as I grappled with all this:

Out beyond ideas of wrongdoing and rightdoing there is a field. I'll meet you there.

I bloody love this field. To me it is a realm of our human experience beyond the tired and angry competing and trolling and ghosting and gaslighting. It's where we stop disputing issues and instead discuss values. Soul values.

I had to find a way to this field, through the paradoxes and complexities, Black Swans and 'new normals'. And the title would have to directly convey what we all want to reconnect with, dedicate ourselves to and save, once we arrive there together.

And, so…this one wild and precious life.

7   What began as a three-year adventure in which I interviewed more than 100 scientists, philosophers, psychologists, psychiatrists, poets, artists, activists, teenagers and two nuns, has now become my life. 'You can't unsee this stuff.' 'There's no turning back.' The scientists, activists and artists I met on the way, we'd say these kinds of things to each other.

The whole way, I stalled and tripped, I raged and doubted.

I made decisions I never thought I'd have to make. When Dad referred to it in the family WhatsApp group, he called it 'Sarah's Book of Everything.' I got lost in the nuances, trying to find succinct ways to sum it all up. More calamities struck. More rewrites. But in time, the journey revealed itself. And became this thing you're holding.

In the first part of the book, I tackle why and how we've landed where we are. As I set off, I found I had to pull apart our loneliness and our relationship with technology, as well as the entire neo-liberal model upon which our society pivots, to best understand our disconnect. I also do a face-off with the existential threat posed by the climate crisis nice and early on. Knowing the why and how makes us feel less overwhelmed and more compassionate toward each other and ourselves, I find.

In the second part, I show you some of the ways I found to meet in Rumi's field and reconnect with life.

My friend the Irish poet David Whyte has a technique that I found perfect for navigating such a journey. He has a lovely lilt and an even lovelier way of pausing after a complex thought, or a hoary quandary, looking out to the room of devotees who flock to his workshops around the world, and asking, 'But what is the more beautiful question?' And we are immediately reminded that there is always a more beautiful question that should be asked. I've heard David explain that asking the more beautiful question (invariably the courageous one) delivers us the answer we seek. A question can often be laced with blame or rage. ('Why did he do that to me?' 'Why won't she just learn to recycle properly?') But when we dig a few layers deeper to the more delicate, beautiful question ('What need in me is not being met?' 'How can I better connect with this person?'), we find ourselves going to a kinder, more considered place in ourselves and each other. Which is what we ultimately seek, right? I mean, especially *now*.

And so I will be asking a lot of questions, some of which you have asked me on social media and at public forums, and others that I ask myself. I will endeavour to ask them as beautifully as possible.

In the final part of the book, I explore what we can do once we are fully alive and connected – how we can be of service in an uncertain and upended world.

And then, in the final chapters, we arrive at what I hope will be – for we are yet to get there – a new level of radical, determined kind of hope and a blueprint for living – *really* living – our one wild precious life that we've been granted on this beautiful planet with each other.

Here are a few other things about this book:

This journey is a soul's journey. I reckon you know what I mean when I say this, no explainer required.

Humanity has always experienced times of great despair, pandemics, sadness and bewilderment, yet at all turns there have been wise good people who have nutted out paths forward, via poetry, art, fiction, philosophy. What I'm saying, is, there is legacy; the paths back to life are already paved and no new wheels need to be invented. In *The Catcher in the Rye*,

Holden's former teacher consoles him in his despair. 'Among other things,' he tells Holden, 'you'll find that you're not the first person who was ever confused and frightened and even sickened by human behaviour. You're by no means alone on that score, you'll be excited and stimulated to know. Many, many men have been just as troubled morally and spiritually as you are right now. Happily, some of them kept records of their troubles.'

Where it flows, —
I'll include
names, books
and podcasts
that are worth
checking out.

I draw on these records throughout, specifically Stoicism, existentialism, Greek mythology, Jungian theory, Romanticism, feminism and various spiritual practices. Perfectly, they all emerged in response to similarly turbulent times in history — the Crusades, world wars, revolution, the civil rights struggle, the Cold War era and so on. Having said that, I would never want to limit your journey to these sources alone. I won't be limiting mine.

I provide sources (with hyperlinks) for all political, climate change, spiritual and psychological claims online at sarahwilson.com. I also include a list of additional references; I figured you might enjoy being able to access the reading and listening materials (books, podcasts, op-eds as well as scientific papers) as much as I did.

I've tried to write this as a conversation, and one that will continue beyond these pages. Active conversation is a most sustaining way to reconnect. And so I don't write in a normal writerish way. I ramble, I layer, as you and I would in an IRL chat. There's no other way to talk about an itch so vast and nebulous.

I've used wide margins — partly because I like to include little notes for you, the reader (to point you to extra info that might be useful), and partly so you can write your own notes as you go.

— This wide margin, here.

Finally, I walked this book. At the outset it was the only way I could deal with the overwhelm and fear I felt. I hiked to get clear and to feel and to connect. It became my salve. But it was also my *way*. I developed most of the ideas, did most of my experimenting, and explored the biggest, boldest theories while putting one foot in front of the other on trails around the world. Or in daily walks I did from my apartment when I'd gone too far down research and writing rabbit holes. Again, there is legacy. Many philosophers and thinkers throughout history hiked for the same reasons. Friedrich Nietzsche, for whom I have a very soft spot, claimed, 'All truly great thoughts are conceived while walking.'

— I share the more detailed information of each hike at sarahwilson.com.

So, I follow in some of their footsteps. I also tread paths made by ancient cultures that have outlooks to offer us today, mostly pivoting from their spiritual — or otherwise — connection to walking. Sometimes, as I say, I just walked out my front door. And in the movement, in the practice, things began to unfurl.

That was a long introduction, friends. Onward.

our

crisis

of

connection

all

the lonely

people

8 Right, so first I needed to identify this disconnect. To say it's an itch, a nebulous feeling, was not going to cut it.

It often presents as loneliness. At least that's how we tend to describe disconnection – it's an accessible entry point. You can point at loneliness, study it. Also, there is no denying that just navigating this gargantuan topic – the everythingness – is lonely. How many times have I called out during a sleepless night into the dark, is anyone else feeling this existential clusterfuck as I am? Is anyone seeing what I am, willing to question things as I am?

PS Clusterfuck is a military term from the 1960s. It refers to a chaotic, complex situation where everything seems to go wrong.

9 'Loneliness is a populated place,' literary critic Olivia Laing wrote in *The Lonely City: Adventures in the Art of Being Alone*. In just a few short years, however, the joint has reached bursting point. It's now an epidemic, say the headlines. In the 1980s scholars estimated 20 per cent of people in the United States felt lonely; now it's half of all Americans. The UK government has a Loneliness Minister. The position was created following news that the UK ranks the second loneliest place in the world. Australia has a Coalition to End Loneliness and I read Dutch supermarkets have a 'conversation' checkout where people can chat to the cashier to combat the issue. Which is so Dutch, and really rather lovely.

One study found loneliness is 'contagious'. People are 50 per cent more likely to experience loneliness if someone they are directly connected to feels lonely. A causation that is just a bit ironic, you'd agree? And, goodness, it gets worse. Loneliness now kills twice as many of us a year as obesity does. One report found that smoking fifteen cigarettes a day is a healthier option than living on your own, a state of being sociologist Hugh Mackay calls the 'global warming' of demographics.

But then we learn that 60 per cent of married people feel lonely. Seemingly we are all lonely, regardless of the number of up-close humans in our lives. Indeed a 2019 study rated Australians as the third most 'socially connected' people in the world, yet we are feeling lonely at unprecedented levels with millennials reporting both the most 'connection' *and* the greatest loneliness globally.

— As Anton Chekhov wrote, 'If you're afraid of loneliness, don't marry.'

But then, funny creatures that we are, we increasingly claw over one another to be on our own; we actually seek aloneness in a hectic, hyper-socially connected world. The Pew Research Center found that 85 per cent of adults seek more aloneness. One major international travel company reports that more than half of its bookings – more than 75,000 – are solo travellers. Nearly 10 per cent of US travellers are married people with kids wanting to get away on their own. I read the other day that in Japan a growing number of car share app users don't actually drive the car they've booked. They hire them to simply sit in them. Alone.

And just to muddy things further, when given the option to be on our own, we freak. A series of studies by University of Virginia and Harvard University psychologists found that the bulk of us will opt for an electric shock over being left alone with our own thoughts for as little as 15 minutes. In the study, participants were given the option to break the discomfort of merely sitting solo in a chair in a room, with no phone and nothing to read, with a self-administered painful jolt. Two-thirds of men and a quarter of women in the study chose to press the button.

So where do we land? All those pandemic lockdowns aside, we are feeling lonely, possibly more so than ever before. But this isn't about not having enough humans around us. Not any more. What we're feeling is deeper and more original. And wonderfully nuanced.

10   And so I think the beautiful and courageous – and richer – question here becomes: what are we lonely from?

The magnificent artist Patti Smith wrote, 'A new-born cries as the cord is severed, seeming to extinguish memory of

THIS ONE WILD AND PRECIOUS LIFE

the miraculous. Thus we are condemned to stagger rootless upon the earth in search for our fingerprint on the cosmos.'

Yep, we start out alone. We die alone. And we spend the time in between trying to reconnect to this memory of the miraculous oneness from whence we came. I like this. For me, this memory of the miraculous is a knowingness that life is big and meaningful and precious and that everything is awesomely, unfathomably, satiatingly connected.

We share 60 per cent of our DNA with a banana. The first living cell emerged four billion years ago, and its direct descendants are in all of our bloodstreams. We are literally breathing molecules right now inhaled by Buddha, Marie Curie and Beyoncé. We die and decompose and replace ourselves — every cell — every seven years. We are the Earth. We are space. Our fates are inseparable. You pull the cuticle on my little finger, and you can move my entire lumpen frame. The spiritualists teach us this, but we know it viscerally, too.

It's miraculous and true. And yet we're not living it.

So, what are we lonely from?

For most, it really isn't from lack of more connections with humans, per se. No, we're lonely from lack of *meaningful* connection to each other. And to life. I learned recently that 22 per cent of millennial men in the US with less than a bachelor's degree reported not working at all in the previous year. Why? The study put it down to video games. But, wait! It's not that these young men couldn't find work so figured they might as well game to kill time. Nope. The study found they were not working *because* they're gaming — gaming

Of course many in our community who are wholly disenfranchised — the homeless, the elderly, the underemployed, new parents, the mentally unwell — suffer terribly from lack of human contact.

provided more meaning and connection for these young men than the disenfranchised entry-level jobs available to them. I found my heart opening when I viewed the 'problem' through this lens.

11 We're also lonely from ourselves.

Those people in Japan who rent cars to sit in them on their own (where they knit, write or just close their eyes and be with their thoughts) are finding a way to reconnect (at least more peacefully) with themselves. I had an agent when I was working in TV who faked business trips to sit in her aloneness. She'd book a motel room down the road and order room service and sometimes just sit in the bath and cry. It's a gorgeous oddity of our existence – our loneliness is not caused by being on our own. Indeed, loneliness is best cured with aloneness, which is to say, a meaningful connection to ourselves.

All of which presents a veritable triple-pike paradox, the full glory of which played out during the corona virus lockdowns. We were all forced into isolation, which for multi-person households stripped its members of alone time, leaving many lonely for a meaningful relationship with themselves, for 'a room of one's own'. While for the 20–60 per cent of us living solo in the western world, who'd had to do lockdown with no human contact, our connection with our communities was severed, forcing us into a particularly biologically grim, catch-22-like loneliness.

36

You see, in times of crisis the human species is genetically programmed to seek out other humans to survive. Human touch sees us down-regulate our autonomic nervous system, which in turn enables us to overcome the fear and helplessness and fight for our survival with all our smarts on. And yet solo dwellers were denied this primal response during lockdown. Of course, at the same time, isolation itself triggers the flight or fight (anxious) response, which roots us further in the very crisis we are programmed to try to flee.

Former US Surgeon General Dr Vivek H Murthy's book *Together: The Healing Power of Human Connection in a Sometimes Lonely World* was released just as the US death rate from COVID-19 started to accelerate (Murthy had no inkling it would land in a world of enforced isolation). He wrote: 'Over millennia, this hyper-vigilance in response to isolation became embedded in our nervous system to produce the anxiety we associate with loneliness.'

We breathe fast, our heart races, our blood pressure rises and we don't sleep – all signals to seek connection. Cut off from our ability to attend to such urges, those of us who are generally not lonely in our aloneness suddenly feel a horrible kind of severance from, well, life. As Robin Wright, a writer who lives solo in Washington DC, penned in *The New Yorker*, 'As the new pathogen forces us to socially distance…life seems shallower, more like survival than living.'

The upside of such a unique scenario, of course, was that our fundamental need for reconnection was exposed; so too just how removed we've become from what matters to us. It held a big fat mirror – nay, a magnifying glass – to so much of where we'd been going wrong. And to all the complex and beautiful paradoxes and uncertainties of the human experience, actually. But we'll get to that shortly.

12 Just as I set out to write this book, I was sitting in a café facing onto Ljubljana's central square. A woman, I'm guessing in her late thirties, was sitting alone opposite me. She just sat there, watching. There was a heatwave on this day in Slovenia, and a public holiday, and the square was suspended in an eerie abandon. You could hear church bells from across the river; roller-doors were down.

On days like this in cities around the world people like me – nomads who tend to travel a little wider and weirder to find their connection with the miraculous – will come out to sit alone in the only café that's open to wade in the abandon.

This woman sitting on her own wore all red. A red skirt, a red and white striped t-shirt and red Birkenstocks, her hair tied low in a knot. Her legs were crossed and her hands rested in her lap and I really just dug her. She was not reading a book, not looking at her phone. For 45 minutes she just sat there with soft eyes in a chosen stillness.

Caffeinated and craving the connection particular to talking to strangers in foreign cafés, I reached over. 'Do you mind if I ask…what are you doing?'

She smiled. 'On special days I like to sit and think nothing.'

By special days she meant public holidays.

I asked if I could take her picture and post it on social media. I told her she looked happy and that I was aware that sharing her stillness was a bit wrong in a binary kind of weighing up of things. She laughed and I wrote out our conversation in the post, pretty much as I have here with you. I wonder if she ever saw it. In the photo she's smiling.

The post prompted an interesting reaction. I've been stopped in the street and asked about it, months – years – on. 'Did she tell you how she could just sit there like that?' Some said the picture made them feel sad, that it reminded them of something they used to be able to do, but no longer could, like doing cartwheels into pools. In the comments, people wrote, 'Goals! I want to be able to do that again!' and 'I saw this photo and thought, we're not allowed to do this any more…NOT ALLOWED…WTF?!'

She was not touching her phone, not scrolling, not distracted, and to me, this was like sticking two fingers up to the pressure we feel to be doing something on a public holiday. Her soft, calm smile suggested she was not lonely. And I think this is probably the real juicy point of what she represented. She was meaningfully connected – in this case to herself and to life. To our collective memory of the miraculous.

It's like we're jealous of this ability, almost angry in the face of it. How dare she not be distracted while we must battle the incessant suck-hole. What makes her think she's allowed to ignore the stimulus, the requests? And how dare she not succumb to the modern fear of missing out. But we're aware, aren't we, in these moments that no one robbed us, no one forced us to become so distracted and so trapped, so unable to sit still and quiet and not need more likes, more feedback, more action, more 'more'. Which is where the unfathomable sadness comes in, right? We have trapped ourselves. And we miss the version of ourselves that used to be able to be like this.

And so what the Lady in Red really triggered was a nostalgia. Nostalgia, I was interested to learn recently, is a Greek word that means homesick.

Yes! We are longing for home. For meaningful connection with ourselves.

I wrote in my notebook, 'Lady in Red does cool aloneness.' Cool Aloneness. It sounds like an Edward Hopper painting.

> I wound up finding the Lady in Red via a tangled Facebook group search. We connected via a Zoom chat, which I recorded for my podcast. Her name is Manca and we stay in touch.

13 But here's the crucial element to all this that brings us right to the nub of what itches at us so despairingly. Without meaningful connection – to others, to life, to ourselves – we also experience what sociologists and psychologists are calling 'moral loneliness'.

Yes, moral loneliness!

Moral loneliness is when the supply cord to connection, caring and doing the right thing by each other and the planet has been severed. If bog-standard loneliness is the feeling you are a lone unit unable to connect to other people or things in the matrix, moral loneliness is the sense that the mains to the matrix have been cut. We can't tap into the point of life, to what matters.

This is the truest pain point of our disconnection, don't you think?

A number of political, cultural and spiritual fractures have rendered us isolated from the values that once provided communion and 'belonging', and our moral compass. Externally we have corrupt leaders, unbridled media corporations that trade in fake news, political agendas and unethical click baiting, and churches covering up the horrific crimes of their clergy. At our own soul level, we are increasingly, I feel (but you determine for yourself), watching ourselves disconnect from our own value system. We struggle to determine what matters any more, and whether our own caring can make a difference. We buy more and more things, throw out food, use the clothes dryer and disengage from the political process because – and I think I have it right, although I'll drill down further later in the journey – our disconnect from the matrix has rendered us paralysed.

And dehumanised. Yes, this is a great word for this disconnected loneliness. *Dehumanised.*

Again, this aspect of our disconnect became blindingly apparent for many of us during isolation. Our culture's greed, individualism and obsession with success suddenly presented as entirely empty and pointless. Our shiny SUVs sat in the driveway, we became dependent on the goodness of others (to stay at home, and to not sneeze on us while queueing 1.5 metres apart at the pharmacy) and it was nurses and delivery guys and supermarket workers, not bankers and lawyers, who were going to save us. I think many of us felt relieved to experience this kind of clarity.

14 In 1956, philosopher and psychoanalyst Erich Fromm described this moral isolation, or loneliness, as more unbearable than the bog-standard loneliness. In *The Art of Loving* he explained that the reason Americans did not rise up against the risk of worldwide nuclear destruction was because they were already experiencing the moral disconnect internally – a 'deadness within'. When you don't know your true north – when you're dehumanised – the disorientation is terrifying. You are suspended in a vague and directionless vastness. You can't sit coolly alone. You scroll. You adopt 'false selves'.

The Greeks argued that this kind of moral loneliness led to acedia – a state of spiritual apathy or listless sloth. The 13th-century theologian Thomas Aquinas described it as 'the sorrow of the world' that emanates from 'the flesh utterly prevailing over the spirit'. It's the numb, 'blah' despair that kicks in when our overindulgence quashes our ability to care.

Me, I abhor this moral 'asleepness'. As I ventured into the early stages of this journey, I quickly realised it was at the root of our disconnect from this one wild and precious life we'd been granted. And that we'd be revisiting it many times over.

15 You might remember that jacket Melania Trump wore to visit the migrants at the Mexican border during that horrible era? The khaki one with the graffitied slogan on the back? It read, 'I really don't care, do U?' I remember seeing it in the news reports and thinking that the brazen insensitivity of the jacket was one thing, but more disturbing was the way it raised the despairing question, is this what the world has come to? Do we just not care any more? Are we that disconnected and lonely and lost? I've seen young people wearing t-shirts with the same slogan more recently. They're not being ironic. They're serious. I know because on two separate occasions I stopped them and I asked if they meant it. One nodded. One shrugged.

16 I want to make this point, though, and might also come back to it a few times. It's an evolutionary response to shut down and go numb like this. When we can't fight or flee from a horrible threat, we lie down and play dead — we freeze. A deer will do it as a last-ditch survival trick when being chased by a tiger. Playing dead might fool its predator into being a bit casual in its final lunge, giving the deer an opportunity to suddenly jerk back to life and escape. Abuse victims do it as a form of self-protection; anxiety sufferers do it in the face of too many decisions and existential overwhelm. And I reckon — it's what we do to survive when we find ourselves living a life that is so removed from the miraculous.

Which is useful to reflect on; it certainly makes me more

My (then) five-year-old nephew Emil and I were video-chatting and he asked what my book was about. I said it's about waking up. His mum asked him what he thought that meant and she texted me his reply: 'It's about coming back to life after you were asleep for a long time.' Kids just know.

compassionate about things when I do. Of course, freezing or numbing out can work as a survival trick for a while, but if we remain asleep, particularly as a society, we face our collective demise.

And I add this. This is not how we want to live. It's not our nature to be so disconnected.

A PUB-TO-PUB WALK:
DORSET-SOMERSET-WILTSHIRE, ENGLAND

I dance a wild trot with loneliness. I'm now a 49-year-old woman who lives on her own. I've been mostly single, with varied deep-but-transient loves, for fifteen years. I work from home doing one of the most solitary things in the high school career handbook – writing. And when I'm not feeling quite alone enough, I fling myself off into the world with one bag of possessions and travel for long slabs. Solo. For eight years I lived on the road: in Greece, Paris, New York and London, and on each return to Australia, in different cities and regions. I wrote the bulk of this book, indeed all of my books, and ran a business during this time.

And I write — on topics that have tended to render me an outlier for years at a time.

You could say I am a pin-up girl for the epidemic. I prefer to say I'm a nomad. Nomads leave home to connect with the world and with others. And with ourselves.

And we walk.

44

And so, 'As I walked out one midsummer morning,' close to the beginning of this journey, to hike in the south-west of England, my plan was to cross the Dorset-Somerset-Wiltshire borders over four days. I'd been in London doing book promotions and was suffocating in the stifling grey of the city. I reached out to several British hikers on the Internet asking for advice on a pub-to-pub hike. There's an art to finding a walk that combines tramping through forest or bush for hours with your own thoughts and then lands you in civilisation each evening with a warm bed, a meal and the rosy-cheeked company of curious locals. I've scoured the world and the Googles for such expeditions. A bunch of them feature in this book.

I set off from Gillingham, Dorset, toward the quaint village of Tollard Royal. On my first day I followed a series of carriageways through private land, traversing Guy Ritchie's estate, and encountered hounds and pheasants, brambles, bleating lambs and gurgling brooks. I arrived that evening at the King John Inn and ate deviled kidneys while chatting to the locals who wore tweed coats with reinforced elbows and riding boots and drank warm pints. It was awfully Jilly Cooper. Or Famous Five. Or something betwixt.

The locals kept their distance at first, until I approached them to talk. Nomads have often triggered discomfort in others. The Latin synonym for vagabond is 'vagrant' and it also has the same stem as vague. More recently I was in Japan hiking solo, and came down to breakfast at the inn I was staying in to find I'd been put on a table on my own facing

— This is the title of Laurie Lee's book about his nomadic journey from the Cotswolds to the south of England and into Spain, where he survived by playing the violin. A gorgeous read.

— We'll come to this hike shortly.

the wall, my back to the rest of the room of couples and families, many of whom had been placed at communal tables with other couples and families. It wasn't cruel. Sometimes the world just doesn't know where to place people like me. I sat and read the English-language newspaper. Page three had a story about some Japanese minister declaring women needed to have at least three children to solve the aging population crisis. Page thirteen had a story about 'no talking' cafés in Tokyo for single people who want to be on their own and 'away from couples'. I smiled to myself. And the wall.

I'd brought along Elizabeth Gilbert's *Eat Pray Love* for this British walk (I'd done a book swap in the hotel in London and figured I'd revisit it a decade after first reading it) and retreated to a corner in the pub after a while to read. Gilbert quotes a diary entry by Virginia Woolf, a nomad of sorts herself. Woolf hiked not far from here, as did Thomas Hardy, who wrote his most famous works walking some of the same paths I was. Funnily, Woolf once fan-girled Hardy. She had visited him at his home not far from where I was sitting and asked him to sign her book before she caught the train back to London. He'd misspelled her name: Wolff.

Ditto Gilbert. —

This is the line Gilbert cites: 'Across the broad continent of a woman's life falls the shadow of a sword.'

On one side of that sword, Woolf had journaled some time in 1925, lies the conventional, 'correct' way, on the other is the life you choose when convention doesn't suit you. On this shadowed side, 'nothing follows a regular course'. She added that choosing this shadowed side 'may bring a far more interesting existence to a woman, but you can bet it will also be more perilous.'

Oh yes. It can be. I have weak moments living this shadowed side, as a nomad. I watch couples sitting opposite me in pubs, sharing a carafe of Beaujolais and navigating as a team where they will head next or what dessert they'll share, and I think it would be so nice to only have to make half the decisions (and to share the joy of the anticipation). Wouldn't it be less exhausting to have a ready-to-go connection available, instead of having to hustle for company? Or to know that you wouldn't be alone on a Sunday night or, if you have kids, that three-quarters of your social life for the weekend was set out for you? This would provide some certainty and security. And when you felt a bit wobbly, there would be sitcoms and social rituals (weddings, christenings, playgroups) that reminded you your path was the 'right' one. If you live outside such structures, as a nomad or as a single parent or a widower, for example, you must wake up each day writing your own guidebook for connection and security, and then hustle for it. Some of you reading this will know what I mean.

The flipside, of course, is that actively hustling for the company of others often takes us to a deeper, more meaningful connection. They are sought out and fought-for connections, not defaults.

Speaking of *Eat Pray Love*, some years earlier I'd visited a shaman in Bali, a colleague of the one Gilbert writes about in her book. 'People like you should not go for traditional relationships,' my shaman told me as his kids and dogs ran around our feet. 'Standard relationships – monogamous marriage – get in the way of relating for you.' This was a tough prophecy to shoulder at the time. But I also knew somehow it would bring a far more interesting existence.

I woke the next morning above the pub in a stuffy cloud of British duvet and, after a breakfast of local asparagus and kippers, set off through bluebell woods veiled in a gentle mist. My footsteps and breathing could be heard with concert-hall acoustics. I passed ancient towns dripping in Domesday history and I saw not a soul – apart from the toffy gents at the pub at lunchtime where I arrived with sodden feet (I spent much of the day squelching through fields in water and mud to my knees). It was a wonderfully moody day and I recall reflecting hard on a question that I continue to pose to myself to this day. Why fling myself off into such solitude? Is this more alone path the right one?

As I alluded to above, humans are paradoxical. We often need to be alone to reconnect to life and to ourselves, which then allows us to connect more meaningfully to others. And we often have to leave to arrive at this deeper, more meaningful connection we yearn. It might mean leaving the 'regular course', stepping away from our culture's preconceived ideas about gender or consumerism or life goals, or it might mean consciously rejecting the collective emotional and intellectual asleepness we feel ourselves sinking into. It might simply entail, like the Lady in Red in

Ljubljana, leaving your phone untouched as you drink coffee alone in a café on a public holiday – you know, to arrive at that smiling knowingness. You don't have to be itinerant or single and unencumbered to be a nomad, just willing to step beyond what does not serve you.

It has taken me a long time fretting in the shadows to realise that this is what I do: I leave to find my reconnection out in the world, often with other nomads, sometimes at a bar in New York or a hotel lobby in London. We can spot each other, sitting alone in transit leisure gear – stretchy layers and sneakers – flirting platonically with the waiters. We love Instagram because we can bear witness – in pictures – to others' lives. And it becomes quite plausible and really not that inappropriate to reach out to a stranger we 'follow' if the geotag says we're in the same city at the same time. Marta, Dan, William, Carla, Danielle, Val, Philippe, Fearne, Octave, Davis, Matt in Athens, Tim, Mel, Susan and the psychopath photographer from Paris…we meet up (often having never even spoken on the phone) to hike, to share a meal and go straight to what hurts, what we think about when we're, well, alone. I've had affairs with men in foreign countries where we don't speak each other's language. When communication isn't fluid, two people keep to the good stuff. It's easier to talk philosophy than dumb minutiae when you have fewer words. I had a two-week affair with a goat herder in Ikaria – Xristos – who spoke no English. We swam each day between his goat duties. We communicated with nods, and expressions in our eyes. He knew nothing of me that relied on a spoken language. Not even my age. But our souls connected.

In the late afternoon I arrived at Buckhorn Weston, a village that is really just a pub. I took up a position in the window seat at said pub and ate a roast prepared with ingredients grown on the publican's farm. A 16-kilometre stroll through bog the next day took me to Corton Denham and the next I followed the pilgrim path to Salisbury. I sat in the beautiful Saxon abbey in the centre of the village and wrote some notes in a pew where the stained glass lit a rosy vibe while I waited for the train back to London.

When I looked back over my notes from this trip, I noticed I'd circled this sentence: *I choose perilous and interesting.*

the scrolling.

the
bloody
scrolling.

17 Let's pull things apart a bit more. We tend to blame technology for much of this despair that I'm labelling disconnection. Again, it's a neat, tangible thing to point at and talk about. We're lonely because of online dating. We are getting fatter, dumber, ruder, sicker and sadder because we are addicted to our screens. I remember Trump (and many others) blaming the spate of teen massacres during his presidency on online games (when in fact there is absolutely no causal connection, let alone any correlation, between the two phenomena). We link screen time to teen mental health decline when the evidence is in fact 'paper thin', affecting only 0.5 per cent of adolescents and only those who spend more than two-thirds of their waking lives online.

 For here's the truth: technology only ever enables.

— Just as guns don't kill, people do.

— Remember to visit sarahwilson. com for the references for these kinds of factlets.

I don't dismiss the insidious, addictive hold that the scrolling has on us (nor the sanity-saving and life-affirming role it can play in a pandemic) but as I looked into things more closely – and at my own horrible addiction – I realised there was a more beautiful and courageous question to be asked: 'What does technology enable?'

18 A few years ago I took to texting instead of calling. Everyone had, hadn't they? I can have a 'conversation' on WhatsApp for 20 minutes using Siri to dictate my messages. I could pick up the phone and get the information across in a fraction of the time, but that seems…harder…and way more confronting. If I text, instead of calling or fronting up IRL, I can hide behind a safe persona that I get to construct before hitting send. I chuck on a wink emoticon and a double X at the end of harsh messages.

Phew. Done. Outta here.

I also watch myself ignore incoming phone calls if I know they might be about a tricky issue. Equally I can pretend I didn't see a text message and thus avoid responding altogether. Because I've turned off the default setting on my phone that displays 'read' when I've opened a message. I read my WhatsApp messages and Instagram DMs in notifications instead of opening them (which alerts the sender that I've seen them with two blue ticks). You too? I know not to go posting messages on social media immediately after ignoring a text. Actually, what am I talking about? I've disabled the setting that allows people to know when I'm online and active on various apps, such is my commitment to avoiding the discomfort that other humans present.

Of course, I share this so I can't be accused of lecturing from a pulpit; we all do it. But what are we doing exactly? We're avoiding the potentially ugly, confronting image in the proverbial mirror that another human always holds up to us when we interact face-to-face or show up emotionally. We're avoiding being vulnerable. We don't like the mirror; exposing our vulnerability is terrifying. But it's precisely this reflection in the other, and in the world, that has always tamed our worst impulses and held us accountable. An offended look on a friend's face makes us recognise our insensitivity. A smile can encourage our commitment to making changes within ourselves. Calling someone back when an issue is in our court, and apologising or front-footing things, sees us rise to our better selves. That's how we grow and become kinder humans.

We can use our devices to take the easy route in all kinds of not-so-admirable ways. A conversation gets dull, we pick up our phone (and scroll). We can preen our Instagram photos, whiten our teeth, smooth our skin, add a tan, to feed our vanity. We humblebrag and virtue signal. We get a bit stuck on a tricky paragraph in a work document, or have to make a hard phone call, so we refresh our feeds to see how 'liked' our last post has been. And, of course, we can troll, sink boots in and have the final word in a Twitter thread and never face the object of our cruelty, or be held accountable in any way because we can keep a hidden profile. We go for the cheap dopamine hits to the reptilian reward-centre of our brains – fast, junky recognition! – and keep going back for more and more – because it never actually satiates. We become chemically handcuffed to our worst behaviour.

So, back to the beautiful question: what can technology enable? It pains me horribly to declare it.

It enables our human smallness. Bugger.

19 I had been sitting in a bookshop café up the road, trying to nut through a writing rut over a glass of red wine on a Friday evening. I like to get discordant when I need a more expansive outlook. Which is to say I like to sit alone in odd places at odd times when most people are doing opposite things like coming home from work, feeding their kids or getting ready to go out for the night. My rut had got ugly and tunnelled. I needed some edge.

A group of three twenty-somethings drinking beetroot lattes were sitting at the same table, holding their phones up close to their smooth faces, flicking and poking their screens. They'd been to the beach and taken selfies; I could see the image on the screen of the girl next to me. She was wearing a bikini and kneeling on the sand in a flattering pose. I watched as she sculpted her inner thigh gap pixel by pixel. The others – a guy and a girl – were also preening their shots. They didn't look up or talk. Once or twice, they showed each other their handiwork. The guy told one of his friends,

'Wow, that's so authentic!' without really looking. I thought about what they'd do next. How, in an hour or so – peak traffic time – they'd upload and share the images with their virtual friends who would 'like' them, perhaps without really looking. They might spend the rest of their night checking to see just how liked it was, commenting and liking their friends' comments.

I sat there watching them and got fully Gen-X-judgemental. On the surface, they were hanging out and being pleasant. So why was I so disturbed? Psychologist Sherry Turkle coined the term 'alone together' to describe this kind of arm's-length connecting, whether it be via WhatsApp group chat or sitting side by side Face-tuning oneself in silent oblivion. It has its pleasant-enough benefits. But, as Turkle argues, it's a form of connecting that demands so little of us. Particularly any kind of vulnerability. This is the issue. I recognised the same cop-out behaviour in myself; that's why I was being judgemental. These young people were holding a mirror up to my own smallness.

As I walked home, I gave it all a name. Connection-lite. Connection-lite is the cheap, diet version of showing up to others and to life. It's when we answer a message with a wink emoticon to avoid giving our opinion or feedback. It's a copy-paste-forward 'How's it going?' text to six people late on a Friday afternoon instead of mindfully asking if they'd like to meet for an after-work drink. Connection-lite can provide us with fleeting, marshmallowy dopamine and oxytocin hits. And a vague sense of satisfaction that, *tick*, we've attended to some commitment or other. But like the diet version of anything, it leaves us hungry for the real thing. You know, full-fat life.

Say, 'I get you'

When we feel disconnected and undernourished, we can often fall into the trap of distancing ourselves further by hating on the nearest person living 'lite' in one form or another (pretending, avoiding, sending wink emoticons). I do it myself. I know a lot of us do as we grapple with the fragmentation going on around us. But I now use my judgey rage as a trigger to get me to come in closer. It goes like this: I feel the hot rage and judgement. Then I stop and I look at the people. I might see their pain, their lostness straight away. Sometimes I imagine them as a little child of seven so I can best see their vulnerability. My anger subsides and I feel compassion in its place.

I try to look into their eyes if they allow me. I make sure I'm smiling when I do. I do this at train stations, when I'm bustling down streets; I do it when I'm confronted by others who don't share my political values or scientific views, a situation that is increasingly causing division among us all. The technique never fails to connect me into our shared humanity. I soften. They soften.

Next, and for extra sturdy effect, I say to myself, 'I get you.'

I get you, young people poking at your devices because you grew up with the phone representing a sort of intimate comfort.

I get you, scared neighbour so terrified of death that you shut down talk of climate change to cope with being a functioning husband or parent.

I get you, acquaintance who makes fun of my passion for not wasting food every time you see me because perhaps you are feeling bewildered and, really, sometimes poking a person is the best way to get the information you need.

I get you. I repeat it over and over until I can feel a warmth come over me.

A lot of people I know are struggling with a disconcerting anger toward those who aren't yet ready to emerge from the shock and overwhelm of where we have landed. They want to connect, but their anger upsets and separates. I started to invite them to try this simple phrase, 'I get you.' They reported back that it shifted their perspective from judgement to compassion in a blink. I also suggested they use the phrase on themselves.

'I get you, vulnerable human, trying to find a way to rally humanity together, but with no handbook in sight.'

20 We might just go back to that café in Ljubljana briefly. On that stonkingly hot day, I was in a fretful place. For a bunch of reasons, which I'll get to. Nika, the gorgeous millennial publicist at my Slovenian publishing house, texted me while I was sitting there. Was I still in Slovenia? Would I like to join her and her friend Janez, a 55-year-old radical journalist and contemporary of the wild socialist philosopher Slavoj Žižek on a gondola ride above Lake Bohinj, an hour or so from Ljubljana? Janez, she told me, had asked to meet me to talk philosophy. I'd been reading Žižek! I love gondolas! Yes, I'm in! Nika came and picked me up 20 minutes later.

As the three of us rode up the mountain to the hiking town of Vogel, Janez talked madly, hair flapping. He's a kind and considered and supremely alive human. When he was younger, he was a nomad. He still has a nomadic spirit.

We talked about awe. 'I've lost my awe,' he said, 'because I'm too much in my head.' He asked me how I maintained my awe. 'I hike, and I accept gondola excursion invites from strangers,' I replied.

It's an extraordinary thing about this country – the genuine curiosity and engagement in the important stuff. There are poetry cafés, for instance, and I often saw teenagers reading the newspaper. I did a TV interview about sugar and I was asked to opine on Brexit. Slovenians still observe a Sabbath in a loose, non-religious sense. On Sundays everyone has picnics. Families hike. And I love their humour. In a government-issue tourist brochure, the intro reads 'Greetings from Slovenia… or is it Slovakia?' in full recognition of the fact that most foreigners get bamboozled by the annexing history of this region. Another pamphlet advises, 'Don't bother learning Slovenian during your stay, as we all know it's a bloody difficult language.' Countries with a history of trauma that have only recently had to redefine themselves beyond such conflict are often open and conscious and alive like this.

Back down the mountain my new friends take me to a

tavern with an outdoor garden overlooking sunflower fields. We order livers and local beer.

It's a perfect and random encounter, the kind that punctuates our stories on this planet with joyous exclamation marks. Humans are capable of this kindness and courage, of being 'big humans'. And it is our nature to reach out hungrily to a visitor and say, 'Come, let's connect!' The epic tales of history involve big souls reaching out to or taking in pilgrims and randoms everywhere from Ithaca to Bethlehem. The nature of travel also tends to more readily expose you to these kind of big human, curious, engaged and meaningful encounters. Paul Theroux wrote: 'Travel, its very motion, ought to suggest hope. Despair is the armchair; it is indifference and glazed, incurious eyes. I think travellers are essentially optimists, or else they would never go anywhere.'

After lunch Janez asked me why we've stopped thinking and challenging ourselves with philosophical thought. I used a metaphor. We are the overweight dude on the couch (or Theroux's armchair if you like). Modern life sees us spend our days consuming and indulging in convenience, without having to move. We order cheap fast food from our phones, we binge on entertainment on our screens-for-one (even watching a movie is no longer a communal experience), we have virtual relationships. And so little is demanded of us. Of course, we begin to atrophy from so much indulgence. We get sugar slumps and become foggy. But by now we are too toxic and dull to move. Or care. It's a bit like how at Christmas you eat so much that you fall into a food coma and when your sister-in-law suggests a walk around the block to get some fresh air, you honestly just can't. And so you consume some more (mince pies and *Everybody Loves Raymond* reruns).

I explained my theory that opulence, particularly in Australia (which had seen nearly thirty years of uninterrupted economic growth), has made us intellectually flaccid and un-vibrant. We are also some of the biggest consumers of social media in the world. A Harvard University study that looked at global economies and innovation found that Australia, paradoxically, was both one of the richest nations and the least innovative,...and that the former led to the latter. In his book *The Decadent Society: How We Became the Victims of Our Own Success, New York Times* columnist Ross Douthat points out that indulgence has led to stagnation: 'America is a more peaceable country than it was in 1970 or 1990 with lower crime rates and safer streets and better-behaved kids. But it's also a country where that supposedly most American of qualities, wanderlust, has markedly declined.

'We used to go to the moon; now we make movies about space.'

I told Janez, 'Modern life has enabled our depressing sloth. We are so fat on our individualism, materialism and vanity, we've fallen asleep intellectually, morally and spiritually.' I stabbed the last liver with my fork, suddenly aware that I'd gotten too ranty. And not so compassionate. And that I'd done what I often do – eat the last thing on the plate without doing the polite ask-around. 'But, you know, this is not how we want to be, it's not our nature to be so small,' I added. 'It

Since the publication of his book of course, gun violence has shifted this perspective somewhat.

Douthat adds that ours is the most medicated generation in history, with most drugs (marijuana and opioids) geared at numbing people out.

pains us. It really does.'

Janez clapped his hands and walked off into the sunflowers for a bit.

21 I'm going to pause now to discuss how this is all playing out in the dating world.

Our connection is arguably at its 'litest', and most cowardly, when we reach out to each other romantically online, which is where most dating happens now. With half the population single, it's applicable to enough of you here to hand over a chunk of space to the issue. And, besides, a lot of people in my orbit asked that I would. Everyone seems to find it fascinating.

Back in the olden days (pre-1990s), the dating stakes were terrifyingly high. Yet it was great! It was exhilarating! Scoring a date entailed procuring the other's number (by actually fronting up and asking for it), thinking through a time when said romantic interest might be home, knowing you ran the risk that their dad would pick up or you'd go through to a communal answering machine (such vulnerability! such courage!), and then making the big brash move of calling. And then (oh glory be) jumping from a great height and actually asking the other person out, concretely setting a time and place, painfully aware they might say no but doing it anyway. Because, as some of you will recall, you really only had one shot.

So, for instance, a bloke couldn't tyre-kick for a fortnight —

I use the example of a bloke here because for most of our history, it was the man's 'job' to court the woman, rightly or wrongly. And I use a heterosexual example to distinguish the two parties in the equation. Interchange for your own purposes!

61

with noncommittal texts like 'Maybe we could hang out?' or 'We should catch up for a drink sometime' or 'Let's try for Friday, but only if I happen to finish my DJ gig early…but let's see how it goes [insert wink emoticon, maybe the one with the love-hearted lips].' He couldn't test waters or hedge bets. Nope, he had to rise.

As a young woman, I was equally alert and scared when a guy 'showed up', but I'd reward his gallant efforts with a yes. I mean, that's what we did, within reason. It was a beautiful, delicate, uncomfortable dance. And once again we grew from it. We became bigger humans.

And now? I was recently on two dating apps, although I've tried most of them. And over the years I've dated men of many ages. And I can report from the front line that it's an entirely different game – 'game' being very operative here.

The cowardice kicks in at the outset. I match with someone. Neither of us make a move. I wait for him. He waits for me. We are all so horribly confused, aside from anything else, partly due to the supposed 'equality' our devices are meant to have bestowed upon us (one of the most popular dating apps requires the woman to make the first move, which totally scrambles the evolutionary equation).

Neither of us has to go out on a scary limb and risk rejection, risk looking the fool. So we kinda, oh, maybe, nah…don't. In the meantime, we keep scrolling. Add to the mix the entirely telling predilection for people to declare upfront in their descriptor that they are, gulp, in fact an introvert. Both men and women are putting their Myers-

I could legitimately say I signed up to the sites for research for a story. But honestly and vulnerably, I'm a hopeful romantic. I seek love and growth.

Briggs classification next to their star sign, although only if
it's an INTJ. I guess it flags to the world, 'Hey, don't expect
me to be the brave one.'

— INTJ is the most
introverted of the
classifications.

The smallness continues once some sort of flimsy contact
is made. We text back and forth. We might even meet IRL.
Millennial men, I have found, will tend to offer a commitment-
lite invite, like, 'We could get a coffee sometime, somewhere.'
Or sometimes just, 'Hey.' My impatience (and compassion)
sees me risk looking the fool (and get full-fat with things) by
suggesting a time and place. Which is often met with silence.
I've got too heavy.

When things in the online dating realm get uncomfortable
(which is what dating is, at its core) we can ghost each other
and never have to explain why.

— Ghosting happens
when one party
goes MIA in
text/ WhatsApp
etc. chats, never
to respond again.
He (or she) will
then unfollow
you on Instagram
for extra
avoidant effect.
This dynamic
tends to be
more of a bloke
phenomenon,
according to
the reports.

If you can bear with me, I'll explain another nuance that
drives home both our desire to connect, and the sadness of
the diet version we are reverting to. A while back someone
shared the meme, 'To all the boys who've wasted my time
and follow me every day on Stories.' I appreciate that this
meme may not resonate if you're not in the dating world, or
not on social media. So I'll explain. A bloke will ghost, then
disappear from a woman's social media feeds. But that same
bloke will then appear at the top of her 'views' in Instagram
Stories every single time she posts a new story, even though
he no longer follows her. Which is to say, her stories would
no longer automatically come up in his feed. He'd have to be
actively going to her profile to view them.

This made no sense to those who were observing the

phenomenon because generally only people who followed you would appear at the top. So, and this is super granular but stick with me, a Vox journalist investigated and found that Instagram algorithms at the time were such that the views were chronological for the first fifty only. After that Instagram prioritised people who viewed your profile the most. Ergo, these ghosters were obsessively visiting the profiles of the women they'd ghosted and had stopped following, presumably because they still cared at some level, albeit in an avoidant, lite, small manner. I can vouch for the phenomenon. At any one time I have a good half-dozen of my ghosts and no-shows at the top of my Stories. As we go to print, I note there are several apps you can buy that will track and expose your stalkers and ghosts. Which adds an even uglier dimension.

This is all a heavily millennial phenomenon. I don't highlight this in a finger-pointing way, it's compassion I feel. This generation simply doesn't know a time before this arm's-length way of connecting. It's not their fault. Similarly, I don't wish to come down on men. Truly. There are complex and very understandable reasons why men are perhaps struggling more than women in a connection-lite culture. And, besides, I notice we all become complicit eventually. This way is, after all, 'easier'.

This is 'small humanness' on steroids. So much so, I think the deeper despair single people are feeling is not so much for the want of another person. They're hankering for something bigger from their fellow human beings – and themselves – than this blancmange of noncommittal answers and uncourageous half invites.

I still use one of the apps. I have a bio that says I promise to engage in curious conversation. And that I don't dick people around. I would always say yes to courageous invites to meet IRL. Ghosts continue to lurk in my Stories. Sometimes they would re-emerge to half ask me out for a coffee somewhere sometime. I always said yes. 'Somewhere sounds great!' I'd say. With corona virus isolation, the acute loneliness experienced by singles, as well as the choicelessness imposed on physically meeting, saw a return to old-school dating etiquette. I read articles about how the virus and isolation actually provided a launchpad for lovely, considered chats about what matters in life. I noticed this, too.

Wonderfully, we're all here wanting to be bigger, more connected, less lonely, more humanised, don't you reckon?

Shall we dig further? Ask more beautiful questions?

the

C-bomb

22 We can swirl around finding ways to explain away our human smallness and moral asleepness, our loneliness and tediously awkward courtship behaviour and how it can be that we live in a world that can track our every consumer behaviour from a virtual cloud but fail to save its citizens from a virus that had been predicted for years because it can't produce enough simple cloth face masks. But eventually all roads lead back to the broken system we find ourselves in.

Ready for the C-bomb? That broken system is capitalism.

23 This is a big, highly charged issue. So let's get down small and close to talk it through.

I was grabbing a coffee from a café around the corner a while back. A construction supervisor was sitting next to me drinking his latte in a single-use cup while sitting in. I took the opportunity to ask him, gently, why he wasn't using crockery.

I should explain that I used to turn rabid when I encountered someone with a disposable takeaway coffee cup that gets used once before ending up in landfill. It wasn't big of me and so I took to using such moments as a radical self-betterment practice – I felt the rage and used it to trigger compassion ('I get you. I get you.'). I know an activist who uses Trump tweets in a similar way.

I guess swapping a single-use, disposable cup for a reusable one, or simply drinking your latte sitting in, represents one of the easiest, 'low-hanging fruit' consumer switches we can make to try to steer the ship right. So why don't we just do it?

By now we should all know that it takes at least 400 years for a coffee cup lid to decompose (actually, we don't know this; every bit of plastic ever created still sits somewhere on the planet, increasingly in the guts of whales, fish and our children, and it's possible that it will never break down), and that most of the cups themselves are also lined in plastic. We also know that most of the lids contain BPA, a known endocrine disruptor (linked to breast and prostate cancer, early puberty, obesity, autism and fertility issues) that has been banned in many other products.

And the recyclable takeaway cups? Well, we should be aware they're not being recycled in much of the world. In 2018 China stopped accepting recycling from the United States, Australia and a bunch of other western nations.

Primarily due to it being so poorly sorted.

The bulk of our recycling is now being sent to landfill or stockpiled until someone can find a solution. Even pre-2018, only 9 per cent of plastic was being recycled.

Oh, and the biodegradable cups? Hmmm, well a University of Pittsburgh study found that the production processes rendered them more polluting than standard single-use cups. There're the fertilisers and pesticides used in growing the sugarcane and cornstarch from which the cups are made; the chemicals used in processing; and the fact that the discarded end product is rarely broken down in proper composting facilities (do you take yours home and dig it responsibly into your compost?). Most end up in landfill or recycling stockpiles, where, deprived of oxygen, they release methane, a greenhouse gas twenty-eight times more potent than carbon dioxide.

And even if we don't know all of this, or we disagree on climate change science or the severity of our situation, we should be clocking that single-use anything will always come with a horrible price. Resources were used, burned, polluted to make it. And to transport it. And store it. All so that we can use once and chuck.

And there I go, using a whole bunch of rage-ish 'shoulds' in the space of five short paragraphs. As I say, I'm working on it.

Anyway. Back to the latte-sipping construction supervisor. This guy was in his late twenties and had a lovely, open demeanour. He was on a smoko, so we drilled things down

Aussie cigarette break —

together. His initial response was that it was just a habit. Which he quickly realised was pretty lame. He threw up a few more excuses. Then he paused and stared into his endocrine-disrupting, morally bankrupt milky soup. 'I guess I have to accept I just don't care enough.' He sounded sad, resigned, despondent. I felt sad with him.

But his conclusion made sense to me. When we care enough, we do tend to fire up and change our behaviour. But I'd like to suggest something here. And I hope the dude reads this one day. What if it's not that we don't care enough. What if, instead, something was preventing us from caring enough, caring as much as our hearts are longing to, whether it be about landfill or giraffe extinction.

— I just learned his name is Caine. He sang out to me from the other side of the street to tell me he now owns a KeepCup. I told him he features in my book.

Another drop of the C-bomb: I pose really rather unequivocally that this something is capitalism.

24 Me, I grew up wary of capitalism. Dad would voice his criticisms to my brothers, sister and me, although not in a ranty way. We'd discuss the goods and services tax at the dinner table over goat goulash. Or he'd explain to us why he moved us out to the country to live a semi-subsistence life (with goats for milk and eating). He said it was because he thought – or hoped – capitalism was doomed. He abhorred suburbia and consumption, and Thatcherism and Reaganomics. He was still stuck in the system, though. He rode a motorbike into town each day to work a desk job. It was the middle of a drought back then and we had to buy water from town when the tanks ran dry. Ironically, it was this reality that tipped the family over the financial edge and sent us back to suburbia when I was in my teens.

But it wasn't until I stepped out on this journey here with you now that I got a feel for how deeply unhappy and disconnected from life capitalism is now making us.

And how reluctant we all are to talk about it. Which, I realise, is why we stay so entrenched and lonely and overwhelmed.

I mean, for a long time, like most people who grew up in the shadow of the Cold War, I got awkward just dropping the C-bomb, even in passing. As in, 'That's an interesting capitalist perspective.' It conjures images of unwashed types charging around university campuses in Violent Femmes t-shirts. It labels you 'extreme' and even deluded. Perhaps a 'raving inner-city lunatic'. But that's the real power of a regime or cult – its ability to render its power unquestionable, or worse, invisible. At times, I've observed myself on social media chickening out of dropping the C-bomb. I often temper my anti-consumer opinions lest I appear too extreme and unwashed. I'll chuck on a cute emoticon at the end of a spiel. We're all good, yeah?

But I began to see a shift. A growing skepticism. A pervasive pissed-offness that invariably emerges within a system when human freedom is squeezed too far. And, of course, when COVID-19 struck it became a frothing what-the-fuckness, for there is nothing like a crisis to expose a system's weakness. I met Teena, a 32-year-old mum who'd

A line from Australia's Deputy Prime Minister, — referring to those of us who wanted the government to discuss the recent Australian bushfires as a climate change issue. And, yes, the same guy who made the 'exploding horse manure' comment on page 15.

70

seen some of my emoticon-ed rants and approached me in a bookshop to say, 'I'm glad you're talking about it.' By 'it', she meant capitalism. She couldn't actually bring herself to utter the C-bomb, either. 'We need to be shown the words for it,' she told me.

CNN recently reported that 66 per cent of Americans aged 21–32 have nothing saved for retirement. Not because they're being irresponsible millennials. Nope, they think capitalism will no longer exist when they're sixty. The young people interviewed said they expected a massive collapse of the system in the coming decade or two. A Harvard University study found the majority of Americans across all age groups, apart from the baby boomers, were against capitalism. A UK YouGov poll found that 64 per cent of Britons believe that capitalism is unfair; in Germany, 77 per cent of people are skeptical of it.

The distrust and despair are most palpable among the generation down from the millennials. Understandably. These are the kids following Greta Thunberg and the school strikes and who greet those over fifty-fives in that Harvard study with the dismissive, 'Okay, boomer.' These are the kids who are looking squarely at what the more-more-more setup means for their future, and they have no room in their souls for awkwardness. The slogans on their placards directly name and shame capitalism.

One of my favourite sports is to witness erstwhile free marketeers wake up to capitalism – often middle-aged men who go on to write books and start podcasts about their awakening. Angus Deaton, a 2015 Nobel Laureate in economics, recently wrote that capitalism is 'visibly sick', and that a push toward socialism or democratic socialism is growing in America. Marc Benioff, chief executive of cloud computing company Salesforce, has declared that 'capitalism as we know it is dead'. Ray Dalio, the hedge fund billionaire, recently wrote an essay on LinkedIn declaring that capitalism 'is not working well for the majority of Americans'.

A few years back, Paul Krugman, an economist and *New York Times* columnist (and Distinguished Professor of Economics at the Graduate Center of the City University of New York) began publishing columns asking 'But I've been wondering, exactly how discredited is socialism, really?' In another article he asked, 'Have we really established that markets are the best way to do everything? Should everything be done by the private sector? I don't think so.'

As central banks struggle to predict and manage inflation, many more rationally minded economists have been forced to question the mechanics and modelling they'd relied on. The interruption was rude.

25 Capitalism is not inherently evil. I suppose it started out as a force for good. It has brought better democratic processes, health and prosperity to a lot of the world. But, as with many regimes after some time, it's wound up failing us.

I have to confess that, prior to COVID-19, I'd struggled to find a way to convincingly expose and describe the stinking disaster that capitalism had become and the threat it was presenting to our survival on this planet. It's hard to show something is broken when you're in it. But then we were unceremoniously plucked from the spinning cogs and suddenly, from our pared-back, isolated outposts, many of us were able to view things with fresh eyes. We could see the system for what it was – a brutal yet fragile construction that had largely landed us in this viral mess. This prized market system saw us define ourselves by our careers, which were suddenly yanked from many of us. It saw healthcare run on purely economic concerns, leaving hundreds of millions of us as vulnerable as 14th century peasants during the plague, while globalisation and long supply chains left us without simple face masks.

From our little subsistence cocoons, suspended on 'pause' from all the shopping and running around trying to keep up with each other, we were also afforded this unique and stark opportunity to see how unjust and cruel capitalism had become. Our survival depended on the victims of the exploitative system – the UberEats cyclists delivering meals, and grocery workers and bus drivers who had to keep working, the migrants and racially marginalised communities who care for the elderly and our kids, and the underpaid health workers, teachers and scientists. So we had to take note. We had to observe how these fellow humans at the front line (whom we cheered from balconies and dedicated Instagram tiles to) were also the least protected – often with no health insurance, no income protection, no savings, and often with compromised immunity.

A disaster doesn't so much break a system as show how broken it already was. As the actor Danny Glover said of Hurricane Katrina, 'When the hurricane struck the Gulf and the floodwaters rose and tore through New Orleans, plunging its remaining population into a carnival of misery, it did not turn the region into a Third World country, as it has been disparagingly implied in the media; it revealed one. It revealed the disaster within the disaster; gruelling poverty rose to the surface like a bruise to our skin.' Oh yeah!

But like I say, we need to get granular with something so pervasive. Shall we do it with some simple math?

As a reasonable person walking around the planet today, you can probably see that the very premise of capitalism's more-more-more model no longer stacks up, if it ever could. The supply-and-demand system casually assumes the availability of infinite resources for a never-ending and exponential cycle of consumption and growth. But we're reasonable and we know how to add and subtract. We know that if you consume, consume, consume, stuff runs out.

We currently consume the resources of five planet Earths. Some estimates say seven and a half planet Earths. This is clearly not a sustainable model by anyone's books.

Apparently, goes the capitalist promise, we demand $5 T-shirts, so the fast fashion stores supply them. In this tacit arrangement, the stores churn out more and more cheap tees to be able to pay for the cotton, the chemicals, the water and wages to keep up with demand and the low margin.

Perfectly, these tees are made from poor-quality cotton, so look like rags after just a few washes and we feel the need to buy more. More demand. More supply. Of the materials flowing through the consumer economy right now, only 1 per cent remains in use six months after sale.

It all appears to work to a swimmingly succinct equation, even if it does seem a bit hectic. Except, um, hang on, stuff runs out. Plus, the fashion industry produces 20 per cent of global waste water and more carbon emissions than all international flights and maritime shipping combined. If nothing changes, by 2050 the fashion industry will use up a quarter of the world's carbon budget. And the cotton in that $5 tee is the world's single largest pesticide-consuming crop, using 24 per cent of all insecticides and 11 per cent of all pesticides globally.

But here's the thing. We keep buying the fast, cheap tees.

We've also seen the videos online of turtles knotted up in beer can ties and dead whales with 40 kilograms of disposable beach toys and shopping bags in their guts. We know that by 2050 there will be more plastic in the ocean than fish. And that we ingest a credit card-sized amount of plastic every week through our drinking water, seafood and fish. Plastic doesn't break down and a third of all plastic ends up in nature in micro form, and we eat it up.

— Although I should flag that even before corona virus, fashion retail had taken a dive, see page 390.

Yet a recent study shows that as awareness of plastic pollution increases bottled water consumption has in fact gone up globally. Ditto single-use coffee cups. Oh, and the purchase of oversized cars. As I posted on an Instagram tile,

'When the apocalypse comes, we'll all be driving SUVs.' And this rant doesn't touch on the chemicals that leach from the plastic into the water, or the fact that in many countries bottled water contains more toxins than the local tap-water reservoirs it's taken from, or the carbon miles involved when we insist on shipping it from Fiji, or the fact that one-third of Fiji's population has no access to clean water as a result, and so on.

What is going on? Do we not care? And why were we not talking about this, like, really loudly?

26 Okay, so let's unpack things a little more. It may be a bit dry and confronting, but let's do it anyway. I ran this chunk of the book past a young guy I met at a vegan smoothie bar in Mammoth Lakes, California, where I was writing. The kid was drinking some sort of modern sweet beverage (vegan) from a single-use plastic bottle and was unlucky enough to sit next to me, exposing himself to one of my (gentler) confrontations. He was cool with it and asked to read 'more of that stuff you just banged on about'. I gave him the very rough draft of this chapter. When he was done, I asked if he found it too dry, too confronting. He didn't.

Right then.

We are communal beings. We need to belong to a tribe to survive and thrive. Yet we are also inherently selfish. And we tend to veer toward rampant self-interest if given a fifth of a rampant chance. Albeit to survive and thrive. So we live within an interesting evolutionary tension. Or paradox.

But being the smart mammals that we are, we've found ways to traverse this paradox. Throughout our evolution we have put in place structures to keep our individualism in check. We invented wonderful myths and mores, helpful religions and political doctrines, to encourage kindness and generosity – via a bunch of moral codes – so that we didn't destroy the community and the fabric of our culture and immediate tribe.

Gods and heroes steered us from wrong to right by example. Spiritual leaders – Buddha, Jesus, Lao Tzu, Mohammed – wove a code of behaviour through parable and commandment. Religion told us to not kill each other and applied basic lifestyle edicts, such as observing a Sabbath. An enforced day of rest protected us, gave us space to connect with each other, ourselves, with life and our spiritual core. Shops stayed shut on Sunday and half of Saturday.

We also had trade unions, human resource departments, charities and community associations that enforced our collective moral code. Governments implemented universal education and healthcare and set up competition watchdogs and tribunals to protect us from inequality. Oh, and an independent judiciary and media that kept all the bastards honest.

These structures served as our moral umpires on the footy field of life. They blew the whistle on too much greed, they white-carded corporations that crash-tackled a minority group, and sin-binned polluters.

And it all served to save us from that dreaded moral loneliness, or acedia.

Then capitalism joined the game.

It kicked off in the late 17th century and hit its stride during the Industrial Revolution in the 19th century. As I said, capitalism, like religion or communism, isn't intrinsically bad. It started out with the intention of freeing us from the strictures of religion (which had become corrupt and was thus failing in its moral umpire role) and conservative social norms and did largely raise incomes, life expectancy, literacy and equality to some extent.

Cut to the 1960s and 1970s and capitalism stepped up a notch, primarily in the United States, United Kingdom and also Australia, playing out as neo-liberalism. We saw the 'free market' mindset extended to every part of our lives. Competition and individualism were regarded as the defining characteristics of human relations and citizens became consumers whose democratic choices were best exercised by buying and selling.

Neo-liberalism became focused on kicking the moral umpires off the field, or at the very least confiscating their whistles, so individuals could do as they needed. Umpires, particularly those funded by governments or 'taxpayer dollars', got in the way of the free market. So, neo-liberalist policy got rid of parks, libraries and other services that united us as a community. We've all seen this happen in our lifetimes, it's not unfamiliar, right? Corporate dollars convinced governments to switch from being providers of universal healthcare and free tertiary education to promoters and enablers of markets and competition. Academics and scientists, once respected for their objective 'rightness', were devalued as 'the chattering class', the 'intellectual elite'. We were told to play the game as 'free' individuals, no holds barred.

To bring back in the moral disconnection we're exploring here, according to historian Fay Bound Alberti in her book *A Biography of Loneliness*, modern loneliness is the child of capitalism, a direct product of individualism and secularism that saw privacy become something you buy. She highlights this fascinating point – loneliness didn't exist as a word or concept in our culture until the 19th century. 'It is not a coincidence,' she writes.

So here's the bit I've been working toward. In proactively encouraging individualism, capitalism eroded our sense of society, and with it our sense of connected belonging. In 1987 Margaret Thatcher declared, 'there's no such thing as society'. And that was that. Most of us today grew up with this neo-liberal flavour of capitalism, which proclaims that we succeed when we pull ourselves up by our bootstraps and that getting rid of Medicare and public-run utilities and telecom services is a win against what was once called fair governance but now disparaged as the 'nanny state.' And that growth is king, and we have to keep consuming and consuming to arrive at our better life.

27 The rising tide of more-more-more was meant to lift all ships, we were told. The market system, comprising individual consumers left to their own devices, was to bring increased opulence to everyone. Yeah. Well. We know how that went. With each year, the rich are getting exponentially richer and the poor poorer. During the pandemic the ten richest men on the planet doubled their fortunes, while the incomes of 99 per cent of humanity fell. Since then, as the cost-of-living crisis deepens, the world's 1 per cent have captured 63 per cent of all new wealth.

Studies show that neo-liberalism has directly caused misery and despair and sharp declines in physical – particularly via obesity – and mental health for the majority. Yes, the majority. (We should bear in mind that capitalism and globalisation also landed us in the COVID-19 crisis. There is also an intersection between these forces and the issues that the Black Lives Matter protests brought to light. And it cannot be ignored: capitalism was built on the unpaid labour of enslaved workers.)

And if that's not enough, the meritocracy, bootstrap-pulling nature of the system meant that we blamed ourselves for not coping and for not being rich and famous and self-actualised, for not being 'happy' and successful people. The message is entrenched. Cognitive scientist Steven Pinker leads a crew of commentators determined to push the 'life is good, you're just choosing to be miserable' line. In *Enlightenment Now*, which Bill Gates cites as his favourite book of all time, Pinker helpfully provides a tirade of factlets, including how more of us have access to the Internet, fewer of us are enslaved, we live longer (um, if you're willing to ignore the generation dying of those 'diseases of despair'), how we're all less likely to be killed by a bolt of lightning than we were a century ago and how time spent doing laundry has fallen from 11.5 hours in 1920 to 1.5 hours in 2014.

But of course, we are human. And we yearn to live – not just survive – in a connected world among a tribe. It's in our nature, as I've said already. So, when the evolutionary tension between self-interest and community welfare gets out of whack with all those rampant individuals running around the field buying up towns, knocking down public libraries and killing coral reefs, we cry out for the umpire. Surely someone is meant to step in and do something? We do the same when Big Food takes over the school canteen system. And when the banks cause a worldwide financial meltdown and those in charge not only get off scot-free but also expect to be bailed out. And after other such corruptions and hypocrisies. Who's at fault here? Who's meant to fix this?

Ah, well, according to the neo-liberal individualistic model, the answer to that one, comrades, is the individual – you and me. Having gotten rid of the moral umpires, the neo-liberal system has left the gargantuan role of navigating these kinds of mammoth quandaries squarely on our shoulders. We are expected – as individuals – to do the job that massive institutions used to do. All while trying to keep roofs over heads and meals on tables and coping with being human. Oh, and dealing with the overwhelm, guilt and blame.

This is despairingly, panic-raisingly too much.

I've fallen for this 'we're to blame' mindset. Take my takeaway coffee cup rage. I've let myself be convinced that we – the consumers – are responsible for solving the climate emergency by recycling, and using reusable cups, when 71 per cent of carbon emissions are contributed by 100 corporations, and governments are failing to provide infrastructure (like building large-scale recycling facilities) to support our various earnest efforts. I observed the soft drink industry a few years back, when finally forced to face the fact that their products were killing us, introduce the 'calories in/calories out' argument. The industry paid for 'studies' that showed too much sugar might be a bit of a problem (!), but if you burnt off the calories doing exercise, there was no problem. Getting fat and sick? It's your fault; you're not going to the gym enough. Which we might be able to stomach except the calories in/calories out science was a complete fabrication. Seriously, it's faux science funded and disseminated to dupe us into feeling guilty. It was a stupendously deft neo-liberal manoeuvre and we fell for it, convinced obesity was about a deficiency in personal willpower.

And what about when a global pandemic strikes and suddenly people lose their jobs and then a cost-of-living crisis hits, and we discover one in three Brits lives pay check to pay check, with a quarter of households unable to pay for food and electricity, and suddenly – like overnight – we are being told our survival now depends on principles of solidarity and uniting in community… Who's meant to fix *that*? Which community leader, which moral principle will 'bring us all together' just like that? Which village square are we going to gather in?

And what about when the salve – our survival – depends on the very community structures and 'umpires' that were decimated by neo-liberalism: broad-based welfare, universal healthcare, mental health support, scientists with proper funding whom we now rely on to invent a vaccine?

How do a bunch of isolated, competing individuals navigate such a collective clusterfuck?

28 *New York Times* columnist David Brooks was a raging market economist and conservative for most of his life. Then he published a book about his own awakening to the capitalist con. In *The Second Mountain*, he argues that this privatisation of meaning – the requirement that we map out and enforce our own moral code – is impossible for the average human. 'Unless you're [philosopher] Nietzsche,' he writes, 'it's a homework assignment that none of us can complete.'

And that's at the best of times.

So we turn acedic and revert to our default position – being entirely, rampantly individualistic. That delicate evolutionary tension – between our self-interest and our need to belong to a community – is totally thrown. Brooks argues that we wind up 'following our unrestrained selfish desires to our unhappiest conclusions…online bullying, the rape and pillage of the planet, the gunning down of schoolchildren.'

And, you could — argue, fighting over toilet paper in supermarkets.

Capitalism has caused the moral aloneness and asleepness we are feeling. Capitalism dehumanised us and led to our behaving as small humans. Capitalism has disconnected us.

Rallying together to save our lives – from a virus, from cruel inequalities, from those diseases of despair, from the destruction of the planet – will require some wild imagining and creating and becoming beyond capitalism.

Boom! C-bomb dropped. From a great height!

THE HEIDIDORF HIKE: SWITZERLAND

When I was six, Santa brought me *Heidi* by Johanna Spyri. Dad covered it in plastic and wrote my name on the inside cover. It was my favourite book. Orphan Heidi (the story goes) was fobbed off by her career-focused aunt and sent to live with her gruff grandfather high in the Swiss Alps. The two of them drank goat's milk together and ate warm bread and imbibed the sweet mountain air. Heidi ran wild in the meadows and didn't have to go to school. To me, the pages of the book smelled of ripe grass and goat hair. And freedom.

I need only think of the book, or encounter a goat, and my heart turns light. A mere whiff of mountain air triggers a cosy nostalgia. So, a few years ago I set out to experience this smell, in its full verdantness. The book, I learned, was set outside a small village called, I'm not kidding, Heididorf, not far from St Moritz. It gets quainter. While on the Googles trying to find the place, I zoomed in on a nearby village in the Fex Valley, about an hour's walk away, where no cars are allowed. To this day the only way to get in and out of the village is by foot or horse and carriage. On the map, a web of hiking trails spin out from the valley and up and across narrow and inviting contour lines.

I arrive in the small cobblestoned town of Sils Maria and walk an hour to an inn in the Fex along a winding path. The farmhouses along the way have thatched roofs and window boxes bulging with flowers. Gingham curtains tied with bows drape from the tiny windows. The rolling hills are iridescent and sway with buttercups – a veritable *Blütenmeer* (sea of petals). I'm in Heidi territory and I'm greeted at Hotel Sonne Fex (run by four generations of the same family) with schnapps and a plate of goat's cheese and warm bread. I want to tie my hair in plaits! I want to run through a meadow!

I spend the next few days setting off from the inn following paths up to mountain-top lakes and lookouts. I'm joined by the familiar apple-green and fire engine-red Gortexed leagues of couples in their fifties and sixties who go at a hill with a Nordic trekking pole like Prince Charming to a wall of brambles. They descend upon you in alpine country around the world, all tanned sinewy calves, jangling with aluminium bottles and carabiners. For decades I've watched them, giving a hiker's nod and smile as I pass in my decidedly amateurish getup, my snacks and mobile phone stuffed down my bra.

This breed of hiker, I like to think, is a study in what the hills can do to a person. You head off, kitted out, a strident, striding human, top of the food chain, in charge of your destiny and determined to conquer the world with your carbon-fibre accoutrements. You charge at the mountain, your Apple Watch ready to count your caloric achievement. But then something happens. After a few hours – or maybe it takes a full day – of wrapping along its contours, absorbing its geometric rhythms, you succumb to the mountain. This behemoth, this original thing, doesn't exist to be conquered. I mean, who do we think we are? If I were to describe how I feel once this succumbing happens, it's like the mountain wants to hug me. Really it does.

As I wind around the switchbacks, a centrifugal force pulls me in and envelopes my being and my thoughts. Suddenly I cease focusing on the exertion and resistance. I stop thinking about arriving or my fatigue or when I should stop to eat more chocolate. And the raw energy of this original thing steps in. It's colossal. And it is always there, just waiting for me to shut up and join it.

I reflect on this while I climb the peaks above Fex each day. I get to the top and sit for a while, looking out over a vast expanse, across to the next thing hundreds of metres away, and it feels like my mountain is sitting alongside me, quietly, majestically watching the same expanse. There are few such truly solid moments in connected experience that can compare to watching distance with a mountain.

A mountain's not going anywhere and invites you to do the same.

In the village back down the mountain at the end of day, their jumble of Nordic poles propped nearby, the Gortexed tribe are transformed. They're soft in the face. The blood in their cheeks looks jolly as they drink hot chocolate and beer. I love that everyone experiences the same connection when they hang with a mountain long enough. We nod at each other in mutual understanding. That's why we keep coming back.

My friend Libby joins me to do the Heididorf hike at the end of my Fex Valley stay. We've known each other since our late teens when we'd do awkward shopping mall fashion parades together. She now lives in Zurich. We meet in Sils Maria early to have coffee and a pastry then set out around the lake to a path that heads upward to Grevasalvas and then onto the Via Engiadina.

Libby and I connect once every five years or so, but more frequently in recent years. She had kids young and we meet in our mid-forties in a similar place, wanting to discuss similar stuff. How shall we make life richer? How can we best be of service?

Those of you who have read the book will know that Heidi's A-type aunt eventually forces poor orphan Heidi back to city life in Frankfurt to be schooled in the home of a rich family. Capitalism-fuelled industrialisation is in full swing and Heidi is miserable conforming to city life, rife as it is with pollution, alienation, inequality and greed. She becomes psychologically sick and stressed, and the doctor suggests that she returns to the mountains to heal and to, indeed, return to herself. This was a common salve in the 19th century. I'm always reading about philosophers or artists from this era being sent off to the countryside, mostly the mountains, and often in Switzerland, to recover from some illness (psychological and/or physical) caused by the city (read: industrialisation). They were prescribed constitutionals (healing walks).

I realise as we hike around Heididorf that Heidi was probably my first introduction to the human yearning to reject the alienating more-more-more system. And to the power of the mountains as the antidote; of nature as healer.

As we come over the final rise of the day, we see Heididorf nestled in a dell below. It looks frozen in time, all wooden barns and cobblestones. Libby yodels for me. It's a melancholy, primal sound, a yodel. It reaches the churning confusion at our core and draws it out into the open air. It's best gurgled outdoors where it can connect us to the awe of the mountains, the expanse of the sky, the depth of it all.

We head back down the hill to Maloja, and to the bus to Sils Maria.

On my last day in Sils Maria I noticed a cottage in the centre of town where German philosopher Friedrich Nietzsche had lived when he wrote *Thus Spoke Zarathustra* – his seminal work famously (mis)appropriated by the Nazis to form the philosophical foundation of their Aryan race ideology.

As it happens, Nietzsche came to Sils Maria in 1881 to heal from his particularly nebulous illness (a combination of migraines, psychiatric disturbances, neurosyphilis and stroke). And to hike. Each day he would do long walks in the mountains – along the same trails I'd been wandering the past week or so – carrying a notepad and pencil and composing much of his work while in motion. 'All truly great thoughts are conceived by walking,' he famously wrote, as I quoted earlier. The cottage is now a very earnest museum housing a bunch of his letters and notes. And it literally sits at the start of the path to the Fex Valley. I'd missed it in my haste to walk.

I find it perfect and wondrous that at the same time *Heidi* was being penned, Nietzsche was channelling a similar collective angst from just over the hill. I'm not sure if this juxtaposition has been highlighted by others, but I love that this young girl (Heidi) and this cranky philosopher both felt the deep existential despair that had descended from the social and moral upheaval across 19th century Europe. All the old ways – Christianity and bourgeois hierarchies – were being dismantled and the more-more-more malaise was in full centrifugal spin. It could render a kid like Heidi sick and mad. Nietzsche and a number of intellectuals including Rousseau and Voltaire were scrambling to articulate the despair and how to cure it. All three hiked, by the way, as they did so.

'God is dead,' Nietzsche famously declared in 1882, as

— Fun fact: Nietzsche's writing room in the cottage overlooks a chalet where – wait for it – Anne Frank would visit her 'great aunt' around the time the Nazis were poring over *Thus Spoke Zarathustra*.

SARAH WILSON

a simultaneous conclusion and explanation. This death was
to his mind a good thing. Religion had given us all a leave
pass on moral responsibility and stopped us thinking for
ourselves.

Now that it was disintegrating as scientific thinking
took hold, we humans were free to create our own moral
doctrines. Hoorah! We would be masters of our rights and
wrongs!

But the end of religion was also a bad thing, according to
Nietzsche, mostly because he believed the average human
was incapable of creating their own moral code and applying
it, as Brooks described more than a century later. Nietzsche
fretted we were too feeble and too wired toward selfishness
to pave a way to 'right' rather than 'wrong'. And so, he
predicted, we would be left with a moral vacuum. This idea
saw Nietzsche slide into a wild panic on our behalf.

The guy then — very literally — developed a premonition
of where we are today. Check this for size...

He foresaw a terrifying 'rootlessness' and loneliness that
would take hold in the absence of the 'guardrails' that religion
once provided. He wrote that we would abandon the task of
doing the right, productive thing and descend into numb
and avoidant mediocrity. (Imagine his horror to see us scroll
and scroll as the planet burned...)

We would 'invent happiness' to avoid the tough decisions.
(Indeed, happiness has become an industry and generally
serves to bypass facing the painful bits of life, but more on
this soon.)

His desperate rants referred to a 'meek mindlessness' and an absorption in 'little pleasures', even an obsession with health. (The guy was visionary!)

He termed this meek, resultant being 'the last man'.

'"What is love? What is creation? What is longing? What is a star?" thus asks the last man, and he blinks,' he wrote. Sound familiar? When confronted with the beautiful questions, with nuance, with depth, the last man shuts off and goes numb (you can bet he'd have scrolled if he could). Nietzsche termed it nihilism, describing a world where the question 'Why?' finds no answer. 'I describe what is coming, what can no longer come differently: the advent of nihilism… For some time now our whole European culture has been moving us toward a catastrophe.'

It really is quite uncanny that 140-odd years ago the guy foresaw the coming of the Instagram influencer who wears a 'There is no Planet B' sweater while drinking a green smoothie in a plastic cup with a plastic straw and who loudly declares they're not interested in politics.

Nietzsche also predicted that we'd be too scared to question it all, to drop the C-bomb. 'No shepherd and one herd! Everybody wants the same, everybody is the same: whoever feels different goes voluntarily into a madhouse,' he wrote.

Again, I find all this enlivening. And wonderfully (albeit oddly), it allows room for much-needed compassion. Nietzsche's prediction, and the beautifully confronting debate many commentators are now having around capitalism and its ability to guide us forward, confirms there's a reason why we are feeling morally alone. It's not our nature to be this way, which suggests, equally, it doesn't have to stay this way. And, you know what? This triggers a fire in me. We actually might be able to bust this popsicle stand! As US author and essayist Ursula K Le Guin declared: 'We live in capitalism, its power seems inescapable. But then, so did the divine right of kings. Any human power can be resisted and changed by human beings.'

29 In an op-ed for the *Guardian*, British writer and activist George Monbiot made a point that has stuck with me and that I come back to over and over: 'To be at peace with a troubled world: this is not a reasonable aim.'

Monbiot continued: 'If you don't fit in, if you feel at odds with the world, if your identity is troubled and frayed, if you feel lost and ashamed it could be because you have retained the human values you were supposed to have discarded. You are a deviant. Be proud.'

A *deviant*.

Wow. I wasn't quite sure what to make of such a wild notion at first. But I smiled reading it, like I always do when a brave soul puts words to a thing that resonates at an awkwardly private level. It felt deviant to just consider that I might be a deviant.

We've been well-behaved economic units for so long we've forgotten that this is actually what humans do. You know, deviate. When systems create suffering for the majority, we buck them and evolve. Dr Martin Luther King Jr stood up and changed the course of history. Rosa Parks, a 42-year-old Black mother and seamstress, sat down and issued the now famous line, 'knowing what must be done does away with fear.' A 13-year-old French peasant girl woke up and led her country to freedom. 'I am not afraid... I was born to do this,' Joan of Arc is said to have declared.

These moments in deviance go down in history, they define our sense of morality, belonging, society.

Over the course of this journey, the appeal of being deviant became stronger and more vibrant for me. We can feel proud, not bewildered and ashamed that we are anxious and despairing. And we don't have to feel alone. Because we are meant to buck this despairing wrongness...together.

30 Before we move on, I'm going to pick up on something I've flagged a few times, perhaps a little offhandedly and even self-consciously (because it is deviant to even suggest such an idea).

Capitalism is like a cult.

Actually, I'm going to own this fully deviantly.

Capitalism *is* a cult.

We've become so ensconced in it, however, so blind to its power, that it's hard to see it as such. Which is how a cult is imposed on people. I mean, we can't fathom that there could be any other way of existing and we defend it even when we can see it is no longer working for us.

I sat on a ferry heading into the city through Sydney's iconic harbour as Australia headed into Stage 3 shutdown and we could only move about to buy essentials and attend medical appointments. I always sit on the outside benches, no matter the weather. I looked across the water at what we'd created. Massive homes lurching over huge pools, layer upon layer. Towers and antennas. Garages the size of homes, housing cars. Cars. We once lived happily without them. Then we drove them only when we really needed to. Then it became completely normal to drive them to the gym down the road to sit on a stationary bike. Then drive them back again. And we don't even question how mad this is. Nor how mad it is that we buy air freshener (which pollutes the fresh air with dangerous chemicals) or buy diced fruit in plastic pouches because we're told it's perfect for lunchboxes (when an apple or a banana already comes in a lunchbox-ready skin). We don't question dryer sheets or the notion of pumping our lips and faces with toxins manufactured by a drug company, because the pumped-up look has been deemed desirable by, um, yep the drug company. We don't fight back when handheld device behemoths change the hole that your earphones go into, forcing you to buy new ones.

I looked at the beautiful gardens and ancient fig trees and palms. The boat ramps, the boats that cost as much as a home and are sailed a few times a year (if at all). And the boats used by the caretakers of the boats that are out on the harbour, polishing the boats (that don't set sail). It was all beautiful and absurd. From a ferry, with the Pixies' 'Where Is My Mind?' playing in my earphones, the beauty and absurdity was appreciable. And my thoughts expansive and free-roaming.

And I reflected...we can easily point to the stunts employed by cult leaders and other dictators to keep the masses unquestioning – the drugs, the militia, the gurus and the unrealistic promises of salvation. But we struggle to see that the capitalist system does the same. Like any cult, we can't see we're in one. We genuinely believe ads (propaganda) that tell us we need a $3,000 handbag or oversized black SUV (to be saved from irrelevance, emptiness). We unquestioningly accept messages (brainwashing) that success is about 'getting ahead on the property ladder', that we are 'worth it' – 'it' being a whopping great mortgage, overseas trip or sunglasses that cost more than a small car. Then we make payments (sacrifices), often going into debt for said dwelling, adventure or eyewear. Soon enough we're thoroughly beholden (to the credit card repayments and lock-in contracts). Other characteristics of a cult, according to Dr Robert Jay Lifton, include economic and sexual exploitation, a culture that quashes nuance and leaves followers feeling they can never be good enough.

In his bestselling book *Sapiens*, Yuval Noah Harari traces much of our blind acceptance of the capitalist model to the agricultural revolution, when we started to farm (and produce more than we needed). Harari calls this so-called revolution 'history's biggest fraud', for the more-more-more model put millstones around the necks of farmers. As more food was produced, we stored more, and more communities stopped wandering about and instead settled in one spot. Then more kids were born, producing more mouths to feed, thus creating more demand for food. More, more, more.

It all created more work and less leisure. And less wellbeing. Sicknesses set in due to more people hanging out in their stagnant detritus and fewer kids being breastfed (more mums had to work out in the fields to keep up with 'demand'). More famines struck (single crops meant more folk were susceptible to droughts), and we all convinced ourselves that if we worked a bit more (and squirrelled away more of our crops to fend off more famines), then things would get easier and we'd arrive at what we were promised.

And so it came to pass that we ran around like rats in cages.

The Industrial Revolution, the advent of large household appliances in the 1950s and the invention of personal technologies in recent years also promised the same – more leisure, more ease – but delivered the opposite – more work and more disconnection.

Why did we let ourselves be conned over and over? Harari argues we weren't paying attention. 'The promise of more-more-more kept us sufficiently distracted.'

Recently, I met a family who'd escaped a religious cult only 12 months earlier and were living in Paris. The wife told me, 'We didn't know we were in a cult because we were too busy feeling indebted and making up for the debt.'

31 Another thing I thought about on that ferry: in Roman times the despotic emperors used distraction to keep citizens from revolting. The term 'bread and circuses' was coined to describe this seductive coercion technique of handing out cheap food and entertainment to peasants, such as arena-style bloodbaths. Capitalism does the same today. Cheap, addictive, instantly gratifying 'things' are dangled from every direction by multinationals instead of dictators or despotic gurus. They have kept us distracted, indebted and wholly non-deviant. But for how much longer?

To be honest, when I properly reflected on this stuff, I was able to answer perhaps the most perplexing question of this journey: how did we get to where we are right now? How did so much power get handed over? The answer (we got distracted) alleviated my shame and the blame I was hurtling outward at construction supervisors and Kardashians and whichever idiot it was who decided to re-release Snapple in plastic bottles ('New! Now in plastic!'). I'd journeyed from feeling lonely and fearful to ashamed (of myself) and angry (at everyone else) for not caring enough. But I saw now that the issue was systemic. And that we were, in fact, all in the system together.

Which meant I actually had a chance in hell of not shutting down – going acedic – right when the world needs us fully alive. And it allowed me to ask myself, and all of us here, the more beautiful question, 'Are we finally ready to do this differently, to imagine, create and become beyond the system that is destroying us?'

the

elephant
in the
room

32 Rightio. It's time to get real about the whopping great elephant in the room. Which elephant? Oh, just that unfathomably large mammal that has taken over the whole room, nay, the entire biosphere and our sense of selves as humans.

We turn psychologically blind to elephants in rooms, pretend they're not there and talk around them because of – and in spite of – their hugeness. But it's impossible to walk and talk around this one now.

For this elephant is the very fact our life on this dear Earth is in peril.

We were warned for decades, more than a century actually, that capitalist consumption would eventually wind us up in a global warming-led climate crisis that, if left unattended, could kill us. And here we are. We're losing life on Earth at a pace that hasn't happened since an asteroid struck 65 million years ago and wiped out half of all living forms.

Now, some of you reading this might differ from me in your acceptance of the climate science and the exact role humans play in the crisis unfolding around us. And indeed, the yawning divide between what Yale University, in their 'Six Americas' study, call the 'alarmed' (the most climate science-responsive segment of the population) and the 'dismissive' groups (those at the other end of the spectrum who deny it) remains just as wide, no matter what (natural) disaster strikes. Similarly, following the devastating Australian bushfires in early 2020, an Ipsos poll showed no spike in concern about climate change and that skepticism about climate science actually rose compared with the previous survey two years earlier.

But whether we are a climate activist or climate skeptic, privileged or disadvantaged, we can all see we live on an overcrowded planet that can't feed and house us all. We will not be able to avoid the food and water shortages, droughts, crop destruction, fires, wildlife extinction, job losses, new diseases and refugee explosions. We will not be able to ignore the rising waters submerging Bangladesh, Calcutta and New York; or that rice, avocados and 85 per cent of wine crops will be gone by 2050, ditto 30 per cent of the English coastline, taking with it 200,000 homes.

We can't viably argue, when we cast aside ideology and other cognitive biases, that we don't understand the simple maths of extracting more resources from a finite system, nor the simple physics and chemistry of trapping heat in a closed

SARAH WILSON

atmosphere with increasing CO_2 concentrations. We can't claim those images of burning koalas and starving polar bears don't exist.

We'd been getting away with turning a blind eye to the unsustainability of so much destruction and disruption, but in many ways corona virus planted the elephant on our laps and said, 'Here, deal with it.' Climate scientists predicted such a pandemic as one of the many life-threatening outcomes of the emergency. I'd been reading about it for years. And a number of researchers from across disciplines argue the destruction of biodiversity via mining, hunting, logging, factory farming, as well as bulging populations, is what created the conditions for COVID-19.

David Quammen, author of *Spillover: Animal Infections and the Next Human Pandemic*, wrote, 'We cut the trees; we kill the animals or cage them and send them to markets. We disrupt ecosystems, and we shake viruses loose from their natural hosts. When that happens, they need a new host. Often, we are it.'

Then the rising waters and temperatures of the climate emergency see such viruses spread exponentially; ditto pollution, which also causes faster mutation. Research by Harvard University that looked at 3,080 US counties showed that pollution contributes to much higher COVID-19 death rates. Inversely, and ironically, cleaner air that resulted from less driving and industry activity during the global lockdown led to 11,000 fewer deaths in one month...in Europe alone (!!) according to the Centre for Research on Energy and

Clean Air. A similar study demonstrated that cleaner air was likely to have saved twenty times the number of lives in China that have been directly lost to the virus.

33   When I spoke to the dozens of climate scientists interviewed for this book, I asked if they thought they'd die from climate change-related causes (disease, pandemic, famine, war). Nearly all replied yes.

Goddamn, it's hard committing that to paper.

I'm very aware of not wanting to write it. As if leaving it out might make it less true.

For sure, humanity has faced tough times before…but not like this existential spiral. It has been said that what we face with this climate crisis is harder than winning World War II, achieving civil rights, defeating bacterial infection and sending a man to the moon…combined.

So let's get super duper clear, my dear friends: *this is a human despair crisis.*

And what we are fighting for is our lives.

As writer Rebecca Solnit wrote in the updated edition of *Hope in the Dark*, referring to the climate crisis specifically, 'The scale is not like anything human beings have faced and journalists have reported on, except perhaps the threat of all-out nuclear war.' She then added the whopper caveat that nuclear war was something that 'might happen, not something that is happening.' I add this: With nuclear war, we all agreed the threat was real and we talked about it openly. We weren't fighting the science on it. Oh, and it wasn't deemed our fault or responsibility. Ronald Reagan and Mikhail Gorbachev were the only ones with access to the red buttons.

34 Now, if we were sitting in an earnest emotional support circle, I'd be getting up from my stackable chair and saying, hand on my heart, that what's on our plate is unfathomably, tear duct-piercingly huge and hard.

Many in the environmental movement (and beyond) argue that talking the scary facts is too much for most and for years have instead taken softer approaches, such as highlighting the potential extinction of cute animals as opposed to the extinction of *us*. I toyed back and forth with this myself. But as I spoke to scores of experts, activists and psychologists, and young people, it became obvious that facing the elephant is crucial to our actual survival. Hopeful action can only build on the sturdy foundations of full-frontal truth. And besides, the emergency has arrived. We're in it *now*. It's sitting on our laps. I spoke to Manhattan-based climate psychologist and co-founder of The Climate Mobilization Margaret Klein Salamon about calling out the elephant. 'It's important to feel afraid of things that will kill us,' she said very directly.

With the release of the United Nations Intergovernmental Panel on Climate Change (IPCC) Special Report on Global Warming of 1.5°C in late 2018, the world's leading climate experts and IPCC representatives came out with all truths blazing (see some of the exposed realities below).

David Wallace-Wells, author of *The Uninhabitable Earth*, paraphrased the report as giving us official permission 'to freak out'. The 2021 report saw the UN Secretary-General António Guterres issue 'a code red for humanity'. With each report published, I've watched the poor guy try to find new language to express the worsening situation and to, yes, get us to freak out, or at least sit up straight. His latest effort tells us the planet is a ticking time bomb and the latest report is a 'survival guide for humanity'.

Now, some have argued we should at least protect kids from the starkness of the emergency. But it's young people who are calling for the adults to get fully real. Four in five young people are anxious about climate change. In the United States, a whopping 78 per cent of GenZ-ers and 70 per cent of millennials say they aren't planning or do not want to have children as a result of climate change. A similar UK survey found nearly half of women are delaying having children due to fears about the state of the UK and the wider world.

'The room is on fire and we want you to panic,' 'You get to die of old age, we will get to die of climate change,' and 'If you won't act like adults, we will!' read their placards at the global school strikes they organise to get our attention.

35 So how about we do a rundown of this crisis, in bullet points. I'm not going to get too detailed with the science and politics here; we're on a soul's journey. I'll instead stick to zeitgeisty relevancies, pithy comebacks to unhelpful arguments your recalcitrant great uncle dumps on you at family barbecues and juicy DYKs. And remember that kid in Mammoth with the bottled drink? He specifically requested bullet points. I said I'd do what he asked if he quit his crappy single-use habit. We shook hands on it.

Now, did he stick to his end of the bargain? Because I clearly did (see below). Turns out he did. I hunted him down using Google Earth to find the café where he worked...yada, yada...many emails later we connected and... Lo! Behold!... He'd not only quit his plastic habit, he'd quit all packaging and was living off-grid in the forest. All prompted by our conversation.

You can hear him share the details on my podcast.

In no particular order or hierarchy, because, frankly, there ain't any in this predicament, the promised bullet points.

Check out the late comedian George Carlin's sketch, Saving the Planet – he slices through this particular distraction brilliantly.

- *Sure, we've had climate change before. And, yep, the planet survived.* But this is not the point. No doubt the planet will survive again. There's just one small problem that we get distracted from. This time, *we* probably won't. Or at least, our lives as we know and love them won't. Brutal. But factually so.

- *We are the sixth extinction.* In the five previous 'extinction events,' other life forms, including dinosaurs, were wiped out. Exact timings and the extent of human wipe-out is open to conjecture, but the point remains - human life is what is at stake here! A paper released by the think tank Breakthrough

National Centre for Climate Restoration (and backed by a former Australian military chief) found that by 2050, 55 per cent of the world's population would be living in conditions 'beyond the threshold of human survivability'. Mass deaths are predicted to result from the disease outbreaks, air pollution, malnutrition and starvation, heatwaves and suicide. Other voices argue that the most likely threat will be the mass civil unrest that results from the destabilised conditions. As Margaret Klein Salamon told me, 'Starving millions don't just lie down and accept their fate. They fight.'

- *The science IS conclusive.* More than 97 per cent of actively publishing climate scientists say the warming of climate over the past century has been caused by humans. The fact that humans are causing climate change is at least as settled as the link between smoking and cancer.

- *Besides, regardless of what or who caused the planet to heat and become so degraded, we are the only ones who can fix it.* Put in pipe. Smoke it. Let's move on...

- *Scientists and activists have no vested interest in making this shit up.* How many rich activists do you know? Or rich climate scientists, for that matter, apart from the ones funded by oil or other vested parties and who make up that 3 per cent who deny human causation?

There is no money to be made and no power to be gained from spreading information about the worth of sustainable energy, or consuming less. I said this to someone who challenged me at a dinner party as to my motives behind engaging in climate activism: 'We would much rather be at the beach.' Fair point, they replied.

Which brings us to...

- *The 'science is inconclusive' argument is fabricated.* By, principally, the fossil fuel companies. You might already know this, but I'll include it as a reminder. Science confirmed more than 30 years ago that human-caused global warming was categorically real and advised what we had to do to survive – stop oil and coal production. What? Why didn't anyone tell us back when it wasn't all very close to too late? Oh, well that's because Exxon, the largest oil company in the world, had known that burning fossil fuels contributed to CO_2 and temperature increases by the 1980s. Making deep cuts into its climate research budget, it then launched a blanket campaign to distract us from demanding cessation of oil and coal production, the one that goes, yep, 'the science is inconclusive'. It was a colossal duping that was only revealed in 2015.

- Another tidbit: until the early 1990s, both Democrats

THIS ONE WILD AND PRECIOUS LIFE

and Republicans in the US, as well as both major parties in Australia and the UK, had accepted the scientific consensus on climate change and a price on carbon was in the pipeline. But then Big Oil stepped in again and financed campaigns to lobby against climate solutions. And continues to do so. UK's Margaret Thatcher, in 1990, publicly declared, '*It is mankind and his activities that are changing the environment of our planet in damaging and dangerous ways*' and praised the creation of the Intergovernmental Panel on Climate Change (IPCC). A little over a decade later, in her autobiography, she did a U-turn and denied the science. She cited the work of a bunch of think tanks funded – you guessed it – by Exxon and other fossil fuel companies to back up her new position.

Now for the stark facts on where we must head...

• *To survive, temperatures must not exceed 1.5°C above preindustrial levels.* This emerged from the Paris Agreement in 2015 and the IPCC Special Report in 2018. Thousands of scientists from all over the world contribute to the IPCC and 189 countries signed the Paris Agreement and pledged targets to avoid exceeding this *1.5°C threshold*. As the first edition of this book went to press we hit 1.1°C above pre-industrial levels. Since then, it has nudged up to 1.2°C, and Australia is at 1.47°C above. As I write this, in mid-2023, the UN's

World Meteorological Organisation has announced that the world will breach the 1.5°C threshold by 2027, albeit temporarily, but with 'increasing frequency'.

To stabilise below that point and to meet the Paris agreement commitment, every government in every country must halve its net emissions by 2030.

Then halve them again by 2040.

Then the entire world must reach zero net emissions by 2050.

At the very latest.

- *Now bear in mind, zero net emissions means…*that the greenhouse gases we emit are in balance with the GHGs that are permanently sequestered (stored in trees, oceans and the soil). The time frame that we take to reach net zero, and how many emissions are released in the process, determine how much warmer it is going to get.

- *So how are we looking? Horrendous, TBH.* Most wealthy nations have now committed to at least halve their emissions by 2030. In the lead up to the Glasgow COP26 Summit in 2021 the UK pledged to cut emissions by a 'world leading' 68 per cent by 2030. But, of course, it remains to be seen if these plans and pledges are enacted. The UK is already looking set to miss its lofty target. The United States' prospects will be determined by the next election. Donald Trump has said the US would withdraw from the Agreement entirely if he became president.

Regardless, even if all countries around the world met their existing 2030 emissions reduction targets we would be headed to a dangerous 2.4°C of global warming.

• *And if we continue business as usual?* IPCC scientists, former Executive Secretary of the United Nations Framework Convention on Climate Change (UNFCCC) Christiana Figueres, commentators such as David Wallace-Wells, and a host of international experts have taken the projected data and painted a horrifying picture of what life could look like if emissions continue unabated.

The melting of ice sheets will pass a tipping point of collapse and New York City could be flooded within 30 years. Mumbai, Jakarta, Guangzhou, Hong Kong, Ho Chi Minh City, Shanghai, Bangkok and Manila would be largely inundated and abandoned. Around 15 million people in Bangladesh alone would be displaced.

— And bear in mind, many say that as 'tipping points' compound, the picture could be even bleaker.

There would be 8 million cases of dengue fever each year in Latin America alone.

Across West Africa, tropical South America, the Middle East and Southeast Asia, there would be more than 100 days a year of deadly heat, leading to over a billion people being displaced.

Southern Europe would be in permanent drought. The average drought in Central America would last 19 months and in the Caribbean 21 months. In northern Africa, the figure is 60 months – five years.

The areas burned each year by wildfires would double in the Mediterranean and sextuple in the United States.

Water scarcity would affect 400 million more people, and even in the northern latitudes heatwaves could kill thousands each summer.

In equatorial countries there would be 32 times as many extreme heatwaves, each lasting five times as long and exposing, in total, 93 times more people.

Food production would drop off due to the 'catastrophic decline' in insect populations, weather too hot for humans to survive in significant food-growing areas and chronic water shortages. With not enough food for the world's population, prices would skyrocket. Global grain yields would fall by 50 per cent.

By 2050 vegetables would be 'junk food'. As atmospheric carbon levels rise, plants produce more sugars and fewer nutrients.

We would see at least 50 per cent more conflict and warfare than we do today. Possibly more.

We would also see millions of premature deaths due to air pollution, and horrible spikes in suicides.

I won't go into the cascading emotional implications

that would domino from the above. I think we get the picture. It's not life as we want it. It may not even bear out as life at all.

- *So what do the money people say?* David Wallace-Wells in *The Uninhabitable Earth* cites studies that show a temperature rise of 3.7°C would result in more than $US550 trillion of climate-related damage. This is twice today's global wealth. There is literally not enough money on the planet to fix things if we get to this point. The economists, big business and the insurers get the threat. The world's biggest banks, insurers and investors in control of more than $130 trillion, are variously committing to diverting funds from fossil fuels into sustainable energy projects, saying there's no future for the former.

— Plus, a recent report by economists at three leading institutions flags that the economic situation is likely to be worse than predicted by the scientists. This is because scientists can't include uncertainties likes cascading feedback loops and tipping points, and must leave them out of modelling.

- *Things are speeding up.* Research published in *Scientific American* shows scientists have underestimated the pace and severity of the crisis. The Black Summer bushfires in Australia in 2019-20, for example, were predicted for 2050; permafrost in the Canadian Arctic is thawing at rates that weren't expected for another 70 years.

But! There absolutely is hope!

- *First, the solutions already exist.* The Exponential Roadmap report (produced by an international group of academic institutes and private sector companies) outlines thirty-six of those solutions that have been tested and are already practised in different parts of the world. We just have to put them all in place globally. 'Low-cost solar, wind and battery technologies are on profitable, exponential trajectories that will be enough to halve emissions from electricity generation by 2030,' said Tomas Kåberger, one of the authors of the report.

And we can do this crazy thing with individual and collective action combined.

• *Individual change is vital.* I think one of the most demoralising and destructive arguments out there is that 'anything we do won't make a difference'. Don't fall for it. This is technically bullshit.

I explored a stack of documented examples of this along my journey, but for now it's good to know this: according to the IPCC special report in 2018, fossil fuel companies contribute 89 per cent of our CO_2 emissions. It's a lot, but even if we replace these with renewables (wind, solar), it may only provide about half of the world's demand for electricity by 2050 (unless we see governments worldwide give an almighty push to renewables).

So how do we meet the other half? We halve demand by cutting our personal carbon footprint.

This is actually — the latest denialist tactic – to seed the idea that all is doomed so don't bother trying.

112

Project Drawdown (a US non-profit organisation) has shown that many small consumer-level changes make the biggest dent in emissions. Cutting household food waste in half, for instance, rates as #3 in the Top 100 emission-cutting practices – it cuts more CO_2 emissions than solar farms and rooftop solar combined.

— They've recently updated their list. Now, reducing food waste along the food chain is ranked #1.

• *We in the West must make BIG changes.* We probably need to stop using the excuse that India and China (and other countries with big populations) should be changing before we have to.

I have three things to say:

One, we don't tolerate it when kids use the 'why do I have to do it if Johnny's Mum doesn't make him do it?' argument. We shouldn't tolerate it from adults.

Two, per capita, Australians, Americans and Brits (and most Westerners) emit far more emissions than Indian or Chinese folk. The consumption of the world's wealthiest 10 per cent produces up to 50 per cent of the planet's consumption-based CO_2 emissions, while the poorest half of humanity contributes only 10 per cent (and is the most vulnerable to climate change).

And three, India and China (if we are to stick to the examples that our leaders often draw on) are doing more than us in some instances. China is already the world's largest investor, producer and consumer of renewable energy, which has led to the wonderfully rapid decline in the cost of solar and wind technologies

113

over the last decade. President Xi has announced that China will aim to peak emissions before 2030 and reach net zero emissions by 2060 – super significant given that it's the world's largest energy consumer and carbon emitter. China has also quit overseas financing of coal projects. Meanwhile, the cost of renewables in India has reached record lows and in 2017, both China and India announced plans to end the sale of gas and diesel vehicles. And China has banned single-use plastic bags across its major cities. Yeah. So.

- *Activism is also vital.* The biggest barrier to change is the fossil fuel industry and the governments it funds. As I mentioned earlier, more than 70 per cent of the world's greenhouse gas emissions can be traced back to 100 companies (inclusive of fossil fuel companies). They will only shift when we make enough noise.

- *The 3.5 per cent figure of hope!* The great news is that activism works. Harvard political scientist Erica Chenoweth researched all significant political movements from 1900 to 2006 and found that when 3.5 per cent of the population – yes, only 3.5 per cent is all it took – actively participated in sustained non-violent protest, change happened in every single case. In 1986, for example, millions of Filipinos took to the streets of Manila in peaceful protest. The Marcos regime folded on the fourth day. In 2003, the people of Georgia ousted Eduard Shevardnadze through the bloodless Rose Revolution, in which protestors stormed the parliament building carrying roses.

- *Finally, we've fought big elephants before.* The US switched from a consumer economy to a war economy in two months at the start of World War II. The scale of the endeavour was unimaginable, but the entire country mobilised. Ships that took eight months to build were completed in two weeks. Across the country everyone turned off lights at dusk, paid income tax as high as 94 per cent, took part in car pooling to save on gas and endured heavy food rationing. They got activated and magic happened. This is what we're built for – pulling off the extraordinary at the eleventh hour.

  Food rations and other collective actions were enforced in the UK, and Australia too. — The population in all three nations were the healthiest in their history.

  More recently, we fixed the hole in the ozone layer. The hole was discovered in 1985. The global warming science was accepted and just two years later the world signed on to the Montreal Protocol committing to phasing out chlorofluorocarbons (CFCs). It worked. The hole has shrunk, and NASA has predicted it may heal by 2060.

  The treaty was initiated by — George HW Bush, pushed largely by Republican senators and then signed off by President Reagan, for extra hopeful effect.

  And, hey, look how the entire planet mobilised to fight corona virus!

36 As a small, final thought, I want to raise a question that I've been asked a number of times. Is there a chance that we

This is one — prominent geo-engineering 'fix' that's been put forward. It would work by deflecting solar radiation back into space.

don't really need to change our ways quite so urgently? Couldn't we wait until someone actually manages to invent those space sunshades I keep hearing about? The question is not always posed in so many words; it's often just reflected in the vulnerable inaction of some loved ones in my life. I find it useful to answer by painting a picture of us all as the proverbial frogs in the pot of water on the stove. Things have been getting warm, slowly. It was cosy for a while, comfortable. So comfortable in fact that we started to get a bit sleepy and lethargic. We've thought about jumping out, of course, because we know that where there is heat there is fire. But the thought of leaping into the cold unknown seemed too jolting, too extreme. So we figured we'd just stay a bit longer.

Things start to get hotter, though. *Hmmm, this is starting to feel a bit dangerous*, we say to ourselves in our little frog brains. But the sleepy heat has now rendered us unable to move. We've missed our crucial moment to save ourselves.

Before I over-egg this thing, the point is, it will be too late if we don't jump now.

a path

for

our

souls

a brief

bridging
chapter

Wanderer, there is no path.
The path is made by walking it.
— Antonio Machado

37 I remember many years ago a friend sat with me on my couch and we were trawling through the tangled detritus of my recent failed relationship with some on-again–off-again bloke. The to-ing and fro-ing of the messy grief and blame had argued itself to a standstill, and my friend put down her wine and turned to me. 'And…what are we going to do about it?' she asked.

Her implicit message was brutally and helpfully clear. Be in pain, do the pain. And…move forward. She'd recently done The Landmark Forum. She was all over brutal confrontation. We can always add an 'and…?' to a shit sandwich. We can be in grief, we can itch, we can be overwhelmed, *and* we can choose to do something about it. We don't have to be rendered numb, asleep, despairing. I learned some time back that I could be fretting with anxiety *and* I could choose to live a great life. It was a revelation when I opened myself to this truth. I didn't have to wait for a 'fix' before I got on with living fully.

— Courtesy of His Holiness the Dalai Lama.

And...what are we going to do about it? It's the big, beautiful question for our times.

38 By this juncture I'd nutted out the nub of our human despair crisis – we're morally lonely, trapped in our human smallness and an empty more-more-more cult. I'd got real about the scale and urgency of the elephant in the room. As I say, there was no unseeing any of it, no going back.

And this is where I got horribly stuck. I didn't know what we were going to do about it.

I had been on the road for a little over a year, researching and interviewing experts and writing as I went along, and the truth is the magnitude of it all had engulfed me. I found myself scared for the first time. What if we couldn't turn this ship around in time? Fear turned to guilt and shame, then a raging anger as I flailed in the uncertainty and feelings of helplessness. I wrote in circles for months – about 40,000 words of circles. Meanwhile, fires raged and plastic consumption increased, and Trump threw a hissy fit when he was told he couldn't buy Greenland. We talked about how bad things were and put sad emoticons under pictures of singed koalas ('it's so sad'), but little was shifting. No one was moving forward, no one seemed to have a fix. Politicians spoke in riddles when asked by journalists to explain things. The scientists spoke in emissions tonnage and particles per cubic centimetre, data that sent me in spirals.

I also got anxious, specifically manic, as I tried to take it all in. Some days I couldn't leave the house or talk to loved ones. My head and my emotions were too wild. I was itching like mad!

I sent emails to my publishers. 'I can't find a path through this. I don't know if one exists.' After months of this I could feel myself veering perilously close to giving up in an overwhelmed numbness. Or acedia.

39 Timothy Morton is a British philosopher and environmentalist who is regarded as the most powerful figure in the contemporary art – yes, art – world. He has collaborated with Björk on various projects, performed at Glastonbury and has consulted to NASA as well as Steve Coogan's series *The Trip to Italy*. He also coined the term 'hyperobjects' to describe the kind of ginormous phenomena unique to the Anthropocene period that we are currently grappling with – the Sixth Extinction, global pandemics and democratic collapse.

The Anthropocene is the most recent period of geological history – agreed to span from 1950 to the present – in which humans have transformed the earth.

In his book (titled *Hyperobjects*) he explains that the climate crisis and other human-made clusterfucks of the Anthropocene are now fundamentally too big to wrap our heads around, control or fix. We are trapped in it, part of the unwieldy whole, so it is manifestly impossible. But precisely because we are trapped in such hyperobjects, we are condemned to live with the awareness of them (we are reminded of coral bleaching every time we turn on the ignition in our car, for example). All of which basically causes a messy implosion of our brains.

I describe it as a fear-guilt-anger-despair-overwhelm cycle. This quintet of emotions is probably familiar to many of you. It kicks in when we so much as put a tentative foot on this path to dealing with the hyperobject that is the climate crisis.

Let's pause here and unpack it. (And we must because it is presenting a huge roadblock for many of us.)

First, the fear (and anxiety). The thing is, we *should* be feeling fearful. Our lives are at stake. The climate emergency (and all the rest) is an existential crisis. Fear and anxiety exist to tell us something is not right and when we feel it – and very, very importantly don't ignore it or cocoon from it – it triggers us into life-saving action. We run from the stampeding rhino; we flee a burning building; we roll up our sleeves and save life on Earth. When we fear the fear, instead of bravely feeling into it, we don't move (and risk death).

The guilt is also productive and makes perfect sense. So too shame. Guilt means we are reflecting on our behaviour; shame means we are reflecting on our overall moral inclination. Such emotions lead us to take a good hard look at ourselves. And to see that we're not living a 'right life', that we've strayed from our values. As Brené Brown has explained many times, when our shame is felt into and met with empathy and understanding, it dissipates, and connection and wholeness replace it. All great stuff. Bring on the guilt and shame!

But then there's the anger! I'm angry a lot of the time – at our lacking leaders, at the oil companies, at single-use coffee cup consumers. I have often felt terrible about my anger and tried to quash it. As kids – little girls in particular – we're told to mute our rage should we want to fit into polite society. But here's the thing. Anger is often a very healthy emotion to process rather than bottle up. Crucial, in fact. You might love this as much as I do: the word courage quite literally breaks down to 'rage' of the 'heart' (*coeur* in French).

A raging heart brings us the courage to do what is required.

The despair – or grief – is also very healthy and useful. We grieve what matters to us. Let's recognise this. Climate psychologist Margaret Klein Salamon told me that it was only when she was able to grieve the losses we've already sustained in the climate crisis, and let herself feel the full weight of the despair, that she was able to accept that the climate emergency was real and then attend to it with everything she had (including co-creating The Climate Mobilization group in 2014 at the age of 29, which has since seen more than 1,000 global cities declare a climate emergency.) But grief did something else, too. 'It reminded me of how much I love this world,' she told me. I want to point out, too, that we don't just grieve what we've lost now, we also grieve what may be lost in the future... I realised I was grieving not being able to feel safe in cities like New

THIS ONE WILD AND PRECIOUS LIFE

York, because they'll be underwater in years to come. I was grieving not being able to hike into my old age in unspoiled nature, and that my nieces and nephews wouldn't experience the animals and reefs and wild experiences in the books I read to them. When I thought about it this way, I, too, got very real about my love for this one, wild precious life. And what I would do to fight for it.

Then we get to overwhelm. When we get to this stage, it's usually because we have not felt into and processed the other feelings – the fear, guilt, anger, despair – which now swirl madly, and become too hectic for our little minds and souls and so we shut down, descending into acedic asleepness. Remember that deer chased by the tiger? When things become too much and we feel we can't fight or flee a threat, we can often freeze, go numb (play dead). The emotions get too much, the news feeds are drowning us, so we shut off, stop feeling any of it and say things like, 'I refuse to watch the news' and 'I can't even...' and go back to thumbing through TikTok. But if we stay numb and don't allow ourselves to fully feel the life-saving emotions, we won't be able to shake ourselves into action.

As psychologists tell us, emotions become dangerous when we ignore them or quash them – the irony being that when we block our feelings, we get stuck in them (and the hyperobject). So stuck that we can do nothing else.

BTW, when relegated to our homes during the COVID-19 lockdown, this process of sitting in and facing our emotions became key. Dr Vivek H Murthy argues we are programmed to fear isolation and when we feel into this particular anxiety, we are prompted to seek out connection and attunement with other humans. Anxiety triggers the impulse to come together, just as hunger triggers us to eat and thirst triggers us to drink. Touch and attunement then down-regulates our autonomic nervous system, allowing us to overcome helplessness and a dangerous downward emotional spiral.

A quick trick to turn fear into action

I asked Margaret if she might show us a technique for moving through the overwhelm cycle. She quoted Pope Francis in his 2015 encyclical 'Laudato Si' in which he says that to stop the climate death spiral, we must 'become painfully aware, to dare to turn what is happening to the world into our own personal suffering and thus to discover what each of us can do about it.' Yes, experience the personal suffering! She then talked me through the following. I've paraphrased and added to it.

First, name your feeling (and the situation that triggers it). For example, 'Seeing yet-another-petition makes me feel aggressive.' Or, 'Watching the news makes me feel helpless.' You might like to write these down.

If you're not feeling much, describe that. For example, 'I feel numb.' It also helps to ask where in the body you notice physical expressions of your emotion or lack thereof (tightness in your chest or neck, swirling in your gut, etc.).

Next, notice where the feeling sits in your body as you name it. Does it stay in your gut or ricochet up to your head? If you're not feeling much, ask if you're blocking feeling.

Where in your body are you blocking it? Sit and 'watch' it a little longer.

This must help you, too. I remember a therapist suggested that I treat my feelings as a friend and have the sort of kind, merciful conversations I would have with them if they were feeling pain. I'd invite them gently to share the feeling of pain; I wouldn't tell them to ignore it and shut up.

Then, Margaret suggests building 'affect tolerance and emotional muscle'. Simply writing down the feelings and where they're moving in your body will do this, according to her studies. So does talking about your feelings with others. During the writing of this book I held discussion groups, ostensibly to garner feedback, but they became incredible outlets for accessing a certain sturdiness within. The more I talked about my feelings, the more I controlled them, not the other way around.

Finally, Margaret says to cry or dance it all out. It might work for you to put on loud music and fling around your living room. Or to go for a run. Or even wrestle someone. In all instances you're doing what the deer does after playing dead for a little while – allowing the fear to turn into action. Shake it off! Move forward! Save life!

40 It was around this point in the proceedings that an artist friend–slash–lover asked if he could cook dinner for me. I was told it was on the condition that I just sat on the stool at his kitchen counter and did not share my opinions on how he made the salad dressing or turned the fish. Afterward he asked if I would like him to read aloud to me. The guy ached to connect, and he tended to do it via bodacious and often controlling seduction, a tactic that has rarely failed to get under my skin.

I pulled a book from his shelf. It had a fabric cover with embossed lettering and the mothbally smell of things old and treasured. It was called *A Strange Language*, a collection of Vedic poems and musings written in the 1930s by Pundit Acharya. The artist dude opened it randomly and read from a passage about how lost humans have become in their fleeing from nature:

> *Come, hold my hand,*
> *And we shall run away from the intelligence of man*
> *His intellect is a petrified lie.*
> *We shall go back to life.*

Come. Hold my hand…we shall go back to life.

I asked him to stop.

Bingo!

What if this could be our path to reconnection? To drop the rational, head-orientated right vs wrong dialogue that blocks our feelings and our souls and to simply go back to life? As in, go back to nature. Go back to our nature. And to do it together. We can hold hands.

The idea sang. In an instant I became unstuck and knew this was my way forward.

THE ROYAL NATIONAL PARK HIKE, SYDNEY, AUSTRALIA

The following day I got up early, stuffed a train pass down my bra, tied on my hiking shoes and did what I always do when a breakthrough idea needs to germinate fully – walk.

I boarded a dawn train to Australia's oldest national park, an hour south of Sydney. When I arrived, I started hike-jogging along the Uloola track, an 11-kilometre single track from Heathcote station to Waterfall station. I know to do this when fretful overwhelm grinds me to a halt – to stop, hightail it into nature and just move. The trail wound up and down gullies and through deep prehistoric undergrowth. It passed a series of pools and rocky flats. I didn't stop to swim; I had a surfeit of adrenaline that I had to pump out of my being. The whipbirds were at it, the warm morning exciting them into a chatty crescendo.

I ground up and over rocks and through creek beds and slowly my clanging thoughts began to order themselves, just as a flock of birds formed an orderly V-shape and darted off, moving in a seamless cohesion with no designated leader. I remember reading that naturalists early last century struggled to define this awesome organising force that took a flock to where it needed to be. I thought about it now as I started to find my flow on the trail. In the absence of a scientific

Scientists in 2013 revived the old collective noun for starlings – 'murmuration' to describe this behaviour, in starlings and other creatures, and used principles of physics to map the patterns.

explanation they called the phenomenon 'group soul'.

Group soul. Goodness, what a marvellous term for something so indescribable yet so known and intuitively true.

And it hit me, just as the Vedic poem had the night before: We go back to life by unifying with group soul.

I realise such phraseology sounds awfully esoteric. But what if it isn't? We are a species crying out for connection with ourselves, each other, with all of life. In biological terms, we are life, intricately connected. We are of nature. What if we've made the simple act of reconnecting too complicated, cerebral and fractured? What if we could go straight to where we want to be *now*? Be in it. Be with each other. Do not pass Go.

I lay on my back for a bit under a large eucalypt with amber sap running down its dusty white trunk. I love to do this on a hike. I did it as a kid. After a spurt of exertion, I'd lie in the most immediately available patch of earth and simply allow myself to be held. I felt the ants crawl over me, the flies tickling my ears, and I watched the capillaries in my eyelids lit up by the sun. And many good, fulsome, connected thoughts settled into my viscera as though pulled by a magnetic force.

My heart felt light and expansive for the first time in months, maybe years. I realised, lying there, that this was what was missing from the whole picture – the lightness that comes from connecting with what we intuitively know to be true at our soul level. Ditto that alive thrill and anticipation of a wildly deviant way forward.

Of course, I'd been exploring these themes from day

one – reconnecting with ourselves, with others and with nature and doing it at the collective level. But I'd allowed the prevailing ideology of arguments that focus on *issues* instead of *values*, and the overwhelm cycle, to drag me away from what I knew intuitively. It's an easy trap to fall into.

Back at the station, as I waited for the train to the city, I jotted down my thoughts on the scrap of paper I'd also put down my bra (with a pencil). 'We go back to life. We go back to nature. And the how is taken care of! Then it becomes fun!'

I got home and started rewriting the whole manuscript through this simple, fired-up and hopeful lens.

41 I'll add here that joy became a crucial element in the equation for me. Timothy Morton concludes that the ginormous hyperobjects that dump us beyond any ability to control or fix our fate are best dealt with by – yep! – accepting we are not separate from nature but part of it, as well as enjoyment. He writes that combating the climate crisis is about 'having a disco in every room of your house' (because if, like him, you've converted your home to wind power this is entirely sustainable). My meditation teacher Tim reminded me of this one day when I'd let my fear, guilt, anger, despair, and all the grim facts, CO_2 tonnage, political persuading and exhausting campaigning get to me. I was issuing expletives over the toast we were sharing and threatening to take off with my tent into deep bush until it was all over. 'But Sarah, you love this

— Btw, Timothy has also joined me on my podcast, should you care to hunt down the episode.

journey, you love the wildness you've found, show us how to find the charm!' He was right. In the final wash, coming back to this one wild and precious life has to be more charming than destroying it. It reminded me loosely of a Nietzsche wisdom I draw on very, very often these days. The poor, tortured guy struggled to feel hope and a sustainable love for life on his own existential journey back at the end of the 19th century. His fix was to feel, or seek out, beauty in nature instead. Once we feel into or exist in beauty, love and hope rush in.

42 What follows now is a motley crew of wild practices and experiments that can reconnect a soul back to life, beauty and nature, presented roughly as they unfurled for me...and with the joy with which I have come to experience them, even amid the 'societal shitstorm' that refused to abate as I progressed.

Some I have cultivated over many years. And some entailed being deviant. As in, they involved bucking the system – often by simply 'doing the opposite'. This is a technique I flagged in my previous book. It draws on a Sanskrit philosophy, 'Do what you're not doing.' When things are bad or stuck or just boringly despairing (because I've exhausted all deliberative angles on the subject), I do the opposite. Which is also fun.

cultivate

big kindness

like a Greek

43   This first technique is a cracking start point. Erich Fromm wrote extensively on freedom throughout the 1940s and 1950s as the postwar economy ramped up. He worried deeply about our collective asleepness and disconnection. His antidote was to 'live life as a study in love and work'.

How I love this. Love and work are sturdy and joyous things to cultivate in a lifetime. They take us on a morally straight path to a life of meaning. Fromm wrote in *Escape from Freedom* that this approach was the 'only solution for the relationship of individualised man with the world'. Love and work create an 'active solidarity with all men' and enable us to cope with the frightening uncertainty and overwhelm of our world.

Now, I can work. I have loved work since I got my first job at eleven, packing trays in a nursery. I love that a love of work can so often see me rise to the right thing and bring me into a natural commune with humanity. My coward point, however, is big, fully intimate, vulnerable love. I wrote this to my Instagram friend Adrian in South Africa the other day: 'I love humanity, I just find real-life humans hard.' There's a deep, long story to my resistance to intimate love – there is to everyone's – that I no longer bore myself with.

Not to dismiss the benefits of understanding one's blockages nor the value of therapy and self work. It got me to the point where I can be aware of this stuff and go on this journey.

Rather, I've learned to go straight to the antidote, straight to reconnection, and straight back to life. Specifically, I go to Greece. And its lessons.

Greece has often lured me. It seems to have put its hand up for the job of being my teacher in this lifetime. And vigilant student that I am, I keep going back to have the raw, honest, story-steeped land pummel me with its teachings. I'm Odysseus to a bunch of sirens when it's time for another lesson, mostly in love. Actually, always in love – kind, big, fully human unconditional love. My Achilles' heel.

Eleni, a tough Ikarian woman roughly my age with scars over her face from motorbike accidents, who became a lifelong friend, said to me, 'Greece either catches you, or spits you out. It's up to you.' There are many lessons in this alone…

44 But let's chat about philotimo, the greatest of all Greek lessons. And a lesson for our times, I feel.

It technically means 'love of honour' and equally, 'the honour of love'. Yet, as a lecturer in Ancient Greek philology at the National and Kapodistrian University of Athens told the BBC a little while back, 'The word cannot be translated precisely to any other language. All the same, philotimo has become one of the building blocks of the Greek disposition.' It's no surprise to me there is no translation for this word. It's really only comprehensible, and lived out, by the Greeks. It is Greek to the core.

I came to fully understand it on a hike in Greece. And it brought me back to life and what mattered in an instant…

THE SAMARIÁ GORGE TRAIL, CRETE, GREECE

I'd been lured this time to Crete, Greece's biggest island. In large part because it is harsh and mountainous and threaded with challenging hikes. Also, Crete's wild terrain has spawned heroes since before the gods. I love the Greek heroes, heroines, goddesses and gods, primarily for being so flawed. All Greek myths are told via some big Greek character stuffing something up and being weakened by a force truer than themselves, often the Furies or nature, before fighting their way to victory with an even more heroic truth. During World War II the impoverished, starved Cretans famously risked the death penalty to rescue and hide British and Australian soldiers (by running them over mountains). *New York Times* bestselling author Christopher McDougall wrote a detailed book about it, *Natural Born Heroes*. Zorba,

SARAH WILSON

my favourite literary hero, dances his wild dance to freedom and love of fellow humans in Crete.

In the middle of the island is the famous Samariá Gorge hike, an epic five-hour descent from the White Mountains that runs through the centre of the island to the Libyan Sea. Crete is almost impenetrable from north to south due to these rugged mountains. For eons, traversing the island had to be done on foot, which bred a type of running/clambering fitness in the Cretans that human biologists have spent decades studying. The Cretan mountaineers managed to defeat Hitler on several occasions by simply outmanoeuvring his soldiers over this range.

I set off early one morning on a 90-minute bus ride from the north-western port town of Chania up to the start of the hike. I had an old I Quit Sugar tote bag, faded to full scruff, containing two peaches, a water bottle, my phone and a copy of Henry Miller's *The Colossus of Maroussi*. Miller 'got' Crete. He walked it, too: 'There are so many ways of walking about and the best, in my opinion, is the Greek way, because it is aimless, anarchic, thoroughly and discordantly human.'

I was wearing my friend Brad's shirt (I'd retrieved it from his bin before I left Australia — he didn't like the spacing of the checks. Or his husband didn't) and the green shorts and baseball cap I'd worn on every hike for the preceding seven years.

The sun was even starker and the sky bluer at the trailhead. I pulled down my cap and headed to the ticket stall. The entry fee for the park was €5. Cash. I only had a credit card.

I had a pair of green shorts that I wore for eleven years. I'm wearing them in almost every hiking shot I post on Instagram, and in many of my cookbooks. I would get recognised via them a lot.

134

I skipped the stall and headed straight to the entry gate up the hill, trusting that something would work out. Something always does in Greece – if you're willing to ride some chaos. Chaos, I like to say often, is a Greek word. They revel in it and enable it. And they have a robust disdain for any rule of orderliness should it hinder human connection.

I began explaining my predicament to the uniformed dude at the ticket gate when Giorgos appeared. 'This is her ticket,' said the 28-year-old engineer from Athens and the most comically novice hiking rookie I've ever met. He was dressed in engineer-geek getup and carried two heavily padded computer bags crisscrossed over his chest. Giorgos had seen me at the ticket stall. 'You made me laugh,' he told me later. 'You spin around, pull your cap down and march off like you were going to sort the world out,' he said. 'So I buy you a ticket.' I thanked him and suggested we hike together.

We set off down the rocky track through cypress pines and glaring white gorges. Giorgos had packed bundles of foil-wrapped sandwiches, a frappé maker, two packets of cigarettes, a jar of Nescafé, three 1.5 litre bottles of water, flipflops and two towels. And his computer. There's fresh running water the whole way down the gorge, I told him. I shared this and other Things to Know About Hiking as we descended. We also talked philosophy and politics and marriage (his, impending).

We spent the next twelve hours together. And the day ranks in my top ten ever.

I asked Giorgos why he helped me. He shrugged. 'It's

philotimo.' I'd heard the term before. During the early years of the Syrian refugee crisis, Greek locals on the island of Kos became famous for dropping everything and helping the Syrians with whatever limited resources they had. Three locals were nominated for the Nobel Peace Prize for their work and I remember reading the term 'philotimo' in the news articles at the time.

One of the Kos locals – a fisherman who went out every day to rescue fellow humans, foregoing income – told the media, 'We may not return with our nets full of fish, but our hearts are warm.'

Giorgos explained that it's simply the Greek way. We tried to break it down in our limited shared languages. It's similar to 'karma'. But more noble. It's not motivated by a sense that you'll be compensated for a kind act later. Instead, it stems from a recognition that you've already been looked after, and you're grateful, and so you feel obliged – a responsibility, a desire – to give to another, mostly a stranger. Indeed, Greek mythology is full of stories about strangers arriving at doors in strange lands and being fed and cared for, no questions asked. It's the Greek deal.

Now that I think about it, 'obliged' is probably the wrong word. Indeed, the sentiment that I heard over and over when I talked about it with other Greeks in coming weeks was that it's a chosen 'honour' to reach out in connected love to another. It's grace without strings. It's risk with heart. It's radical kindness without the individualistic catch. If you are about to tread in a dog turd, rest assured at least three Greek strangers will reach out to steer you aside.

There's no jingoism around it either. The Greeks don't wear philotimo as a badge of honour, adding it to advertising slogans on tourism billboards at the airport. That's not the essence of it. And this makes it all the more beautiful, don't you think?

A local yoga teacher, Panos, wrote on my Instagram feed when I posted a picture of Giorgos and me, 'Philotimo is not a word, it's a lifestyle.' Yes! A way of living that you can cultivate.

The knee-grinding descent finally flattened out, and we passed through a narrow gorge to arrive at Agia Roumeli. We swam and ate the rest of Giorgos' sandwiches. As the sun lowered, we boarded the ferry that would take us along the coast to a bus back to Chania. We lay side by side on the deck, staring up at the purpling sky and listening to Cretan music on his iPhone, an earpiece each.

I wrote an email when I got to my stone cottage another 40-minute ride on my motorbike from Chania late that night: 'Dearest Giorgos, I had such a great day today. Your kindness – philotimo – from this morning will stay with me a long time.'

He replied:

Dear Sarah, it wasn't generosity. You give out positive energy and therefore it was all your work. I am sure you gonna find what you really seek to those adventures you dive in and then, you'll get relaxed with that love you find at the surface.

Every Greek — is convinced all women will marry a Greek man.

Because you will wrap one Greek eventually and he is gonna regret the years that have passed without knowing you. But he'll be there for you. The act I made today, that kindness you say, pass it over to others.

Which is how philotimo goes.

Giorgos and I still write to each other every few months. I love the guy as much as I've loved any soul.

45 I should probably mention I'd also come to Crete to get

Chania, it turns — out, has one of the best insemination clinics in Europe.

pregnant.

It's been a bumpy and unconventional journey, this pregnancy business. In my mid-thirties various specialists told me I'd never be able to have kids. I was going through premature menopause, they said, a side-effect of my Hashimoto's, an autoimmune disorder that attacks the thyroid. But then I managed to reverse all the antibody markers over ten years of work on my health and got pregnant in an eleventh-hour anomaly at forty-two with a man I'd loved. Then I miscarried. Then we split.

I ached to have a child. Through two decades of friends having their first then second kids and sharing their joy and fatigue. Through relationships with men who liked the idea of a woman who wasn't gunning for kids, then one day, a few months in, not liking the idea of a 'barren woman'. Through the building of a business that might be able to leave a meaningful legacy in a different way.

This ache is particular. It's love that longs to give unconditionally but is denied its object of outpouring, so it expands and expands and sings out into the vast vacuum of the night. And you can do all the self-love work and crystal healing or whatever you like, but that aching love only ever gets bigger.

So of course, having fallen pregnant once, I felt I had to respond to the weirdness of the opportunity and give it another go.

But then I couldn't find sperm. It's not such an easy thing to come across, despite this sense my coupled friends have that it pours down streets. Most of my male friends are married or felt they were now too old to take on fatherhood, even if it was in an all-care-no-responsibility kind of way. Some considered doing it 'anonymously'. We like the thoroughly modern notion of a man anonymously donating semen to a capable woman. But when it comes down to the messy details, some serious evolutionary conservativeness kicks in. In two instances these generous men balked when the clinic counsellor I introduced them to asked if they wanted to be the next of kin should I die; they generally did, which made them, understandably, reconsider both being anonymous dads and their involvement in general. Plus, Australian laws surrounding sperm donation are some of the most prohibitive in the world. Making it nigh impossible for a single woman over forty-two, as it turns out, to buy it from randoms.

So at the eleventh hour I got resourceful. I went online, found a way to slip between the various conflicting international laws and bought some semen from a 21-year-old poetry student in Denmark to have it inserted in Crete. Before it was all too late.

And, no, this is not how I thought my life would turn out.

The day after my hike with Giorgos I was to be inseminated. It was to be my last hike for a while.

'Our dear Sarah,' my doctor, Dr Daphnis, had said. 'Please. Please. Please, no more hiking. We want an egg not an omelette.' He would have rendered me housebound if he could. In Greece a pregnant woman is regarded as a very special kind of invalid. I saw Dr Daphnis every other day or so while I was there. The clinic got me to pop in, sometimes for no medical reason I could discern. I later learned from one of the nurses that it was because they knew I was doing this on my own and they didn't want me to feel lonely. More philotimo.

I was having a straightforward insemination, timed with my ovulation. The 21-year-old Danish poetry student had written on his form that his mum's best friend had had a baby using a donor and he'd wanted to make another woman happy in this way. Dr Daphnis was to essentially perform the classic 'turkey baster' job with the student's offering.

It was over in seconds. I said deep prayers down to my loins, and my beautiful doctor came around the table and clipped my cheek with his thumb. He had wet eyes. 'Good luck, our dear Sarah.'

The following day I was attacked by two dogs while walking (not hiking!) along a track behind the cottages I was staying in. One hooked its teeth deep onto my biceps, another into my shoulder blade. When I got back to the little village, the neighbours all came out to greet me and sent me off to a pharmacy to get tetanus shots. A few days later, I was eating dinner at the taverna in the village 20 minutes away, when the weather-beaten old shepherd who owned the dogs saw me. He followed me on his motorbike as I walked back to my cottage through the dusty olive groves. He had two knives in his belt. I probably should have been scared. He insisted, awkwardly in the dark, with his eyes and by pointing to my bandaged arm, on giving me a lift up the goat track. He was trying to say sorry. He did the gentle nod-blink that says, 'It should be this way.'

46 The etiology of philotimo is telling. It emerged in Athens at the same time as democracy – around the 4th and 5th centuries BC. But it came to the fore in the Late Middle Ages, when the Greeks were enslaved by Ottoman rulers and had to revert to subsistence living. Says the National and Kapodistrian University of Athens philologist I quoted earlier: 'While the West was developing modern states that tied together individuals under the rule of law and an abstract sense of responsibility, the subjugated and inward-looking Greeks were bound by pride, localism and interpersonal relationships.'

The Greeks cultivated philotimo during a despair crisis. We are equally in a despair crisis and need to do the same.

I go back to Erich Fromm's wisdoms quickly. He wrote that to cure a world of its individualism and to survive uncertainty (in his case he was referring to the threat of nuclear annihilation) we need to cultivate *an active solidarity* with each other. Solidarity is not the same as mere social 'connection'. It's way deeper and more satisfying. It's a moral commitment to the common good, to the bigger, broader preciousness of our lives together. It's a moral togetherness in a world suffering moral loneliness.

The climate emergency, our collective despair playing out in those suicide and opioid death rates, the pandemics that we are told will continue to strike over coming decades and the crises playing out over social injustice, gun violence, the trans debate and so on, require a very active solidarity.

But we also need an active solidarity at a soul level.

The crises we are embedded in have exposed the underbelly of what neo-liberal individualism has done to humanity and the planet. And our resulting vulnerability (and shock) has made us aware of what I am sticking to with my utmost conviction – we don't want to live in a world where we are so split apart and cruel. It is not our nature.

Crises strike hardest at those who've already been most disadvantaged by the capitalist system. In Michigan, where the corona virus hit early and hard, African-Americans make up just 14 per cent of the state's population but 40 per cent of the dead; while in Las Vegas authorities painted rectangles on an asphalt parking lot to get homeless residents to sleep six feet apart. In the UK, 76 per cent of nurses who died from

COVID-19 were ethnic minorities. The billionaire David Geffen posted on Instagram that he planned to ride out the crisis on his 454-foot yacht, adding, 'I'm hoping everybody is staying safe.'

I could go on...

But as the Greeks say, philotimo is also inherent in us, it's a tendency. And the corona virus crisis showed us this, if only briefly at the outset. As the markets failed and governments struggled to steer us through the pandemic, human solidarity stepped in. A US Navy captain sacrificed his career to protect his sailors; in Wuhan, as soon as public transport was — suspended, volunteer drivers created a community fleet, transporting medical workers between their homes and hospitals; Italians sang opera from balconies; communities in Johannesburg made survival packs for people in settlements; students in Prague babysat the children of doctors and nurses.

He was fired shortly after and the first sailor under his command died from corona virus less than two weeks later.

This solidarity sparked a joy I think many of us have rarely experienced. As George Monbiot wrote in the *Guardian* in March 2020, 'One of the extraordinary features of the response to COVID-19 is that, during this self-isolation, some people – especially elderly people – feel less isolated than they have done for years, as their neighbours ensure they are not alone.' We recognise this joy, because it's our nature.

Going forward, we will need exponentially more of this radical compassion and solidarity. We will need kind eyes to navigate our neighbours' complex responses to their fear and to accept their voting preferences or cognitive blindnesses. We will need it to consciously, mindfully and effectively respond to the needs and rights of our BIPOC (Black Indigenous and Other People of Colour) friends, colleagues and neighbours. We will need to step out from our selfishness into the collective to do what our system has shown it cannot.

My friends, as the system increasingly splits us apart, I believe philotimo can join us back together again.

47 Many countries have a culture of kindness. It serves as a moral guardrail to keep its citizens connected and to ward off loneliness, cruelty, despondency and overwhelm. But the Greek version has always resonated for me. I think it's the wild fun it generally comes with. Whenever I hitchhike or ask for directions there, Greeks will always go an extra, almost comical mile. They don't point lefts and rights. They grab me by the arm and lead me about 75 per cent of the way there. Many years ago in Athens, when I asked a local for advice on a great restaurant to eat at, Natassa – I still remember her name – took my arm, texted a posse of friends and walked me to her favourite place where we all ate sardines and horta.

Louise Hay taught me this approach to shifting a heart – simply doing a bunch of small, everyday but moral acts that add up to a good life.

Mostly guided by my experiences in Greece over the years I've played with a few techniques – little right moves – that have helped me hone this particularly honourable human quality. It tested me. It will test me for the rest of my life.

Ask of others, how is your heart?

This is a particularly divine technique to practise. The Arabic version of 'How are you?' is *Kayf haal-ik?* In Persian it's *Haal-e shomaa chetoreh?* Both of which roughly translate as, 'How is the state of your heart, in this breath?'

When we ask, 'How are you?' we are generally met with the equally flat 'Not too bad.' The whole thing becomes a go-nowhere 'connection-lite' interaction.

The Arabic and Persian versions, however, lift everyone to a bigger, kinder place in the mere asking.

If I reached out and asked you right now, 'How is the state of your heart, in this breath?' I'm already connected to you. In the asking, I find myself genuinely engaged with whether your heart might be aching for more love, or whether it's heavy with the burden of being so mortal, or whether there's a lightness of possibility fluttering in you. And that I go there, and that you go there, too, necessarily injects kindness and throws a bomb under the blah-ness that keeps us from being meaningfully connected.

The 'in this breath' part brings us into nowness. When I've asked friends, 'How is the state of your heart, in this breath?' I've been aware that both of us come into the moment. I listen fully. So does the other person, so their answer is always wonderfully heartfelt and generous. We both get kind together.

Try it with a loved one, or even a work colleague. And perhaps take note of how it feels to be so present to them and what matters. I feel my whole body relax toward the other person and many of the complexities and annoyances going on in my life fade, because for that moment I'm taken to Rumi's field, the one beyond all the rights and wrongs. It's a bloody relief.

Ask an adversary for help
Inventor and founding father of America Benjamin Franklin wrote in his autobiography about being trolled by a rival legislator. Rather than retaliate, he reached out with a letter to the rival troll asking if he could borrow a specific and rare book from his library. Flattered, the troll sent it over to Franklin right away. Franklin then returned it a week later with a thank-you note. The troll henceforth became a fan, forever ready to do a favour for Franklin.

Various people have written about this phenomenon – why and how it works. Once compelled to do a favour, a hater needs to justify their action to themselves. They couldn't possibly do something kind to someone they hated, so they must switch to becoming a fan to avoid internal dissonance.

I've played with this to see what happens. I'll ask a grumpy looking stranger for directions. I go straight in with kindness – with the expectation of connecting. Their demeanour changes in an instant. They go overboard to help. They don't want to be grumpy and isolated. It's their nature to want to connect. I swear, it's never once failed to transform a scowl. And I wonder if it can't be a technique we can apply globally?

Ask yourself, do you want to be right or to love?
Our disconnected culture deals in polarities – in right and

wrong. Every individual must assert their right, and anything in their way is wrong. Our legal and political systems pivot from the notion that the right of the individual trumps many other moral concepts. We are programmed to fight for our right to be right, because this is deemed…right. But rarely has anyone ever felt right from fighting such a fight. Mostly we are left feeling empty and alone.

I was in a 'But, I'm right' loggerhead a while back. It was a horrible professional scenario in which I felt a work peer who'd become a friend had hung me out to dry in a swirl of contingencies and psychological interplay.

My meditation teacher Tim asked me this astonishingly beautiful question when I talked him through it: 'Do you want to be right or to love?'

The swirl abated immediately. In just asking the question, the answer became very clear: I want to love. I will always want to love. Once again, it takes us to Rumi's field.

And it reminds me of an exquisite poem by WH Auden, 'The More Loving One.' Google it!

So I chose love. I took the fall and kept my mouth shut. And my friendship with this colleague deepened.

Do you want to be right or to love? It's infinitely more beautiful and courageous than asking horrible, spiraling go-nowhere questions like, 'But why can't he see I'm right?' or 'How come she gets away with it?'

Again, I wonder if it can't be practised as broadly as possible now as our leaders negotiate policies that must operate beyond ideas of borders and trade agreements. We start with ourselves, we take the approach to boardrooms, community meetings and it spreads exponentially.

When I first started cultivating this approach, it felt tenuous. Sometimes you have to wait in Rumi's field on your own for a very long time before the other person meets you there. Sometimes they stand at the fence slinging arrows and you have to wait even longer, holding the space in that field on your own.

Why would we do it? Because we want love. We always will.

become

a soul
nerd

48 I didn't grow up literary and cultured. I used to do speed art – dashing through a gallery between the blockbuster pieces, in a bucket-list way. And when lines of poetry were quoted in a book, I'd skip over them. But it was actually while researching this book and wading curiously into dense essays and texts, following a thread and then applying myself mindfully to big, wise words and expressions which had to be understood with the heart, that I got a feel for how the considered study of life could also dial me directly back into life.

Evolutionary psychologist Jeremy Sherman explains that there are two 'standard' ways in our culture to connect to the spiritual essence of things. There's Western religion and there's the Eastern traditions that we have turned to more recently. But he writes of a 'third way' to connect. He calls it soul nerding. Soul nerding is about studying our predicament with considered curiosity by 'absorbing evolutionary biology, intellectual history, philosophy, anthropology, and above all, literature.'

I'd add poetry and art to this list, as well as music, particularly classical.

Voltaire called it cultivating our garden.

This connection to our garden is found not necessarily in the literal meaning of the words of some philosopher, or the landscape an artist presents in gouache. No, it's the connection we feel in the stillness and attention required to appreciate a creative expression by a fellow human.

It's in these mindful 'spaces between the words' that I came to practise touching the vastness of the universal, our nature, and our place in nature. Nerding out on matters of the soul also reveals we've been asking the same questions for millennia. We are not alone with our concerns. In fact, our collective yearning to meet in these mindful spaces could be the whole point of it all.

In the Hebrew — Bible, these spaces are marked out and given a name – *selah* – to remind the reader to pause in the space after a really good phrase.

THE LAKE DISTRICT HIKE, CUMBRIA, ENGLAND

I'd met the Irish poet David Whyte a few times. I'd come across his poems via podcasts and some mindful websites I subscribed to, and then got to meet him when he came to

Australia to do his poetry readings. It was through his work that I finally 'got' poetry. I understood that its beauty is in allowing your heart to open in the gaps between the words.

— ...and was also introduced to the notion of asking more beautiful questions!

On one of his visits to Australia, David and his wife Gayle invited me to dinner and told me about a poetry and hiking trip they run in the Lake District of England. Entirely challenged by the idea of an organised hike in a group, I left it to the last minute to book in. It's a juvenile habit of mine, allowing the universe to have the final say in decisions I find too difficult to make myself. It turns out the organisers were able to squeeze me into an 'embarrassingly small room'. 'You have to have the cupboard and drawers shut to open the door', they warned. It suited me perfectly. For some perverse reason, the fancier the experience, the less I enjoy the main event. The higher the linen thread count and the better the view in a hotel, the less likely I am to sleep, for example.

We were a group of thirty from around the world, although mostly from the States where David has a fan base desperately seeking more beautiful questions. We all arrived with our stories and idiosyncrasies. Each morning we'd wake in our farm-stay lodgings, eat a big British breakfast and then meet in the stables to chat deeply, via poems. After lunch, David would lead us on a hike over tarns and crags and peat bogs around Grasmere, following somewhat in the footsteps of William Wordsworth. It was the poet and his sister Dorothy who introduced the British tradition of rambling dells and fells, through heath and heather, to find, as he put it, 'a not unpleasing sadness'. The two of them were mad walkers and are said to have clocked close to 290,000 kilometres in their lifetimes, about 10 kilometres a day from the age of five.

The Romantic era began in this part of northern England. It led on from the social upheaval of the French Revolution going on across the way and wrestled the human soul from scientific doctrine back to nature. Naturalism, and the environmental movement, spawned from it. Turner and Constable painted the Lake District and 'the nature as teacher' conversation then crossed the Atlantic and eventually inspired American naturalists John Muir and Henry David Thoreau.

Wrote Wordsworth:

When from our better selves we have too long
Been parted by the hurrying world, and droop,
Sick of its business, of its pleasures tired,
How gracious, how benign, is Solitude;
...Come forth into the light of things,
Let nature be your teacher.

On day two we set off from our base on Coniston Water to climb some crags. In the car on the way there a couple of the other 'meaning-yearners' and I were talking about the stuff you and I have been chatting about here on these pages. We drilled down to the despair we feel as a culture, flaying about without a moral code, which has left us in this state of overwhelm and asleepness. Andy, a dad from South Carolina, asked me what I thought was the path forward. 'Do we return to religion? Do we look for new leaders? We need something.'

Funny you should ask, Andy. I've only been preoccupied with this very beautiful question for months, nay years!

As we set off around Grasmere lake, the air was nostril-bitingly crisp. The rolling hills, crisscrossed by a labyrinth of dry-stone walls and dotted with sheep, looked like they'd been set-designed just for us. Warm familiarity and a sharp wildness were suspended together, and we were treading into it, single-file. After about half an hour of walking, David recited his hiking poem:

— I've run the whole poem here so that we can all practise this sitting in the gaps between the words.

Just Beyond Yourself

Just beyond
yourself.

It's where
you need
to be.

Half a step
into
self-forgetting
and the rest
restored
by what

SARAH WILSON

you'll meet.

There is a road
always beckoning.

When you see
the two sides
of it
closing together
at that far horizon
and deep in
the foundations
of your own
heart
at exactly
the same
time,

that's how
you know
it's where
you
have
to
go.

That's
how you know

it's the road
you
have
to follow.

That's how
you know
you have
to go.

That's
how you know.

It's just beyond
yourself,
and
it's
where you
need to be.

— **David Whyte**

49 As he recited the poem, David pointed to two stone walls that started out wide and converged at the top of a grassy hill. One was where we came from, and the other what we would become. They united on the horizon with a small opening between them.

He didn't need to explain why 'just beyond ourselves' is where we need to be because poetry goes straight to the heart and our deep knowing. David says it often. Poetry gets us out of our way so we can just touch the knowing, the thing we yearn for.

I turned around to find Andy. 'Andy, our moral code… maybe we don't need new leaders, new structures. Maybe we can go straight to our collective deep knowing.'

'How?' asked Andy from further back in the group.

'With poetry. And hiking together.' Andy gave me a thumbs-up and a wide smile.

We were given a day off from hiking and the rest of the group went shopping for Beatrix Potter paraphernalia in the twee villages dotted around the Lakes. I got a lift into Ambleside and set out for a climb up a mountain, solo. I looked up from the little town square, saw what looked like a challenging trail winding its way up a-near-enough range, and started walking.

I wrangle with mania 1–2 weeks of any given month, although never that predictably, and that day it was tickling at the seams and needed to be grounded (before it imposed itself on the group, leaving me awkward and repentant). I hike to simultaneously express and ground my mania. I had three hours before the car was heading back to the farm, so I switched gears to a whole-body scramble. I got to the first ridgeline and could see down to Ullswater lake. I climbed up another saddle and over to another ridgeline where the landscape suddenly became almost alpine and barren. I figured it would wrap back down to Ambleside eventually.

On clear days like this the depth of a mountain's contours are not apparent; sometimes you need what Wordsworth called the 'vapors' to nestle in and around the crevices for you to see that you are in fact two saddles and another climb from the main mountain, as I was. I met a couple coming from the other direction. They told me I was doing a seven-hour hike (which I was endeavouring to complete in three hours) and that I was now climbing toward Kirkstone Pass, the highest pass in the Lake District.

In the evenings back in my tiny room I'd been reading *The Living Mountain*. A millennial at a bookshop near the train station back in London had told me I looked like someone who'd love it. I was killing time before the train up north; she'd gone and got it from the shelf and handed it to me. I've come to honour such spontaneous outreaches from strangers; I bought the book.

The Living Mountain was written during World War II by Nan Shepherd, a woman who never married and climbed the Cairngorm mountains in Scotland her entire life. She swam in their streams, slept under the stars and set out each time to 'be' with the mountains as one visits a friend.

What a wonderful concept, to be with a mountain. I do think this is how I've come to relate to mountains. I allow them to hold me, to show me. I sit with them and gaze out to valleys with them. The book is a poetic meditation in returning to our senses via the mountain, and 'living all the way through' to ourselves. Shepherd had scary moments –

almost falling down a ravine, almost treading on an adder – that shocked her into a 'heightened power' of herself. Fear became something that 'enlarged rather than constricted the spirit'. 'When walking for many hours on a mountain,' she wrote, 'the body deepens into a fulfilled trance, the senses keyed,' and she discovers 'most nearly what is it to be. I have walked out of the body and into the mountain.' Oh, yes, the knowingness of the mountain. I know such a knowingness.

I reached the top of Kirkstone Pass and the muscles in my legs and abdomen were clawing for mitochondric energy. The wildness in my head had settled; it'd seeped out through touch, smell, sight, sound. The sheep looked at me, impassively. The sky reflected perfectly in an alpine pond surrounded by reeds. I felt a hermetic completeness. 'Everything is as it needs to be.'

50 Deep reading – fiction or nonfiction – is another wholly soul nerdish practice.

I got around to reading Aldous Huxley's *Brave New World* recently. My soul nerding has seen me work through various 'Top 100 Classics' over the past few years. *Brave New World* has had a revival, hitting the bestseller lists for the first time since it was published in 1932. There's a bunch of dystopian fiction classics from the same era – Ray Bradbury's *Fahrenheit 451* and George Orwell's *Animal Farm* and *1984* – as well as Margaret Atwood's *The Handmaid's Tale*, written in 1985, that are being re-read en masse. They were written at a time when the scope of technological and market advancement was starting to scare us, but they've suddenly become bewildering portents. In *Fahrenheit 451*, the government burns all books. In *Brave New World,* the government bans them and all other access to knowledge that might cause someone to question the world. Huxley writes, 'You can't consume much if you sit still and read books.' To this extent, you could say reading is a form of deviance!

— A *New Yorker* cartoon captured this perfectly. It depicted a bookshop where an attendant is carting huge piles of these books from the fiction section over to the nonfiction section.

For me, when I read deep, I am immediately reconnected with a shared knowingness – in a group soul kind of way. To see that what you've been feeling has had words put to it triggers a sense of congruence. Also, to see that an artist has turned your perplexing pain into a thing of beauty…well, that can see me air-punch in celebration.

I love that there is such a thing as 'bibliotherapy'. It can be traced to the Ancient Greeks. Above a library entrance in Thebes was the inscription 'Healing place for the soul'. Sigmund Freud used literature in his therapy, and in post-World War I America libraries were issued with a prescribed course of reading for traumatised soldiers. It included Jane Austen.

I also love that deep reading improves us at a biological level. Neuroscience shows that when we learned to read 6,000 years ago, particular circuits were formed. These circuits sparked vital processes, such as internalised knowledge (which I take to mean 'knowingness'), fair reasoning, the ability to be empathetic and to have insight.

Worryingly, the same research shows that the kind of skim

reading we do now is shutting down these crucial processes. As one of the researchers noted, our inability to deep read is seeing us fail to 'grasp complexity, to understand another's feelings, to perceive beauty, and to create thoughts of [our] own'. Studies show young people now struggle to be able to read university texts, as well as life-affecting contracts and information relating to their political responsibilities (um, Brexit!). In essence, skimming has made us sleepy, with all the now-familiar repercussions. As one researcher put it, 'It incentivises a retreat to the most familiar silos of unchecked information, which require and receive no analysis, leaving us susceptible to false information and demagoguery.'

Which is precisely what we can't afford right now.

(Re)learn long reading

Reading deep articles and nonfiction, as well as good literature, cultivates focus and reprograms our neurons. The stillness and time required for a long read (anything over 3,000 words) also allows our minds to formulate our moral position. This is like building a muscle.

You might like to try my approach.

I set aside time. Sunday afternoons work for me. I take that lull period between morning social activity or chores and the end-of-weekend dialing down and own it. I carve out an hour and sit on the couch. I make a pot of tea. It's a ritual. It must be a ritual. I know a bunch of life-hackers and writers who set aside time in the morning before the pull of the day draws them outward. They make a coffee. Again, they ritualise it.

I turn my phone off. This is key. If mine is on and nearby, I tend to turn to it when a passage gets tricky or a concept requires deeper enquiry. I seek a quick reward hit. Which totally interrupts the muscle-building.

I pull long reads from curated sites and save them in one spot. I subscribe to a bunch of e-newsletters and follow op-ed and feature sections in respected papers from around the world. I draw on a number of Substack newsletters, *The Atlantic*, *Quillette*, *The New Yorker*, the *Guardian*, *The Monthly* and the *New York Times*. Some people use document-saving programs. I simply open each article in a designated window on my laptop throughout the week and on Sunday work my way through each one. I turn off wi-fi on my laptop, enter full-screen mode and dive in. You might use an e-reader. Or print versions (which have been shown to further increase the mindful experience).

— I also find soul-nerdish nonfiction via reviews or analysis on brainpickings. com and literaryhub.com and the podcast series *On Being*. Or by browsing a bookshop.

When reading, I start slowly and allow my natural reading rhythm to speed up when it's ready. Sometimes I breathe deeply to relax into what is an uncomfortable space – being still and focused like this is uncomfortable for our brains, which are so used to racing ahead to the 'point'. That's okay. I feel along with the writer's commas and parentheses and absorb myself into their rhythm. This helps. When my mind darts, looking for a reward, I gently bring it back to the words. The words on the page are like the mantra or the breath in meditation. It's the repeated, gentle, present and firm bringing the mind back to the page that cultivates this antidote to the distraction that plagues us.

Often, I write notes in the pages of books or on a notepad. It's good to coalesce and bring my own take to the writer's thinking or idea. It allows me to formulate my position. Sometimes I think that a lot of our despair stems from simply not engaging in practices that allow us to wrestle with our moral positioning and work out what matters to us. To have an ethical 'home base'. What about you?

51 I had to kill a day in Madrid once. It was a hot Sunday in a big city, and I had a heavy case of the blahs. I wandered fretfully; nothing appealed to me. I busied myself trying to find a loo for an hour or two. I walked into a cool building, an annex to some big palace-looking joint. At the end of a corridor was an exhibition of Edward Hopper art. I had never heard of the guy, but I walked in. It was free, for some Sunday-ish reason. I followed a tour group for a bit and got some background information on who I soon realised was one of the most iconic American painters of the 20th century. Then I went off on my own and just looked at his art. My philistine naivety served me wonderfully. I didn't know what I was meant to be looking at. So I was able to fully sink into the symbols and impressions. I sat in front of *Hotel Room*, a depiction of a woman who's arrived in a tiny, lonely hotel room and stripped down to her underwear to sit and contemplate something in her hand – a note, a map, something that she must attend to. The unpacked suitcase, her slouch, her obvious familiarity with being in a hotel room on her own (when you regularly do hot schleps across cities, you just know to strip down to your knickers upon arrival so you can have a good regroup with a map or some such) – I got it immediately. Even the manila–folder–yellow of the walls in the room. I knew her. A woman quietly preparing herself for something that needs to be done. I felt an instant 'This is vast! And I get it! We get it together.'

Engaging in art takes our confusion, our moods, our vague understandings of what it might be that we yearn for and that we're missing, or what might be making us lonely, and edits them down into something simple and recognisable. Amy E Herman, author of *Visual Intelligence*, has shown that engaging in art, and analysing our emotional reactions to it, makes us smarter and also more empathetic citizens: 'Learning to thoughtfully move past these reactions can teach us more effective ways to contend with the economic, political, and cultural injustices that we face today.' As Alain de Botton wrote in his delicately poetic book *Art as Therapy*, art delivers what we're feeling, 'better than it was before, so that we feel, at last, that we know ourselves more clearly.'

I think classical music can do the same. Actually, all music can – drum and bass, death metal, all of it. Like poetry and art, there are no didactic instructions included for why some trill goes off over here or why a particular crescendo gets us all thinking of an impending storm or some sort of doom. It grabs your spirit and deposits it right on top.

At eighteen, I passed through Prague and Vienna when

both cities were holding a Mozart festival in their national opera houses (I think I managed to follow the festival from one city to the next). They issued the tickets last-minute, standing room only, for a few dollars. I queued for several hours then once inside I snuck down an aisle in the dark and found a step to sit on. I shut my eyes and off went my heart and my soul and all my collected memories and desires in a swirling dance. Every now and then it would all land in a spot where I knew Mozart went to when he wrote it. I sat crying in the dark. After, I emerged into the late afternoon heat, bewildered but stinging with love.

But perhaps this is the most nourishing notion: poetry, deep reading, art, classical music – they all demand that we are not passive. They make us participate, bringing us back to life!

52 Perhaps you like this explanation of how soul-nerding can work as much as I do? Krista Tippett interviewed American writer and art historian Teju Cole on her podcast and they discussed the role of the artist being 'to get people to concentrate more'. Cole said, 'The artist raises a palm as if to say hush and listen and let's be still.' This considered line, too, takes us straight there, don't you think?

That said, I think Alain de Botton, once again, best explains the way art can reconnect in an instant. He argues that certain phrases we read, or an image in a painting, might take a memory and make if feel more precious. I dig this explanation: 'Art reminds us of the legitimate place of sorrow in a good life, so that we panic less about our difficulties and recognise them as parts of a noble existence.' A noble existence, there's something in that...

go
to your
edge

53 So it turns out on that hot morning in a café in Ljubljana –
the day I spotted the Lady in Red, and then later travelled to
Lake Bohinj for a gondola ride – I was pregnant. The Danish
donor's offering had taken root. Although I didn't know it
yet.

It was exactly two weeks after I'd been inseminated in
Crete and surreally the sum total of all my choices as a
woman in her mid-forties had been funnelled down to this
pointy end of the situation – down to this café in this square
in this city on a stifling public holiday.

I'd done a urine stick test (99 Per cent Accurate Up to
Six Days Before Your Period is Due!!) that morning. Twice.
It came back negative. I rang my doctor in Crete and he
ordered me to do a blood test. But, as you might recall, it was
a public holiday and not a single clinic was open.

Now, what I didn't mention earlier was that I was also

meant to be heading off that very same morning on an epic, personally tailored hike – crafted over many months with a hike nut I met on an online forum – into the Julian Alps. You see, I'd put in place a Plan B should I not be pregnant. It was all finely calibrated. Of course, if I was pregnant, I couldn't hike. It was stinking hot and everyone knows the dangers of heat in those first few weeks. And the only way out if I landed in trouble was by helicopter once I set off. Besides, Dr Daphnis would probably send out Greek military rescue teams to retrieve me if I did.

— Actually, I didn't. But I do now.

So there I was. In the café. Kitted out with harnesses and a helmet, with a complex schedule of arrangements to pick up water and food, and bookings for various beds in huts high in the mountains. All perfectly aligned like Tetris bricks, but with a public holiday technicality that had blown the whole pile to pieces.

I was feeling perilously adrift, trapped in a dreadful catch-22. And so you can see why the Lady in Red, and that gondola ride invite with the socialist philosopher, were such gifts.

Anyway, the next day, after much Googling and calling and hustling, I took an Uber ride over two mountain ranges to the only clinic in Slovenia that could do the test for me.

The nurse rang a few hours later. The result was positive. My instant reaction was to laugh – the nurse laughed, too – at the ludicrousness of it. The pseudo-medical percentages that our awkward culture likes to apply to the madness of a woman falling pregnant made it particularly fun. At my age,

I had a 1 per cent chance of falling pregnant with straight insemination (i.e. no IVF). And there was a 1 per cent chance that my urine test would be inaccurate. I was living in the slivers of the bell curves.

I was also living in a no-man's-land. Where in the world would I go now? Dr Daphnis didn't want me to fly until I'd reached three months. I was *old*, he reminded me; the risk of miscarriage was too high. It was the middle of a European summer; all accommodation was booked. I couldn't hike. My harness and helmet had to be returned. I was swirling. I was now pregnant, and, if I am to be truthful, I hadn't thought for a millisecond about how this might look or feel, or what the next twenty years might look like, or about the fact I might need to get a home with real furniture. And all the rest. I guess I couldn't actually believe the chances would bear out.

I was also on the other side of the world and had only told three people where I was at. Honestly, in that moment I felt a girl could not be more alone. Pregnancy, at the least complicated of times, is a radically alone experience. You are suddenly a woman confined with yourself and an unknown being, with a call to rise to your strongest self as the only certain thing ahead of you.

I did what I do in such predicaments. I sat down on the grass with some ducks and had a good chat with myself. And what I said was, 'Sarah, you are at your edge. And this is good. This is where you need to be.'

I was learning as I went further down this path how important our edge is right now. Our edge is where we get

THIS ONE WILD AND PRECIOUS LIFE

jolted out of acedia – our collective asleepness – and pushed into bigness.

I came across a study that showed that an organism's genes turn on when it puts itself in a new and extended situation. A lot of our selves lies dormant, the scientists argued in the report, until triggered. We come alive when we go to our edge; we become when we go further. Parenthood takes many people to their edge. It can push many men and women into a bigness they didn't know they possessed. Sickness can do it. Going into battle, near-death experiences and a global pandemic definitely take a person to their edge. The edge is at the exposed outer limbs, far from the comfortable trunk our small human selves tend to cling to. The edge is where the elements knock you around, where you're battered by the winds of truth. But it's out at the edge you are also forced to flex and fend. You have all your faculties on, you are alert. 'Out on the edge you see all kinds of things you can't see from the centre,' wrote Kurt Vonnegut in *Player Piano*. It's at the edge that you fully come alive. You experience the sharp air, the harsh light, you see and smell and feel everything. It's not easy or comfortable, but it's definitely alive. And it's definitely where the truly big, noble, creative and meaningful stuff in life tends to happen for humans.

54 Pema Chödrön is an American Buddhist nun who has lived a full life, having turned to spiritual service following two difficult divorces in her twenties and thirties, and advises actively going to one's edge to reconnect. 'Life is a whole journey of meeting your edge again and again,' she writes in *The Wisdom of No Escape*: 'that's where, if you're a person who wants to live, you start to ask yourself questions like, 'Now, why am I so scared? What is it that I don't want to see? Why can't I go any further than this?''

Beautiful questions, right there!

She explains that just going to your edge, wherever it might be (and your edge is going to be different to mine in any given scenario), is all that needs to happen. At the point of our resistance, we become aware we're resisting, avoiding, shutting down. And that awareness is the openness, the softness and compassion we need. We meet ourselves. Bam! Connection!

55 After *The Beast* came out I was hit with enquiries about anxiety in young people. I'd not focused on kids or teens in the book. At signings and public talks super-concerned mums and dads would raise their hands. Their 17-year-old son was self-harming, or their youngest had been doing school refusal for two semesters. Many of my friends were sharing similar stories. Over half of teenage girls and a third of teen boys in the UK have mental health problems, a major survey found in 2022. And in the United States, teen suicide rates have doubled over the last ten years.

One could write several volumes on the possible causes of this 'epidemic' of anxiety in kids, though on the flipside, some say it is partly explained by over-diagnosis. Where there is less conjecture, however, is around the fact that kids are increasingly unable to cope with anxiety, suggesting we have a lack of resilience epidemic rather than an anxiety epidemic. I'd argue the former is just as worrying, if not more so, than the latter.

We should be specific here when we talk about resilience. One leading residential clinic for anxious teens in New Hampshire defines anxiety as 'the overestimation of danger and the underestimation of ability to cope'. Lynn Lyons, an author and psychotherapist who works with schools and parents across the United States, says, 'Anxiety [in kids] is all about the avoidance of uncertainty and discomfort.'

Which is to say an avoidance of their edge.

So, it's not just that kids lack resilience for dealing with anxiety. They are not building the resilience to cope with everyday life, which as we know is brimful of uncertainty, doubt, discomfort, flux, delays, irritations, anxiety and myriad other edges. Which means when big stress strikes, they are in exponential trouble. They are an open wound with no ability to form a scab.

How's this playing out? Badly. And this breaks my heart.

Avoidance of the edge sees young people miss out on the connection and vibrant living that the edge provides. It sees young people, for example, avoiding getting a driving licence – but not for the reason you might think. Studies show they'd rather stay home to avoid the discomfort of IRL interaction, connecting-lite on their devices instead. They're avoiding sexual connection, too. In Japan almost 50 per cent of people

— It's not just fear of the test!

under thirty are virgins. They literally don't know how to talk to the opposite sex. Dr Jean Twenge has led seven large surveys of 8 million American teens and has found today's adolescents are two and a half times as likely to be abstinent as Gen Xers were. The reason? Young people are concerned they haven't developed the skills they need to read other humans in live, face-to-face situations. Blimey!

I read a *Highline* long-read that explored the reasons why the number of millennials choosing to become nuns has spiked. The reporter found that the sisterhood was a retreat from flux and uncertainty for these young women. Blimey, again.

A decade ago, the average age of new entrants was 40. It is now 24.

Meanwhile, a recent study from Wales showed that people with high resilience in childhood are less than half as likely to develop a mental health condition than those with low resilience. I think it's interesting to note an Arizona State University study found that privileged youth are far less resilient and comfortable with the edge than more disadvantaged youth and are the most emotionally distressed people in America.

In contrast, we have Exhibit B: the Dutch. The Dutch do childrearing differently. It's like they haven't left the 1980s. (I saw a meme the other day with two lists. Under the first list, 'Parenting Today' (and I paraphrase a little): 'make sure your children's academic, emotional, psychological, spiritual, nutritional and social needs are met while being careful not to overstimulate, under-stimulate or neglect them in a screen-free, processed food-free, GMO-free, negative energy-free, pesticide free, nurturing home preferably with 1.5 siblings spaced at least two years apart…also don't forget the coconut oil.' Under the second list, 'Parenting in 1982,' was a single entry: 'Feed them sometimes.')

Witness the Dutch summer scouting tradition, known as 'dropping'. It sees kids dropped into the woods in the middle of the night, left to get lost – go to their edge – and to find their own way out. This is not some fringe thing; it's perfectly commonplace. 'Of course, you make sure they don't die,' one parent said to a horrified *New York Times* journalist, 'but other than that, they have to find their own way'. I had to dig around for Dutch anxiety figures among teens. Sure enough, the place doesn't have a childhood anxiety problem – in report after report, the Netherlands tops OECD countries for high life satisfaction in young people.

56 It's not just kids who are lacking resilience. Sadly, we all are. Our culture actively shields us from going to our edge, rendering it an entirely stigmatised and highly charged place. Instead of embracing it, we are cocooned from it, with signs that steer us from tripping on a bump in the pavement, safety nets around trampolines, security walls around estates, 'hygienic' plastic wrap on fruit, technology that saves us from all kinds of discomfort (having to wait, not knowing how long our pizza delivery will take, awkward IRL dating) and trigger warnings on just about everything.

It's quite the irony, hey. Individualism and the market

My favourite: the University of Manchester has trigger warnings about clapping at events. Silent 'jazz hands' are encouraged instead.

system were meant to bring us freedom and openness. And yet, unfettered by the safety net of social structures, stripped of a social fabric to wrap ourselves in, denied the moral guardrails that steadied us as we faced death, we then allow ourselves to be controlled in the most life-limiting ways, with the security walls and trigger warnings, and edge-avoiding apps. The double irony being that such controls have only made us more fearful and less open. And certainly less alive. My heart gets so heavy as I become aware of the phenomenon. The corona virus played fully into all this, exposing and amplifying the double irony. Without adequate public healthcare and social services that connect us better, without the sturdy social fabric that looks after its disadvantaged, market-based states (most notably America) found themselves vulnerable and ill-equipped and thus had to defer to more heavily controlled lockdowns (with police edicts and fines, and surveillance) than those with a trusting relationship with their governments, unions and other social structures, such as Iceland, New Zealand, Kerala in India and South Korea.

The fear. The guilt. The anger. The despair. The overwhelm. Yep, that's also the edge. And we flee it, block it and paradoxically wind up stuck in it, rendered small and numb by it. But like I said earlier, we truly do have a responsibility to not let this emotional cycle defeat us. We must fight the urge to look away when the truth being shared on the news is tough to witness. It's not enough to comment, 'It's so sad what's happened to the koalas' in one post and then 'I can't even' in the next.

As Pema Chödrön reiterates in *When Things Fall Apart*, my favourite of her books, the edge is 'where we need to be'.

Each time I have reached my edge, when I felt myself resist and start to ask the unbeautiful questions like, 'Why me? Why is life so unfair? Why isn't anyone else fixing this?' I stop and ask, more beautifully, 'What if this pain is just life, and I'm being brought back to it?'

Chödrön again: 'We use these situations either to wake ourselves up or to put ourselves to sleep.'

57 *Doesn't being awake to the climate crisis and everything going on make you anxious?*

I get asked this a lot. Here's a good spot to cover it. When I've thought about it, I've realised that the more I go to my edge with our predicament, the more my own fear abates, and with it my overwhelm cycle. Remember Rosa Parks? As she put it, 'knowing what must be done does away with fear.'

— From back on p93.

I have found myself using this edge to ask a bunch more beautiful and critical questions.

Do I get resilient and join life where it is?

Or do I fight the edge and retreat to fear and control?

I mean, what kind of *life* do I want?

I want to say a bit more on this. I did a series of Instagram Live videos where I answered my community's questions about anxiety at the outset of the COVID-19 shutdown. I quickly learned that there were a bunch of us with so-called disordered anxiety who were feeling really rather calm (not everyone, but a sizeable and suitably surprised crew of us). Some of us had lost our income, some were still working in healthcare, some of us were living solo, with no touch and little connection. But we weren't freaking, not like we sometimes do when life is coasting as normal and we fall apart in the toothpaste aisle, paralysed by having to choose between fresh mint and cinnamon.

Why? I think it's because we had a sense that as highly sensitive types this is where we are meant to be. A crisis calls us to be hyper-alert and it's like we come into our own (as per those genes that scientists found get 'switched on' when an organism is put in a new, extended situation). A large proportion of wartime leaders, it has been shown, had bipolar or some sort of diagnosed anxiety 'disorder'. You might recall the work of Dian Fossey, which I cited in *The Beast*. She studied chimpanzees that displayed characteristics similar to humans who've been diagnosed with obsessive compulsive disorder – heightened hearing and smell (which could alert the clan to danger), and hyper-vigilance. When she removed these jittery chimps, the clan died out within months. In stressful times we anxious types, with our alert senses, come into our own.

Similarly, the scary edge at which we find ourselves on this planet thrusts us into the present. It's been shown – by forensic psychiatrists as well as Eastern spiritual types (and Eckhart Tolle) – that we actually can't be anxious in the present. Anxiety exists in fretting about the future.

Also, you might find this interesting. We talk a lot about the trauma caused by a tragedy or trip to the edge. Yet psychologists recently found that only a small percentage of people actually develop post-traumatic stress disorder (PTSD), despite the discourse around it. And up to two-thirds of trauma survivors exhibit, instead, what's known as post-traumatic growth. The psychologists found that after a crisis, most people acquire a newfound sense of purpose and develop deeper relationships. The experience of going to our edge sees us, in the main, seek meaning…and then find it in the precarious preciousness of life.

Fittingly, I read Albert Camus' *The Plague* during this time. It explores the ultimate edge – confronting death and the fact that it can strike any of us at any time – which, he and many existentialists argue, renders our frightened, desperate grip on life meaningless and absurd. However, awareness and acceptance of this absurdity – walking toward the edge, not away – actually frees us to get wild and play in love with our fellow humans – and ourselves. And to choose values such as decency and solidarity as a way of being. In the absence of external, permanent meaning, we can get super awake and wild and create our own. As Camus wrote, in a time of plague, we learn that there are far more things to admire in people than to despise.

As I ventured further on this path, I was repeatedly taken to my edge. At times I wanted to run back to the cocoon and say, 'I can't even…' But I practised staying and trusting that this is where I need to be. And I found myself feeling like

I'd arrived in a very knowing, still place. My anxiety had
actually reduced to but one dip of the teabag in the cup. I
started to sleep for the first time in, honestly, thirty years.
Over the course of eighteen months, I went from four to
five bad nights of sleep a fortnight (and any 'good' nights
requiring medication), to a mere one to two bad nights a
fortnight (medication-free). My inflammation abated – my
doctors looked at my blood test results and asked, 'What's
changed?'

'A lot,' I said.

I was often manic. But it was a solid, knowing mania and
I didn't collapse in a heap of self-doubt and self-flagellation.
I felt it was appropriate and purposeful to be thinking wild
ideas, to be feeling unbridled love for humanity, to take up
risky conversations with people that pushed them, too, to
an edge. In response to criticisms that she was not fit to
lead a global climate movement due to her Asperger's, Greta
Thunberg responded that before she got climate-engaged
she self-harmed, suffered horrible OCD and had become
mute, talking only through her father. 'Before I started
school-striking, I had no energy, no friends and I didn't speak
to anyone. I just sat alone at home, with an eating disorder.
All of that is gone now, since I have found a meaning, in a
world that sometimes seems meaningless to so many people.'

As Nietzsche said, when we have a why we can handle any
how. And I suppose this is where I – and many others – have
landed.

Get into trouble

Said artist Chuck Close (putting aside his horrible history of sexual harassment – which I do not in any way intend to celebrate – I have always been inspired by this quote):

> *If you get yourself in trouble, you don't have the answers. And if you don't have the answers, your solution will more likely be personal because no one else's solutions will seem appropriate. You'll have to come up with your own.*

I had to get myself into trouble to write this book. I needed to come in close and rise higher at times. It was a fun, joyous resilience-building exercise that got me increasingly cool with the absurdity of the new 'non-normal'. Life has sped up, I told everyone around me. It's game on. I knew the edge was where we had to practise being. I figured it might help if I shared a few examples here. And you could apply the ones that could work for you. Or adapt them to fit.

When I had a case of the blahs, or felt disconnected from my aliveness, I set off on a hike that would require having to navigate a crazed shortcut or even hitchhike. When you hitchhike you get pushed to connect with others – I'm at my edge, they're at theirs.

I also took up ocean swimming. I'm a weak swimmer. And only a few years ago I balked at the ocean.

But one day I was heading to the ocean pool to do some tame laps and just decided to jump off the rocks at the end of the beach, swim out behind the surfers, in line with the shark sensor, and struggle my way through the currents to the other end of the bay – about a kilometre. I saw octopuses, schools of fish, stingrays. I kept pushing myself. I tried unfamiliar beaches, choppier waters. 'Are you looking for trouble?' my friend Nicho asked me once. I realised I often am.

I find going to my physical edge an effective way to connect, possibly because I'm stuck in my head so much. Perhaps, for you, going to your edge might entail doing your first hike. Or your first solo hike. Or perhaps it's not a physical edge. Maybe you say 'yes' to a course or an event that scares you a little, for the sole purpose of meeting life. When you do, try feeling into the awareness and aliveness. Does it feel good? True? Stay out there, in a bit of trouble. You're building resilience. It's entirely purposeful.

Perhaps you make the first move on a dating app. Or you could take a conversation to an awkward place. A friend of mine has taken to answering the ubiquitous, 'How are you?' with, 'My mother is dying of Alzheimer's and I'm going through menopause.' She knows it will make her work harder, and lift others in the conversation, too.

The edge. Out there. At the front line of life. And death. It's scary, it's uncertain, it's overwhelming. But it's all okay. It's where we are all meant to be.

Move things in your brain
We experience primal fear in the very primitive amygdala. And we experience the anxiety of uncertainty in the slightly more developed prefrontal cortex, which tries to process

information and create a bit of a plan. We tend to feel a lot of our anxiety when our prefrontal cortex doesn't have enough information to create a plan forward (and it will frantically search for data to fill in the gaps, not all of it helpful).

Of course, we experience both — fear and uncertainty — at our edge. It's a double hit.

A helpful technique for managing this in a productive, connecting way is via a simple re-framing exercise.

It goes like this. When we feel fear, we name it, label it, talk about it. This 'processing' consciously and deliberately moves neural activity from the amygdala — the centre of emotion and fear — to the prefrontal cortex, which is frantically looking for data to plan and process.

We literally talk to ourselves and to others using language like, 'I'm currently noticing that I have the feeling of fear.' Or, 'That unsettled feeling I have is probably because I've not made a plan for my day. So let's make a plan.' Or, simply, 'I want to run, but that's because I'm at an edge. So — breathe deep and take in that oxygen you poor old brain — this is where you're meant to be.'

Similarly, positive psychology pioneer Martin Seligman suggests pivoting your explanatory styles — the way you might frame things in your head when anxious at the edge — from internal to external, from global to specific and from permanent to impermanent. So when you talk about what's going on, you might say, 'This is an issue that's happening as part of the planet's biological response to globalisation and, yep, we are at our edge, so how are we going to respond?'

— Which is why many of us obsessively read news scrolls during a crisis, for instance.

This shifts the locus of control from something you can't do anything about, to something you can change, namely your response. Make sense?

THE JULIAN ALPS HIKE, SLOVENIA

So I wound up doing my plan B hike. Sort of. It took me to an edge, the one where I'm rendered choiceless and can't do what I want (hike hard and high).

I was four weeks pregnant. But I had nowhere to stay, so I hired the last rental car I could find in Slovenia and connected with my 'epic hike that never was' on the other side of the mountain range. There were huts that I'd booked there, so I could stay and, um, twiddle some thumbs while I worked out what to do next.

I walked the stretches of the route over the other side of Mount Triglav, out of the midday heat and in small, frustrated segments. The walk descends into the Soča Valley and I meandered up and down beautiful mountain paths with waterfall stop-offs. The terrain is a mix of all the areas that surround Slovenia – the austere beauty of the Tatras and the verdant and neat lushness of its neighbours Italy and Austria. I slept in the mountain huts and was served big bowls of pork and cabbage soup. In the Soča gorge I jumped into turquoise rivers so clear that the riverbed, metres below, seemed only an arm's length from the surface.

On the final day, I watched a family with two teenage kids do a crossword puzzle together, piled on top of each other on a picnic rug, jumping up to dive in the river every now and then. They smiled at me. 'We're a weird family,' the dad said. 'I don't think so,' I said.

I then headed to Hiša Franko, the famous Michelin star restaurant run by Ana Roš and her husband, of *Chef's Table* fame. Roš was named the World's Best Female Chef in 2017 at the San Pellegrino restaurant awards. She taught herself to cook when her husband's family's restaurant needed a chef. I'd saved up to eat here; it was a very special highlight of my trip.

I was seated on her front patio (the restaurant is in their home). I saw another solo diner. I invited her to join me. She was also called Sarah, and together we enjoyed sourdough made from a four-year-old starter fermented in apple peels; fermented cucumber with curry, rabbit and peanut butter... and violets and cheese lollipops. The other Sarah had been travelling with her fiancé. But decided to do a leg of the trip on her own. She'd never travelled solo. And never eaten alone at a restaurant. We had wonderful chats about love. And pregnancy. And decided to not swap numbers and leave our meeting as an isolated special – and edgy – thing.

hike.

just hike.

After you have exhausted what there is in business, politics, conviviality, love, and so on — have found that none of these finally satisfy, or permanently wear — what remains? Nature remains

— **Walt Whitman**

58 What's the most direct way to connect to life, to our big bold true nature, to ourselves? Being in nature. More specifically, walking in nature.

I've been hiking the whole way through this journey. But I've left it until now to really flesh out the hows and whys. Things needed to build for a bit.

We emerged into human-hood walking in nature. Our human brain evolved because we got upright and walked. Our sentience and awareness – the stunning and special stuff

THIS ONE WILD AND PRECIOUS LIFE

that sets us apart in the animal kingdom – evolved to the rhythms of walking and in response to the patterns in nature we saw when we quit schlepping around on all fours and began looking upward.

Hiking brings us back to our nature because hiking is how we know our nature.

59 Let me explain the backdrop to what we're trying to do here. Remember that elephant that is literally sitting on our laps, breathing in our ear? It's there to tell us that life is at risk and that we want to save it. The life of this planet, the life from which we emerge and that brings us sunrises with gold fingers that splay through sea mist, moons that smile at us and birds that deliver us to group soul.

The joy of walking in nature – biophilia as it's sometimes called – also reminds of us what we're fighting for. As an eco-activist tool, little beats it.

The other boon is that walking goes in the opposite direction to neo-liberalism. It always has done, ever since the inception of the more-more-more model in the 19th century. Witness Nietzsche and Heidi in the Swiss Alps, the Wordsworths in the Lake District. In Paris the intellectual elite took to walking in public parks. In the States there were the naturalists Henry David Thoreau, Walt Whitman and John Muir who were also vocally anti-capitalist.

– See my exploration of the flâneur, page 335-336.

In a system that disconnects us from ourselves, each other and what matters, that reduces us to small productive units –

cogs in a machine – and goes at a madly, pointless, distracted pace that has us running down a hill too fast for our legs to connect to earth, walking sticks two fingers up at the whole damn destructive, conformist lot. In fact, thinking about it just now with you, to walk is to commit a most deviant act!

In a system that rapes and pillages the planet as though it were separate from and subservient to us, walking in nature is an act of radical correction.

I love *New Yorker* essayist Adam Gopnik's description of walking in Manhattan as an expansive connection, 'a happy opening out to an enlarged civic self rather than a narrowing down to a contemplative inner one; a way of scooting toward the American Over-Soul, in sneakers.' He speaks to a particular freedom, for which people in big cities are yearning deeply at the moment, particularly cities gridlocked in dated neo-liberal market values: 'when we walk in New York, we always hope to randomise our too neatly gridded city existence. You go where your feet take you. Buses follow routes and subways have schedules, but someone on foot goes wherever he wants.'

I remember Helen Gurley Brown, the founding editor of *Cosmopolitan* and my mentor during my time at the magazine, teaching me how to walk in Manhattan. We were sitting on the leopard-print carpet stairs of her Central Park-side penthouse apartment, our shoes off. She was in her late-eighties at the time. 'Don't stop walking,' she told me, tapping my knee with her arthritic forefinger. 'When you set out, just head in the direction you need to go and move with the green lights.' She explained I should keep zigzagging my way through the grid system. 'Never be stopped.' It was a brilliant metaphor for almost every bit of go-girl advice the magazine ever put out.

It can also be as simple as this: while we're out walking, particularly in nature, we don't consume. We choose our own way to use our leisure time. The billboards, the targeted text messages and the Facebook ads don't reach us out in the woods where more often than not there is no reception. The faux baked-bread scents that pump through malls have no pull on us.

The Cynics of ancient Greece walked as a way to scorn conventions, and the status quo. You could say Western thought is rooted in deviant thinking developed in motion.

When you walk, instead of drive, you are also, very visibly, *not* buying into the all-supreme imperative of the car and all the isolation, disconnect and ecological travesty that comes with it. You take to the streets. You pass traffic jams, you weave your way, your feet agile and moving to spirited beats in your headphones or to your own jibe, naturally. You arrive on foot and you are already in your body, vibrant and present and really quite defiant.

When you think about it, to walk has always been a mode of protest. Jesus walked across a desert. Gandhi walked roughly 18 kilometres a day, twice around the Earth in his lifetime, often as a form of protest. Dr Martin Luther King Jr marched to get legislation changed.

Walkers disrupt. We take over the streets – significant

modes of cog-ish productivity. And we get heard. In London, street protests saw the United Kingdom declare a climate emergency in September 2019 and more than six million people in 160-plus countries joined Greta Thunberg and the school students in their global climate strike, which finally put the emergency on front pages and political agendas, while the Black Lives Matter marches triggered significant symbolic and legislative shifts.

Walking, despite being vagrant, is generally respected. I know when I walk in sneakers to a fancy dinner and sit in the gutter out front to swap into fancy shoes the vibe from the security guard standing nearby is distinctly 'bravo'. Ditto when I cross Manhattan to a meeting and decline the client's offer to book an Uber. I explain it's faster to walk according to Google Maps and show them the screen. Everyone likes the primal good sense that walking makes, and the freedom it denotes. In Japan on the various pilgrimage trails, and on Spain's Camino de Santiago, locals still give coins to the hundreds of pilgrims who pass through their villages each day. It's good luck to respect what a walker is doing. Which in the case of pilgrimage is moving toward bigger moral and spiritual goals that can't be reached with the mind. As Rebecca Solnit writes in *Wanderlust: A History of Walking*: '[Walking] unites belief with action... We are eternally perplexed by how to move toward forgiveness or healing or truth, but we know how to walk from here to there.'

60 And so – and perhaps this is a slightly esoteric leap – to walk is also moral.

When we walk, we have the emotional space to discern where the hell right and wrong land for us. Also – and I just adore this factlet – the rhythm of walking is the same as the theta brainwaves that govern intuition and our 'gut judgement'. Theta cranks up when we walk because it is needed for spatial positioning. Once cranked the parts of our being that steer us to good, to better, to love, they all attune. Walking is a forward motion. Love, yearning, and all the optimistic endeavours of the human experience are also forward motions. When we walk we attune to these positive forces.

I think it can also be convincingly argued that walking in nature generally makes us nicer humans. I'm certainly more pleasant after I've thrashed out my impatience and hypocrisies in some rocks and dirt. Sometimes I hike before — A top introvert's hack!
a party. Seriously. So that I'm less awkward company. Dog walkers are apparently nicer than the rest of us (by virtue of being in parks, walking). I also learned that trees can lower murder rates in cities. An Illinois study looked at housing projects with lots of trees versus those without, and found much lower crime rates and aggression in the former. It's not an outrageous leap to make – trees created an environment where neighbours spent more time outside talking to each other, thus fostering a sense of belonging, community and trust.

I was also interested to learn that Frederick Law Olmsted

(who famously designed Manhattan's Central Park and dozens of other greens spaces in the US) vocally pushed the need to plonk city dwellers in nature to be their best selves. He distributed flyers to doctors' offices in poor neighbourhoods all over New York City: 'Please tell your patients to go to Central Park because it will help them feel better!' With much the same aim, South Korea set up forest therapy camps a few years back for teen bullies. The government literally buses kids out to nature to become kinder humans.

Nature becomes, if not our moral umpire, our moral guru.

'The human being is, relatively speaking, the most bungled of all the animals, the sickliest, the one most dangerously strayed from its instincts,' wrote Nietzsche in the late 1800s. The only cure 'for the disease called man' is a 'return to nature'.

In roughly the same era – and suffering, too, from chronic ill health and torment – Robert Louis Stevenson wrote of walking in nature: 'You sink into yourself, and the birds come round and look at you.'

It's true, they do.

61 It can be a bit tricky to extol the full virtues of walking, or hiking, in words. For years I did it with bludgeoning enthusiasm and demonstration. For my twenty-first I got all my friends to come in party gear and hiking shoes. We carted cheap champagne up the side of a mountain and sat in bushland to watch the sun go down. When I was fifteen, I hung out with some misfits from an alternative school. I got it in my head to take a bunch of them hiking on a scorching summer's day. We were a motley crew. I was in don't-label-me, non-fashion jeans and singlet. There was Jeremy, who worked to a Jim Morrison vibe and who (actually) went off and joined the circus a few years later. Another wore all black with no shoes and had grown his fingernails in 15-centimetre nautilus curves that got tangled in his blue-black hair when he self-consciously pulled it over his whitened face. The third had a good dozen facial piercings that left him with a slight speech impediment and he arrived with two rats up the sleeves of his black woollen jumper. I dragged the crew up a mountain ridge behind my parents' place. They all sweltered on account of their wearing all black. When we got back, Dad came out with orange cordial in toddler cups and Family Assorted biscuits on a saucer. Years later I saw Jeremy in a remote pub in the Australian outback (he was touring the Fruit Fly Circus). It was the 2000 Olympics and we'd both come to the pub – a pile of corrugated iron with a large screen TV tied to a tree – to watch Cathy Freeman run the 400-metre final in that famous spacesuit. He brought up the hike and Dad's cordial. 'I became a hiker from that experience,' he told me.

Bludgeoning enthusiasm...and an Instagram feed full of curated shots of my best hiking moments and tips, is good for selling in hiking (and writing a book that weaves hikes throughout). But facts, science and pointing to the experiences of highly productive and life-giving humans extolling the same is better. How about I bundle it all together, tossing in the details of how I actually go about hiking, in one bulging package.

62 Let's talk about the anatomy of a hike. A hike should have flow right from the start. I will find my perfect walk via hike apps and Googling. I look for circuit tracks, or tracks that are point-to-point where I catch a train to the start and finish at another station or two along the line. The flowy satisfaction of pulling off a train-hike-train maneuver is huge. I'll get a takeaway coffee in a glass jar, which then becomes my water vessel. I drink my coffee sitting on the sunny side of a train carriage winding out of a city and off into the bush and arrive already planted in a meditative, open space.

Packing lighter than humanly possible is also stupidly satisfying. On a day hike I don't take a bag. I shove my credit card, train card and phone down my bra. Often a bit of paper and a pencil, too. You might have active-wear with pockets. Great. (Or you could just take a bag!) If the walk is less than two hours, I will drink a litre or two of water before heading off, then leave my drink bottle or glass jar in a bush to collect on my return (in the case of a loop track). I get my water from garden taps in front yards near the train.

For me, packing light is almost an existentialist pursuit. It's not about the physical weight, it's the psychological weight. Feeling unencumbered adds to the flow. Nomad and travel writer Bruce Chatwin claimed all he needed was a Mont

There are websites in many locales featuring 'hikes accessible by train'.

See page 276 for details of my very versatile DIY KeepCup.

Editor Miriam has begged me to note that all hiking guidebooks recommend taking water for safety. 'What if you broke your ankle and fell down a steep slope into bushland and weren't found for several hours? Or what if it was just hot as buggery?'

Blanc fountain pen and a bag of muesli when he meandered. American essayist Pico Iyer, who's lived peripatetically and minimally for many years (while writing a wonderful book, *The Art of Stillness*, paradoxically enough), says, 'I spend more time thinking about what I don't want to take with me: assumptions, iPods, cameras, plans, friends, laptops, headphones, suntan lotion, resumes, expectations.'

If you're doing a multi-day hike, I recommend Googling videos of people's packing techniques. There is a sub-world out there seeking ludicrous satisfaction from achieving next-level camping minimalism.

There is always something you can drop from your load, which is a motto for life, really.

Swimsuits? Nah, I swim in my undies. More than one pair of undies? Nah, they've just been washed from swimming in them (they dry when I start walking again). Deodorant? Why bother. I'm the only person who can smell me. Toothpaste? I just take the brush (and use the residual toothpaste embedded in it).

What about a map? Well, it's worth asking if you really need one of those, too. I download a route onto my phone. I do screen grabs, too, just in case. Or I don't use one at all. — At which point Miriam has a conniption! Finding where you are helps you find yourself, according to a study from Sweden's Karolinska Institute. Navigating without Google Maps or Navman sees us exerting ourselves spatially, extending ourselves to have a better sense of our relationship to the world, and thus connects us with the part of the brain that craves to know where we are and, thus, who we are. How perfect.

I love Robert Louis Stevenson's take on the freedom of not having a map while hiking: 'you should be able to stop and go on, and follow this way or that, as the freak takes you.'

As the freak takes you!

I also love the concept of 'desire lines', paths that are formed when we abandon the map and go off-piste. They're the single trails that cut a scarring line across a park or go off on their own through a forest. They appear where people wanted to walk, where the freak took them. And of course, someone has studied them. A team at the University of Wollongong in Australia says they 'record collective disobedience'. I love this, too.

It's also a safety — thing. I don't want a creepy person knowing where I am in real time.

Next, I switch my phone to airplane mode.. Partly because having my phone spinning to find signal chews up battery and is probably not an ideal EMF situation so close to my organs. But also because it sanctifies the experience. No calls, no texts, and no imperative to post photos I might take photos as I go but upload them later.

A random line — I found in a random review of a book by Gretel Ehrlich, a nature writer, hiker and cattle farmer in Wyoming.

Then I start walking. At a 'slow, steady trot of keenness with no speed.' I resist a little at first. My bones are wobbly in their joints, stones get stuck in my sock. I can be a bit shitty if I've gotten away late or am sleep-deprived, or if inflammation has rendered me hot and prickly. My autoimmune disease can be irascible this way, but I start walking – in dirt or by the ocean or just on my way to somewhere – and after about 20 minutes the hotness and itchiness drains from my head, my feet and my fingers.

Studies (albeit not overly robust ones) show that walking in nature literally grounds us. Abundant free electrons on the Earth's surface enter our bodies and act as antioxidants, neutralising free radicals (goes the theory). Other studies show negative ions in water – at the beach or near waterfalls – can improve mood and well-being.

After 40-60 minutes, the thoughts stop swirling and fizzle out into the atmosphere. In their place wild daydreamy thoughts drift in. And out. There is no structure to them. Sometimes I like to play a game where I backtrack through the sequence of trippy, daydreamy thoughts. What made me think of that? Then what made me think of *that*? It's fun to witness the wild, childlike stuff that comes up when the clangy, fretty stuff clears away. It's like therapy...the revelations can be really, really interesting and telling. With nothing to distract you, you can reconnect with yourself.

It's around this point that a work or family dilemma might waft into view. Or an emotional or moral issue. In my case, it's often a quandary about whatever I'm writing at the time. The answer to said stuck point will just start surfacing like little bubbles from down deep. They get bigger as they approach the surface. Then pop! The through line or the perfect sentence lands front of mind.

Creatives hike to solve creative problems. Steve Jobs, Mark Zuckerberg and Twitter's Jack Dorsey have all taken to walking meetings. A stack of classic writers say they wrote while walking – Virginia Woolf, Ernest Hemingway, Charles Dickens and Henry Miller, who said 'most writing is done away from the typewriter…it occurs in the quiet, silent moments, while you're walking.' A 2014 Stanford study shows that people are 60 per cent more creative when walking than when sitting still. In one of the tests, volunteers had to come up with atypical uses for everyday objects, such as a button or a tyre. On average, the students thought of between four and six more novel uses for the objects while they were walking than when they were seated. Various studies also show the effect is greatest when walking near trees. There we go!

Walking promotes new connections between brain cells and increases the volume of the hippocampus, the brain region crucial for memory. You also get raised levels of brain-derived neurotrophic factor (BDNF) – which has been described as molecular fertiliser – and vascular endothelial growth factor (VEGF), which helps to grow the network of blood vessels carrying oxygen and nutrients to brain cells.

Another study, published in the Proceedings of the National Academy of Sciences, showed walking in nature reduced broodiness (cluttered and unproductive thinking), explained by less blood flow to the subgenual prefrontal cortex.

Now as a very interesting aside, many famous artists, writers and creatives walked to cure bipolar or constipation or, more often than not, both (because they often travel together). We're talking Henry James, Graham Greene, Jack London, Charles Darwin, Nietzsche, Walt Whitman, Tchaikovsky, Mahler and Kant. Beethoven had manic episodes and would take to the woodlands around Vienna with a pencil and paper; Charles

One of the odder — correlations I learned while researching this book.

Dickens would walk all day and night to thrash out his thoughts, clocking up 30 miles (50 kilometres). All of them mad and 'stuck'. All of them brilliant and perambulatory. As a person with a fiery bipolar condition and related gut issues (one flares as soon as the other ignites in a hot wrestle at my core), hiking has proven the most reliable salve for both. When I hike, all my fast-knotted thoughts will be there, but it's like the left–right–left motion and the soothing 'is-ness' of nature sees them present themselves in an orderly fashion in my brain. I can address them, one by one, rather than have them crush me in an avalanche. At which point the evolutionary response that freezes any slightly superfluous mechanisms (digestion, expansive emotional perspective) when in a heightened survival mode, releases. And, *whoosh*, I can go to the loo.

In Finland, public health officials now recommend citizens get five hours a month, minimum, in the woods to combat depression. And in the United States, there are outdoors programs to help kids with ADHD and veterans with PTSD.

I've always thought that the mere act of moving so rhythmically and naturally through time and space plays a role. So I went digging down some rabbit holes. How's this: attachment theorist John Bowlby found that a distressed baby is calmed when carried and walked at the average pace of an average-sized woman. 'The movement,' he wrote, 'is a vertical one with a traverse of three inches.' Novelist and travel writer Bruce Chatwin added to Bowlby's findings:

'Rocking at slow speeds, such as thirty cycles a minute, had no effect: but once you raised the pace to fifty and above, every baby ceased to cry and almost always stayed quiet.'

That is, — walking pace.

I can also use my walking speed to temper my mood and thinking. Strolling naturally oscillates with our moods and the cadence of our inner speech. When I need to lift my spirits, I walk briskly. Everything gets brisker.

After a while – at the two-hour mark, sometimes a little later – even the daydream thoughts drop to earth and fizzle out. You are but an empty vessel. Hunger or tiredness or some crappy thinking can try to kick back in. But here's the fun bit. Because you are now an ego-less, peaceful, empty vessel, the crappy, clutching thoughts float in and you can actually do that thing that epic meditators bang on about – observe them and let them go.

There's no feeling like returning from a hike. I love to lie on the ground and just let the whole lot sink into my viscera. Hiking guidelines should always come with the instruction: 'Allow to marinate for at least an hour.'

I almost feel drunk as the joy and peace swirl around my body.

Then I eat. I have a ritual on train day-hikes. I don't carry food, I front-load before I head off, along with the water. But at the end I indulge in a packet of potato crisps from the vending machine at the station. And I'll eat them lying on my back on the platform and feel the fat and salt swirl around my body, too. I think I remember almost every meal I've eaten after a big hike: stews on my camp stove,

Yeah, a guilty — indulgence from an environmental POV.

or meals eaten in *auberges* or *gostilja* around the world. I've developed recipes based on these meals and put them in my cookbooks. Adored American food writer Mary Frances Kennedy Fisher once described a Sunday ritual of a long walk followed by a meal at a noisy beer hall in Strasbourg. She'd order a plate made up of 'a large piece of strong runny cheese, a bowl of finely minced raw onion, a smaller bowl of caraway seeds, plenty of good, crusty bread.' You remember and describe food in this kind of post-coital space in the most alive detail.

Lastly, I land. It's a feeling of being filled to the edges with completion. A sense that all is right. A proper exchange of work and reward has taken place and it creates a sturdy, morally re-set foundation in me that I'm able to pivot from in a considered, connected way for at least a few days afterward.

I like this line from Sylvain Tesson, who stayed in a cabin in a forest in Siberia for a year and passed the time walking. His conclusion from the experience: 'In life, three ingredients are necessary: sunshine, a commanding view and legs aching with remembered effort.'

— His book *Consolations of the Forest* is a wonderful read for anyone experiencing the call of the wild.

Oh, yes!

THE WHITE MOUNTAIN TRAIL, CRETE, GREECE

Shall we finish the Cretan adventure from earlier? I eventually returned, eight weeks pregnant. But I'll backtrack a little first.

After completing the Julian Alps hike in Slovenia, I caught the train to Slovakia. Wonderfully, I'd learned that my brother Pete, his Slovakian wife Janka and my nephew and niece, Emil and Milena, were basing themselves there for the European summer. The day before leaving Slovenia I'd accepted a date with a very charming 22-year-old waiter who'd approached me in the Slovenian port town of Piran. He took me out on his friend's speedboat. Being twenty-two, he was not equipped, I decided, to deal with the fact that he was on a date with a single mum-to-be a year older than his own mother. And being oblivious to my condition, he went too fast. The boat got air and came crashing down; I felt my uterus hit the deck, or my kneecaps – something hard and unforgiving.

When I arrived in the mountainous town of Banská Štiavnica in central Slovakia, Pete and Janka suggested I should get things checked out. But Slovakia is a deeply Catholic and conservative country and Janka couldn't find a doctor who'd do an ultrasound on a single foreigner…of my age. You can learn dark and intimate things about a nation via the way they deal with a reproducing woman. After two weeks I got some spot bleeding; I started to worry and to berate myself for being so careless.

My Cretan doctor called a few days later. 'I woke up last night and realised you don't have an obstetrician,' he said, apropos of not much. Such a practicality had not occurred to me. I told Dr Daphnis about the boat ride. 'Come back to us and we'll look after you,' he said.

I arrived back in Chania on a Sunday and Dr Daphnis scanned me that afternoon between church and a family christening. When I heard the heartbeat, I punched him on the arm, 'No way!' It was in this moment that I got what this pregnancy caper was about. As I said, I'd felt numb to it until then, skeptical, tired and a bit whiplashed. Also, when you're on your own, you do twice the worry, and only half the excitement (compared to a couple sharing the experience). But now I felt my being expanding with belongingness. I felt like I had a little mate, a partner in crime. We were going to look after each other.

I hung around in Chania, ate lots of horta and worked on this book. My head was unbelievably clear. I was sniper-like in my focus on what mattered. I mercenarily eliminated anything that didn't. It was a hoot to witness what these pregnancy hormones could do. There was also this: pregnancy hormones extinguished the frenetic buzz of mania and self-doubt that has vibrated in my brain since I was a kid. It had happened last time, too. It was like they were a damper pedal to my anxious sonata. 'Shush, not now,' they whispered to my nervousness.

At eleven weeks my doctor did another ultrasound. It was almost time to go home. I was ready to get real about it all – get an actual lease on a flat for the first time in almost a decade. And actual furniture. And an obstetrician.

But my doctor couldn't pick up a heartbeat. He left it half an hour and came back. Still none. I stared at his face. I busied myself with thinking about what might be going through his head to maintain an optimistic vibe for me as he rolled the scanner around, trying in vain to detect a beat. He eventually stopped and said, 'I'm so, so sorry, our dear Sarah.' An extra test revealed a knot in the umbilical cord, presumably from the little thing doing some odd acrobatics. But who knows? 'She was as overactive as her mum,' he said. I'm not sure why he referred to her as a girl. I had, too, though.

One of the nurses took me out for dinner that night. The next day she walked with me around Chania to find a doctor who'd do the D&C. The Greeks were not going to leave me stranded; I just had to dole out cash under the proverbial table for the anaesthetic. I waited in the hospital lobby until a doctor had an opening. He didn't speak English, nor did the anaesthetist. I woke in the maternity ward next to a new mum doing her first breastfeed. I thought, as I often do when things get comically rough out on solo limbs in the world, 'See the divine humour, Sarah. The divine humour!'

I got dressed and walked home in the blazing afternoon sun. I didn't cry. I ate some figs from a roadside tree. Mum and Dad rang. I was too drowsy to explain the details.

'Dilation and curettage' – a surgical procedure to remove the foetus from the uterus after miscarriage.

The next morning, I woke early and hired a car. I drove up to the White Mountains in the centre of the island. I strapped on my cloth bag containing an orange and my canister of water and I started to climb Mount Gingilos. A wild, determined, almost mesmeric energy fuelled me. As I moved up the track that wound around cliffs and shale drop-offs, I felt like a large goanna, all my limbs alive and in rhythm, my shoulders and hips pivoting to a wild, forward beat. It was more a possessed clamber than a walk. But then every 30 minutes or so I'd stop and lean against a rock face, two hands outstretched, and wail. I wailed from a depth I'd never met before. It felt like a surge of energy, a churning torrent, that had no beginning and no end. It was pure purge.

I wailed until I dry-retched. Then I wiped the snotty dribble from my face and clambered onward. After a bit, the pressure would build and I'd bend over again, my hands on my knees, or I'd crouch down low against a tree, and dry-retch some more. I wasn't feeling sorry for myself. It was just raw pain expressing itself and I knew it just had to do its thing.

I reached the ridgeline. I could see all the way down the Omalos valley, following the goat trail I'd ascended. There was a final summit that required some technical rock climbing. I scrambled up for another 25 minutes. At the top was a metal plate commemorating some woman who had fallen to her death up here. Her name was Sarah. 'We will love you always.' I let the sobs heave from my chest.

63 This pure purge was an interesting thing to go through on my own on a mountain in Crete. It was my own grief, unadulterated by fear that I might subliminally be putting on some sort of show for others who'd expressed their own sympathy and concern.

David Whyte has said that grief is like falling in love. You fall and you fall. You fall toward something, toward the thing you're grieving, the thing that is no longer there. Eventually after you've fallen and fallen and fallen, after you've lived through – or wailed through – the grieving, you land. And instead of landing at the loved one or loved thing that used to hold you there, you land at yourself. When I heard him say this, I knew that was what I was doing when I flung myself at the mountain that day.

I was falling into the grief until I fell through it to myself.

I also knew that this is what I'm often doing when I hike – processing. Trauma psychologists talk of the need to work through the shittiness of pain so that it doesn't get locked in your body and psyche. I've touched on this a little already, but I defer to American somatic therapist Peter Levine to bring it home.

Levine flags that in our former lives as simple humans, fear and stress were almost always a response to a tangible threat (such as meeting an enemy or being chased by a tiger), but we would process the surges of cortisol and adrenaline by fighting or fleeing. And if we won the fight or escaped the physical release and subsequent relief (we survived!) rounded off the experience. The emotion was passed through, with

Or we'd simply – be eaten.

the aid of the physical reaction, and released. Pfft, out of here!

Today, however, most fear is manifested from threats in our heads, or from ginormous hyperobjects where the threat is difficult to cognitise, and swirls around unproductively as we try to avoid and block it; we have no physical release, and so it doesn't get rounded off. We end up storing it in our bodies and psyches. The fear and pain remain 'in our bones', haunting us. We cope by developing neuroses and addictions to mask and numb the pain.

Hiking, then, is a supremely effective, honest and primal way to process our feelings. It whacks a big – and healthy – full stop on the end of them. I hike when I need to fall through an emotional quagmire back to myself. I pass through my heartache and rejection from a failed interlude with a bloke to compassion and acceptance of life by hiking along tumultuous coastlines.

When my mind is going too fast, I go to arid, vast landscapes. My thoughts tumble out into the landscape and there's lots of room and bright light for them to unfurl. The dryness and the honesty of life surviving against lots of odds – roots clawing over rocky outcrops, a flower sprouting from a crack in the earth – provides a great reality check for my thoughts.

Come on, get over yourselves! It's all here. It just is.

I go to forests when I need to find gentleness. Trees are forgiving; they wrap around each other; they cocoon us in a calm, foliaged quietness and so hiking amid them means you can hear the sound of your own feelings and let them ooze

— Even the freeze mechanism sees us process it physically as per the earlier deer example on pages 123-125.

through you and out into the insulating pine needles and fern fronds.

Solvitur ambulando, St Augustine declared. We solve it by walking.

64 The Australian sustainability professor Glenn Albrecht coined the term solastalgia to describe a terrible existential homesickness from nature that has set in as we've witnessed its destruction in recent years. Solastalgia is the upshot of our disconnect from the planet.

It's also been referred to as ecological grief emerging as a very real psychological condition among the humans working on the front line of the climate crisis. Researchers are forming support groups online to help them cope with the serious mental health impacts. Farmers, the Inuit of North America and Australia's First Nations peoples are also feeling this very particular grief. I venture to say most of us are.

Seeing images of the bushland that has held and saved me for decades go up in flames has devastated me. The sound of thousand-year-old tree trunks screaming their oil-drenched fate, the primal roar as the fire tore through hectares of life, was as horrifying as any death scene I've witnessed. Nature scorched puts up a raging, wronged protest. I was on a train from Sydney to Canberra to deliver a talk to a businesswomen's group and passed through country stripped of its webbing, its fibre. Trees were upturned, their roots unable to grip the feeble drought-starved soil. The landscape looked like it had been skinned. It was a scene from an apocalyptic movie – nothing remained. I cried and cried.

'I'm sorry,' I whispered to the land.

The ecological grief we feel is not like the grief we feel for the loss of a human or a baby. Such death is finite. The destruction of nature is enduring. Which I think makes the grief so much harder to process and talk about.

A climate scientist from Labrador in Canada, one of the fastest-warming places on the planet and home to a large Inuit community, was asked by a journalist for her solution to climate grief. She responded:

There's a power and an honour to grief, because it means that we have loved something, and we've had a connection to a place or to species of the planet. We need to find ways to mark our loss and share our loss, but also to remind ourselves that we only grieve what we love. I think new rituals are essential to celebrate that love, and to mark the loss and to come together for loss.

As we covered earlier, we grieve what we love. We also fight to save what we love. More than ever, we need to be in nature, being held by it, left in awe by it, grieving it, loving it. So that we will fight for it.

65 I repeated the purging exercise the next day on another mountain in the Paradise forest near Zourva. I got horribly lost and an evening wind picked up as I tried to find my way back down the rocky goat tracks. I remained calm. It was all part of the process. I got back to my little cottage and poured myself a whisky and I felt that 90 per cent of the grief was passed through. I don't think the remaining 10 per cent will ever go. I can still feel my partner in crime with me most days and I regularly wail out my longing for her into the sides of mountains.

get
full-fat
spiritual

66 And now we come to spirituality. Leagues of humans spanning the eons have turned to it when the deep call to reconnect becomes too urgent and painful to ignore. On this journey I practised spirituality daily, mostly via meditation and mostly in nature, complemented by some fairly esoteric spiritual therapy. In part to provide a framework for processing the pain and grief uprooted by the climate crisis. But also as a touch-point for joy. To keep going, and to be able to perhaps land in a hopeful, connected place at the end, we need reminders of what the hell we are doing it all for, what it is that we love so much and want to save. Those words ring in my ears, 'Sarah, show us how to find the charm.'

But perhaps the most important purpose of spirituality, particularly in difficult times, is as a moral reconnector. The spiritual traditions remind us of, or tap us into, the force greater than our individualistic needs, and guide us to be of service to said greater force. They bring us back into communion with God, The Oneness, or Life, if you like.

67 But here's the thing. So many of the religious and spiritual practices that play out today, particularly in the West, are a lite version of the real thing. Just like connection-lite and commitment-lite, the diet version of the original spiritual texts and wisdoms dodges the hard parts that demand something of us, instead enabling a certain unsatisfyingly indulgent and cocooning smallness.

Sigh. Far from bringing us into communion, they actually work to separate us further.

Allow me to explain.

'Spiritualism-lite', or 'spiritual bypassing' as some call it, is when we cherry-pick the nice, dreamy 'rainbows and unicorns' parts of a spiritual tradition and leave out the chunks that require sacrifice, service and a deep injection of moral courage – the hard stuff. It's taking the forgiveness without confessing. It's being a yoga instructor who preaches 'honouring our bodies when we come to our mat', while wearing leggings made of microplastics that leach into the waterways. It's being a meditation teacher and handing out single-use coconut water cartons at a retreat. It's being a practising Christian and not supporting universal healthcare. It's taking a dreamy sound-bath class where everyone has their eyes closed in gentle self-reflection then scrolling past the Facebook posts calling for donations to bail funds when you get home. It's treating spiritual practice as another consumable that we use to avoid and cocoon ourselves from the bigger and the broader. It's prioritising our own 'feels' over the collective need, and the planet, which is the opposite of what every spiritual tradition actually teaches. And the opposite of the reconnection you and I seek.

But it's tricky. For behind the bypassing is a very real longing. A growing, deeply yearning number of us are drawn to the mushroom lattes and kundalini workshops, the drumming circles and the tarot readings to cope during this human despair crisis and – yes – to connect and be bigger and kinder. I get it. I do yoga, I meditate. I quote Rumi. And all from a highly affluent, comfortable waterside suburb that my privilege allows me to live in. These lifestyle practices can make us softer, more open, more mindful. And they are a much-needed salve for the fear-guilt-anger-despair-overwhelm cycle.

Also, this kind of self-care and inward work was vital for me to work through my anxiety, as it is for millions of people out there. And I really don't want to come across as judgemental toward anyone in that place right now. Because, as I have said often, sometimes we do just have to get through the night to be 'all right.' Boy, do I get it.

— Actually, John Lennon said it/ sang it first.

But once we're soft and open, then what? Are we going to go outward and use it to serve others and the planet, to truly reconnect, like that monk who finally comes down from the mountain and shares his calm learnings?

68 And I'll say this here, italicised for effect, and no doubt come
back to it again: *The times are demanding more of us right now.*

There are periods in history in which this happens. The
Vedic tradition teaches that life works to a never-ending
cycle of creation, maintenance and destruction. We're born,
we live, we die, then we are reborn in some form or other,
and on we go. Physics, biology, quantum mechanics...they
work to the same truth. You could say we've been in a
maintenance phase for decades, if not centuries. But now
things have gotten destructive, as they have before, and we
need to step up from our comfortable lull – our acedia –
go to our edge and serve. It's in such times (of war, famine,
plague, despotic rule) that religion and spirituality tend to
lead us in this stepping up, reminding us of the noble worth
of the hard bits – the sacrifice, the service, the radical faith.

The beautiful questions to ask, then: How are we going
to be of service? What are we willing to sacrifice to live the
teachings of Buddha, Jesus, Mohammed, Gaia, The Universe
– to save ourselves, and the world?

JOSHUA TREE NATIONAL PARK HIKE, CALIFORNIA, USA

For years I'd been busting to check out this protected otherworldly area dotted with those funny looking twisted, prickly trees. I'd seen it on the socials and was sucked in by the sepia-toned, boots 'n' lace vibe of the place. I was in LA for work and figured I could squeeze in a road trip and hike. The Airstreams on Airbnb were all booked out, but I found a room in an equally 'frontier' motel on the main highway and set off out of the city in a hire car with windows you had to manually wind down.

I arrived mid-morning. It was 39 ℃ in the shade and there's no shade out there. But I was in a mood and this — mood needed to be hiked into the dust, so I went hard. In the one morning I did the Barker Dam Loop and Hidden Valley routes. Then I did the Ryan Mountain, Skull Rock and Split Rock hikes later in the day.

By the time I climbed Ryan Mountain, it was late afternoon and my agitated mood had settled. As ever, the desert was able to strip me of a fair whack of my egoic suffering. I've always struggled to do this via those aphorisms (where you witness your ego and stand back from the shards of pain that you've carted around in your solar plexus since childhood, and in the witnessing they dissolve). As I think

FYI a guy I'd met in LA was meant to join me. He'd begged to come along. I deferred to 'yes' in the face of his enthusiasm and booked a bigger motel room. The dude did a no-show. Then ghosted me. It left me hugely unsettled, emotionally whiplashed.

I've said before, thankfully I have hiking. And the desert.

As I skipped up the rocky trail the air was like paint stripper, the light as if under a magnifying glass. In desertscapes the expanse says to you, palm slapping down on the table, 'I am big, get on my level.' You are forced to lift out of your bullshit. It takes you to raw awe. What a boon for a caught-up ego!

Awe is quite a specific experience. It happens when we view beauty amid vastness, predominantly in nature, triggering a deep sense of belonging. Our smallness against a backdrop of immensity reminds us of our insignificance and interconnectedness, which brings about a profound, yet elated, peace. The Apollo 17 team, on their way to the moon in 1972, took a photo of the Earth from 29,000 kilometres away. The photo became known as The Blue Marble and it went on to trigger awe around the world. The impact has been studied extensively – it's called the Overview Effect – and it's credited with kicking off the modern environmental movement. Awe, more than any other experience I know, connects us to the vulnerability, wildness and preciousness of life.

When I got to the top of Ryan Mountain, I sat and looked out all the way to Palm Springs. As the breeze cooled, I felt myself get really, really…insignificant. The view went on and on and the mountain beneath me just sat there being fully solid and knowing and patient and I swear my cells started to dissolve. Soften, release and dissolve.

Then I got up and ran back down the mountain. I was hungry.

Now, here's the odd thing – I saw no one on the trails

that day. Correction. I saw carloads of humans pour out of their reconditioned Kombis and shiny SUVs in the car parks. They walked perhaps 100 metres in and took a selfie and I'm guessing then drove back to their cabin with its outdoor claw-foot bath and drank mojitos. Okay, that last bit was a bit judgey and entirely based on the Instagrammed version of the place. As I say, I was in a mood. But it was more than that. I was frustrated and sad that these fellow humans were missing out on the whole point – the opportunity to grab the awesome precious experience by both hands and devour the full-fat calling to rise bigger and bolder. And to experience the untold joy of the whole enchilada that such an opportunity gifts a person.

I drove out to Pioneertown, 15 minutes away, a town that is as it sounds – desolate, raw, barnyard-littered. I headed to Pappy & Harriet's, a biker dive/diner where meals are cooked on a mesquite fire under the stars out back in the dirt courtyard. I ordered mac and cheese and broccoli and flicked through my phone. As I did, I stumbled upon a video of one of Marianne Williamson's powerful public gospels where she warned America that humanity is the *Titanic* heading for an iceberg. 'We don't know what that iceberg is yet,' she'd said with her infectious urgency. Her jibe was to get anyone aiming for more consciousness to become politically active because something big and scary was coming our way. I felt excited by her rant. It paralleled my fervent hope that those who drove all the way out to a desert might step beyond the car park and reconnect to life's calling. Or just climb the damn mountain.

Two decades earlier, in her book *The Healing of America*, Williamson had criticised the excesses of self-help culture and invited readers to apply the lessons of the New Age to engagement in political and community service. In her more recent book, *A Politics of Love*, she intentionally cries out to 'a generation that has become so sensitive to its own pain' that it is 'desensitised to the pain of others'.

I looked around the dirt diner's rib-eating crowd and reflected on the oddness of our attraction to the desert. The First Nations peoples of Australia and North America often chose desert life when the option to live in less harsh environments had been there. It's not my place to specify the reasons, but I'd be surprised if it didn't have a lot to do with the very connecting experience of raw awe that expands us beyond ourselves.

Today we continue to come to deserts. We take photos from the car park, go to Burning Man and Coachella, and appropriate the wild frontier vibe with the dusty linen and dream catchers. I'm being a smart-arse cynic with all the 'knowing' pop cultural referencing here. But I also trust there's an innocent, raw yearning behind it all. I think the call of 'awe' is being felt by a generation of us hankering for frankness and bigness and the experience of stepping up in full and giving service to something infinite.

A Zen monk might reply: 'Who is asking the question?' — We crave an answer to that inevitable (and beautiful) question: 'What matters if our small egos don't?'

The next day I headed to Palm Springs to sit by the pool

at the Ace Hotel and do my finances. A DJ played circa 1993 House and everyone was drinking cocktails out of red plastic cups, their feet dangling in the water.

A week later, Donald Trump formally announced he was running for president. — And, as it turns out, so did Marianne Williamson.

69 What if instead of self-care we focused on caring for our souls? The original use of the term 'self-care' can be traced back to the self-described 'Black, lesbian, mother, warrior, poet' Audre Lorde. In 1988 she wrote that self-care was a form of self-preservation as a queer black woman, and a way of coping with a world that was hostile to her identity, and thus 'an act of political warfare'. Of course, the idea was quickly – and ironically – appropriated by the masses and became a way to avoid the political. The search results for the term had a massive spike in the months following Trump's election in 2016, prompting many at the activist front line to robustly criticise the modern application of it, along with the spirituality-lite guff.

Caring for our souls is about being aware of 'self-care language'. It entails facing our fears, prejudices and numbness so that we are truly ready for the iceberg we're crashing into. Commentators in this space emphasise the importance of feeling guilty and uncomfortable about our privilege and our contribution to the planet's destruction. And to use these emotions as fuel to act.

70 Caring for our souls and becoming more authentically spiritual also means getting political. A few weeks before I started immersing myself in this exploration I'd gotten an email from Russell Brand inviting me onto his podcast. That sentence reads like it was some wonderful happenstance. Um, no. I'd hustled like a mad person for months and #manifested the living daylights out of the situation to get the meeting. For years I'd been intent on connecting with the wonderfully recalcitrant British comedian. I have loved watching how he navigates his flaws and how he rides some high-octane intellectual and spiritual flow. And so it happened that the day I was due to fly out of the United Kingdom (after doing that Lake District hike with poet David Whyte), I high-tailed it from northern England at 5am and travelled for ten hours on a bus, train, another train and then one more train to get to his farm cottage in the rural outskirts of London.

I will have to add here, however, my admiration has waned in recent years as his rants have taken a narcissistic, 'messiah'-like turn and he has taken to pushing a kaleidoscope of conspiracy theories.

When I arrived in the late afternoon, he offered me some cashews and asked why I'd wanted to meet. I quoted something Brené Brown said to me when she and I had met years ago: 'You lean so far forward it hurts; I knew you were one of my people.'

I've come to realise forward-leaners are my crew, I told him, and that I need them in my orbit more than ever.

I was so tired and nervous I don't remember exactly what Russell and I chatted about. I know we got to spiritualism-lite (I think I called it spiritual materialism), because the grab he used to promote the podcast picked up on this. 'If we're even remotely engaged in becoming more conscious,' I say, 'we have a responsibility to be political.'

I told him that if you've had access to the truth of the way life is interconnected – the Oneness – and you've dabbled in connecting via various time-honoured practices, such as yoga and meditation, then how can you not feel connected to what is going on for our fellow human beings and the planet? How can you not be acutely aware of economic, racial and ecological injustices and wrongs and know that you must stand up to them?

I added that spiritual warrior types will often tell me, 'I'm not into politics,' or 'I don't read the news. It's too heavy.' As I told Russell, I tend to reply to this, while sounding as compassionate as possible (although definitely not apologetic; hey, the times demand some firmness around this), 'Too bad; it's part of the deal.' It's a responsibility. It's non-negotiable. I quoted Marianne Williamson at this point, which generally appeals (her bestselling book *A Return to Love* is familiar to many a spiritual warrior): 'The spiritual has always been political.' Gandhi and Buddha and Jesus were fully political. Marianne is political! As Williamson says in her lectures to the spiritually signed-up, 'We are meant to be the most grown up in the room.'

At this point, I ranted about my minimalist practices, steered by Russell's probing, whip-smart questions. He said to me, 'You're fucking mad.' We vowed to stay in touch.

71 And then there's Sister Joan Chittister. Have you come across Sister Joan? Oh boy. I happily hand the penultimate point to her.

Sister Joan is an American Benedictine nun and vocal feminist and activist who – at eighty-three – had her Australian tour revoked by the Archbishop of Melbourne amid the George Pell sexual allegations firestorm. As the *New York Times* reported: 'The leaders of the church don't like her ideas – especially her call to empower women and laypeople – so they plan to suppress them.' Oprah, on one of her Super Soul Sunday video podcasts, asked Sister Joan why she does what she does. 'I do not want to go to my grave and on that last sickbed say to myself, 'You said nothing!' she boomed.

Sister Joan and I FaceTimed each other one evening; I wanted to pick up on some themes in her latest book *The Time is Now*, one of fifty-odd she's written. She spoke at a fire-and-brimstone tilt. We are a 'globe of isolates', she told me. 'Here we are, hanging out in a spiritual jacuzzi, all nice and womb-like, while the planet suffers.' She directed much of her clarion call at Christians. 'We are worshipping Jesus the healer, instead of Jesus the prophet; we're taking the easy messages, it's narcissistic and comfortable – lazy! – rather than living to the word of God.' She explained that our society is now culturally, politically and spiritually ruptured as a result.

'And so we're as condemned as Sisyphus,' she said, citing the Greek narcissist known for his moral and spiritual bankruptcy who is condemned by the gods to roll a boulder up a hill over and over for eternity.

She told me about the importance of being a fired-up, courageous, deviant spiritual prophet today. 'Prophets speak radical truth,' she told me, and call for change with a 'holy audacity'. Our conversation went deeper. Sister Joan explained that this can mean having to shut down everything that has previously formed you, if required. To be a prophet is not self-serving and often means working in isolation with little recognition. 'You're an agitator in a time of complacency.' You do what has to be done precisely because no one else is doing it.

— I adore this term. You?

'Is everyone meant to step up and be prophets?' I asked her. 'Is that what life is now demanding?'

'No!' she replied. For most of us our obligation is to join the prophetic voice when we're asked to. She explained that our spiritual duty is to support the Gretas of our world. I think this is a wonderful qualification to make. Many around me stall, freeze, sink back into the spiritual jacuzzi when they interpret the calling to mean we've all got to become Jesus or Greta. Christ, no! The most powerful thing we can do might well be to use our spiritual longing consciously and courageously to spin around and face out to the world and join the agitators and activists beyond the yoga mat, the influencers who are sacrificing pride and income, as well as their private lives, to the cause; the writers, the philosophers, the scientists who have given their all. We 'like' *these* prophets' posts, sign their petitions, read their books, attend the strikes they front, heed their guidance, read the political news articles they share. And commit to not shutting down in a sweet swoon of palo santo.

Sister Joan then told me that she had to cut our chat short; she had to head off to care for someone in a critical condition in hospital. Nun stuff. She leaned into her laptop screen and stabbed at my face. 'Wow, I'd just love to be writing this book you're writing. Write fast, Sarah.'

Fatten up your spiritual vibe

Ready to step things up a notch? Try these ideas on for size...

Read, listen to and watch the news. Every day. It's important to know where our wild precious world is at. I make it part of my practice. I keep a small radio in the bathroom and turn it to the news channel as I clean my teeth and get ready in the morning. After meditation and exercise, I read two independent newspapers online (saving longer op-eds and features for my long-read Sundays). I watch the evening news and a weekend news analysis program. In total, it's about one hour of learning about my world per day. I limit it to this so I don't get buried in the drama. I find when you engage with the news of the day, every day, the stories fully form. Gaps in context fill in and we can see what really matters; we can care more deeply. A sense of empowerment replaces the overwhelm. It's a spiritual act to stay caring in the face of the fear-guilt-anger-despair-overwhelm cycle.

Choose better prophets and influencers. We can have a say in the spiritual, connected, life-saving momentum we want to put our 'likes' to in this lifetime. To this end I regularly clean out my social feeds. I'm mercenary. As I scan my feeds, I unfollow the voices that preach the consuming, inward focused ways of the false gods. To apply the Kondo Method, if their gospel doesn't bring life-saving joy I stop being a sheep to their shepherding.

Instead I follow the prophets whose voices bring me the difficult messages and who put care and soul into sharing their words. Care-full wording is a sign of a prophet committed to connecting. I trust the influencers who are brave enough to sacrifice pride and ownership. I bow to those who throw bombs under the situation and light up debate when it's required. Because disruption connects, too.

Play with 'and'. We can contain multitudes, as Walt Whitman said. Play with being spiritual *and* political, peaceful *and* outraged, calm *and* alarmed. This is definitely what our hyperobjectified life is demanding of us.

Make awareness and action your prayer. If you're into crystals, learn about the mining ethics (it's not a pretty picture). If you practise yoga, try not buying into the consumables (the micro-plastic-leaching leggings). If you're a wellness warrior, and your thing is contaminants in water, perhaps switch your efforts from promoting water purifiers to campaigning for cleaner tap water for all. Just ideas…

If you're a 'light' teacher, such as a yoga instructor, you could experiment with being a better prophet, or disciple, by bringing some political clarion-calling into your spiel between asanas.

If you run a yoga/meditation/drumming circle studio, ban disposables. Perhaps rally your community to attend strikes and sign petitions.

Finally, go for a walk through the desert of your own privilege. This is hard. I did this terrifying side-route several times on this journey. I realised I was using certain 'enlightened' or overshare-ish concepts to mask my shame. For example, I often referred to how I came from nothing and got where I am from working hard. It was when I decided to write an Instagram post to this effect that I saw how disconnecting my behaviour was. So I wrote: 'I'm super-white. I've benefited from all the perks of not only being white, and very 'girl next door' in my pink TV sweater (FFS), but also from the leg-ups whites like me who 'came from nothing' and have 'worked to get where they are' and who 'succeeded on their own merit' benefit from. The neo-liberal system can cope with 'disadvantage' that fits into its model of bootstrap-pulling. And it loves success stories. What it can't cope with is nuance and the type of disadvantage

THIS ONE WILD AND PRECIOUS LIFE

that holds a whopping great mirror up to its prejudice. Although, if we're going to stick with this mirror analogy, the system doesn't even see non-whiteness in the reflection.'

When you decide to take this walk, asking a few beautiful (but courageous) questions can help. Like, if you speak of 'unattachment', ask if it's because you are too scared to speak up, or to face the cost of your lifestyle's footprint, or to get engaged in politics.

And when you send 'thoughts and prayers', ask if you are just giving yourself an excuse not to step up and do something. If you talk of manifesting and creating your own reality, ask how you might help create a world where everyone has equal access to the tools and playing field. If you speak of abundance, ask why you are not preaching material sacrifice instead. If you prefer to chill and be Zen, ask if you are shunning the anger, outrage and protest that's entirely necessary right now. Are you gaslighting others who are being honest with their rage?

At every step, I have asked myself, 'Are you practising what you're preaching? Will you use this opportunity to wake up and come back to life and what matters?'

Only I could answer this.

now

we

change

the world

show up

to your

appointment

72 As Anne Frank once wrote, 'How wonderful it is that nobody need wait a single moment before starting to improve the world.' This, from a 15-year-old confined in terrifying isolation in an attic, is particularly marvellous. And motivating.

It struck me it wasn't enough to wake up, reconnect, to meet in that field and hang out for a bit, having more soulful chats and loving on life. We had to get more marvellous with things.

There's a wisdom from Jungian psychologist and prolific author James Hollis that haunts me. He says that eventually, once we're connected and informed enough, our soul will call us to an appointment with life.

Our souls are our knowingness. They perceive when we're off track and not living in service – not actually doing anything to help improve the world – and they say, 'Oi! Time for you, me and life to meet up.' We might ignore the calls for a bit. But as Hollis explains, 'the soul doesn't give up'. We might think we're on track, that we're doing enough, but if our souls have other ideas, they'll summon us again and again.

73 I don't know about you, but as I become more aware and informed of the state of our planet and the inequalities and cruelty we've allowed to seep in on our watch, the same question keeps coming up, 'Why isn't anyone doing anything?'

We know the facts: We can see the planet crumbling, the community is asking for our help, we want to give more love, we are lonely… So why are we staying stuck in a consumer cycle we know makes us sad? Why are we scrolling? Why are we ducking from the truth, from each other, from a fully wild life? Why aren't we mobilising like the world did at the beginning of World War II?

But, of course, there is always an opportunity to rephrase a question more beautifully. What I was really asking, was, 'Why am *I* not doing enough to save this one wild and precious life?'

74 Hollis writes extensively on what matters most in life, mercifully refusing to defer to the pat answers like 'happiness' and having more 'me time'. (British psychology commentator

Oliver Burkeman, also a fan of Hollis, describes him as 'a total downer'.) Hollis' work had been inspiring me for years, so I wrote to him when I arrived at this quandary and asked for his help. He called me the following week on FaceTime from his study in Washington, DC. Hollis is in his early eighties now, with a sweep of white hair, and was dressed in shirt, tie, waistcoat and woolen checked jacket – exactly how I want a Jungian analyst to greet me.

'Our souls are getting louder because the times are dictating they must,' he told me. 'That's what they do when we're off track.' They will inundate our psychic feeds with relentless notifications, reminders, perhaps violent pokes, illness and slap-downs, until we front up to our appointment. At a collective level they might throw a bushfire, a pandemic, a truly challenging president or prime minister at us – appropriate prompts that reflect the state of our off-trackness.

In his book, *What Matters Most*, Hollis writes that the calls can take the form of longings, suffering or dreams. 'Noisy demonstrations are held in the amphi-theatre of the body; streets are blocked in the brain by rebels from the cane fields; dreams are invaded by spectral disturbances; affects riot and tear down the work of years.'

Eventually we must take the call.

Throughout my life, it has generally taken repeated, increasingly violent prods for me to answer. The call first presents as an itch that turns into chronic stress that transmutes into a serious illness that can knock me to the ground. My various autoimmune diseases, my insomnia, bipolar and other anxious 'disorders' have all served to make me stop, pay attention and clamber my way to the appointment. If only because I have nowhere else to go.

And in that moment, when I finally show up, I realise that the most beautiful question of all, the most beautiful question of this whole quest is in fact one I must ask of life.

Ready for it?

Okay, life. What are you asking of me?

75 Most recently, and with more urgency, life has been asking me to get over myself, fire up and act! I asked Hollis what he made of this. 'I think we're all being summoned to fight for this life,' he replied. Not merely our own flesh and blood lives, not even for the planet, necessarily. But for the sense of life we know we come from and belong to. The Oneness. You know, Big Life (that we access best through group soul) as opposed to our little individual 'lower case' lives.

And, frankly, I think we are glad to have been summoned.

76 Two decades after she fled Nazi Germany, existential philosopher Hannah Arendt wrote a famous essay for *The New Yorker* about the trial of a Nazi SS officer instrumental in the Holocaust. She was shocked by how non-thinking the officer was and argued it was precisely his 'thoughtlessness', his can't-be-botheredness to have an internal, connected dialogue about what mattered, that enabled him to commit

the mass murders. It was in this article she coined the term the 'banality of evil'. I think it makes more sense in reverse: the evil of banality. Arendt emphasised that inaction is just as destructive (if not more so) than direct aggression. Other existentialists – Sartre, de Beauvoir, Camus – also pushed the idea that our fundamental moral imperative is to surge forward in action. Theodore Roosevelt famously said in what is referred to as his 'Man in the Arena' speech, delivered at the Sorbonne in Paris in 1910:

Brené Brown — fans would know her book *Daring Greatly* is inspired by this speech.

> *The credit belongs to the man who is actually in the arena, whose face is marred by dust and sweat and blood…who knows the great enthusiasms, the great devotions, who spends himself in a worthy cause; who at the best knows in the end the triumph of high achievement, and who at the worst, if he fails, at least fails while daring greatly, so that his place shall never be with those cold and timid souls who neither know victory nor defeat.*

The existentialists and Roosevelt advocated firing up in the context of a world on the brink of, or embroiled in, war. They railed against apathy and cynicism and self-interest because the times demanded more.

As I've said, the times are demanding we do the same now. I don't say this lightly. We are also at war. Life is calling us to mobilise and fight for our values, democracy, the animals in the picture books of our childhood and for a liveable planet for our children. The time is now. A bit of brutality, and action, is entirely and wonderfully appropriate.

77 So. What's life asking of you? To do your bit?

To make some adjustments?

I can't answer for everyone here, but I have received the very strong message – thanks to my soul dragging me repeatedly to the front line of my consciousness these past few years – that life is asking us to do everything we can.

You could view it like this: everything got us into this mess, everything is affected, and so it's going to take everything to get out of it.

Now, perhaps, like me, you've spent a lot of time debating whether the carbon emissions saved by quitting meat are greater than getting rid of your car. Whether switching to an electric car is worthwhile when the electricity is dirty in your state. Whether you should enforce a 'no devices after 7pm rule' in your home, or campaign to get phones banned at your kids' school. Whether it's worth writing to your local council member when she just supported another coal exploration licence, or switching to an ethical superannuation policy and donating to wildlife groups. I have gotten sucked into all the debates back and forth, justifying my resistance to change with a counterargument here, trying to offset my guilt over there. It became a cerebral slinging match of issues, of rights and wrongs, with an impossible goal – finding The One Thing That Will Fix Everything. The upshot of this approach? We get overwhelmed, shut down and do nothing.

Obviously, this One Thing doesn't exist. And the sooner we accept this, the less overwhelmed and more active we will be. The actual call to arms being issued – that we do everything – is far neater and joyous. And doable.

Just do everything you can. Don't stop. Don't get caught up in granular fights and that dastardly fear-guilt-anger-despair-overwhelm cycle. Don't worry how others are doing their everything. Just keep doing yours and then doing some more. This a beautiful, private journey we are taking. But we must be the change we want to see. And then others may board our bus. As I flag in that bulleted list of climate change factlets, we must all do everything we can all at once – at the individual consumer level and at the activist level – with no one thing being right, but also nothing being wrong. And keep going. For action begets action. And from little things big things grow.

See pages 104 to 115.

THE GROSE VALLEY HIKE, THE BLUE MOUNTAINS, AUSTRALIA

One Boxing Day, I was dark and stuck, so I borrowed a friend's car and escaped the post-Christmas food coma and wrestling competitions with my siblings to go wild camping. I drove up the back route to the Blue Mountains west of Sydney, a region I've always found spooky. Perhaps it's the blue haze from the eucalyptus oil that hangs like a veil over the UNESCO-listed range (providing its name), or the cold valleys created by the uplifted basalt dating back 300 million years. Or just the many stories of people going missing in the dense bush up there. More recently, of course, it's been the scene of mass destruction – 80 per cent of it was burnt in the 2020 fires. I also lost a cousin to suicide in these mountains when I was in my late teens. He was fifteen and jumped from a waterfall in one of the valleys; he wasn't found for weeks.

And yet, I've hiked almost every track in the park over the years.

I passed through Oberon, a town where the only sign of its bygone grandeur is the wide main street. I stop for a milky cup of tea in the one café that's open. I have stuff on my mind. For the past year I've been wrestling with what the hell I was going to do with the I Quit Sugar business I'd built up over six years. It was successful by all measures and had grown fast. I had twenty-three staff, we'd published eleven books, I had a range of supermarket products, and millions around the world had completed the eight-week program we ran. But my soul had been calling me to an appointment with life. You see, to continue running the business I had to scale it up. And to scale meant prioritising the making of money. Which felt inordinately compromising. I had to decide what I was going to do by the time business reopened after the Christmas break.

Some locals at the café were eating finger buns with pink icing, spreading margarine from little plastic punnets with plastic knives. I felt heavy. I looked out of the window and noticed a man sitting on the bonnet of a Jeep. He was thirty-something and dressed in head-to-toe commando camouflage. I paid my bill; he'd gone by the time I left.

I drove up the range to Blackheath where I picked up an emergency beacon and did screen grabs of the route I'd chosen from a map on the wall of the visitor centre, then headed back up the highway before turning down a long dirt road to the Victoria Falls trailhead. It was late in the afternoon, but I knew that the climb down the side of the falls into the valley was only 90 minutes or so; I should have plenty of time to set up before dark.

As I approached, there was only one other car parked in the clearing. Which was weird. It was the Christmas break; I figured the joint would be packed. I got closer. It was a Jeep. It was camo guy and he was sitting on his bonnet again, this time with his shirt off. He didn't look at me – he just sat staring out to the dense bushland.

I sat in the car and fiddled with my bottom lip.

Right. So. Do I add up the weirdness going on here and abort my mission? Or do I just go? My senses were alive and they told me to choose, yes! Go! I had a bigger quandary to rise to and it was calling me to hike it out.

I took a picture of camo dude and his number plate and sent it to my friend Rick with the message: 'Creepy dude. If I don't text in three days, call for help.' I also attached a geo-marker. Then I buckled on my pack and set off. There would be campers at the bottom coming in from the other direction, I reasoned. Plus, I had an emergency beacon.

I scampered down the steep stairs, navigating slippery

rocks, alert to any sign of movement behind me. I made it to the bottom and shuffle-jogged my way through the flats along a winding path, the orange glow of the setting sun lighting up the tops of the eucalypts. I rounded a bend and came into a small clearing beside a river. A few logs were scattered around a campfire. There was no one else there. I looked at my phone. No signal.

Right. So.

It was getting dark. I knew I probably shouldn't stay in the clearing – too obvious. I made my way across the river and bashed through the scrub. About 200 metres from the camp area I found a spot to pitch my tent. I busied myself setting up and chose not to be scared. Because that would achieve nothing. A certain stroppy righteousness can kick in in such scenarios. I will not let fear ruin this experience! I cooked my dinner in my little stove. When the moon came up, I crept back to the river and bathed then I climbed into my sleeping bag to read, my emergency beacon and my knife by my side.

By the light of my head torch, totally in love with the very particular snug joy of lying in a tent with the sounds of wildlife settling into the night around me, I read Sebastian Junger's *Tribe*. Junger is a war journalist and in this book explores PTSD among veterans. He argues that the trauma of PTSD is mostly triggered by homecoming rather than the actual horrors of war. This explains why during the London Blitz suicide rates dropped almost to zero. Ditto admissions to mental wards. Despite the obvious terror of war, the period is remembered by Londoners (according to the studies he cites) as a time of – yes – happiness. Junger writes that hanging out in shelters with strangers saw Londoners thrive. The experience 'thrust people back into a more ancient, organic way of relating.' They felt necessary. He says soldiers more often cope with the terror of war when there is camaraderie and a strong sense of shared purpose. It's the contrasting 'nothingness' of regular life back home that triggers trauma.

'Humans don't mind hardship,' he writes. 'In fact they thrive on it; what they mind is *not feeling necessary*.' Junger adds that our culture today leaves the bulk of us feeling unnecessary. I agree. The disconnection that technology imposes, and the moral aloneness of our guardrail-free culture makes very little that we actually do or care about seem important. My brother Simon and I were walking back from the beach and he was telling me about some plumbers fixing a leak in his apartment block. 'I watched them shove plants around and not care about where they put them, and I thought, where do they start caring, when they get to the leak? Why not just care about every bit of the process?' Totally, Si. I know exactly what you mean.

My italics. —

'Caring begets caring,' I reply.

And if you stop caring with the small stuff (returning texts, never ever drinking bottled water, picking up a chocolate wrapper in the park), how do you get the momentum to start caring about the bigger stuff? Where do you draw the line between giving a shit and giving up? Isn't it just easier to just give a shit wherever you see the opening?

#giveashit. —

I get heart-sick to realise we are a society that struggles to start caring and find meaning. According to a recent Gallup workplace poll in 160 countries, 85 per cent of the population felt 'emotionally disengaged' from their work, finding it meaningless, like 'sleepwalking through their workday'. Increasing automation and the impending AI revolution (and, now, mass un- and under-employment across both white- and blue-collar industries worldwide) are set to disconnect us even further from feeling like necessary members of our tribe, at least while having a successful job is the determiner of our worth in society. And this phenomenon is likely to affect young men most (I think back to those twenty-something men who game instead of work because their online world provides more meaning than the menial jobs available to them), at a time when they are a cohort at heart-breaking risk.

In the morning (after a solid nine hours of uninterrupted sleep), I woke abruptly in my tent to the sound of loud crashing through the scrub. The sun had only just come up. I threw on a singlet and scrambled out of the tent with my knife at the ready, dragging the whole tent from its pegs with my bum as I tried to lever myself vertical. Two men in their early sixties emerged talking loudly about some verse or other in the Bible. They laughed when they saw me and my knife and my tangled predicament. It turns out I'd pitched my tent on the actual trail through the valley floor. Ha!

— I always sleep when camping; it's sleeping in perfectly comfortable beds I struggle with.

I asked them to join me for breakfast. They ate muesli bars sitting on a log while I heated up some porridge and they told me they were teachers and hiked on Sundays as a spiritual thing. Weirdly, they were the second duo of male teachers I'd met on a trail who were 'churchy'.

I had also met Jim and Dave a few years back in the Warrumbungles in New South Wales, where I'd camped on an overhang, and they were the only other humans I'd seen for the three days. 'I'm churchy; he's spiritual,' said Jim, who wore two pairs of glasses (sunnies over prescription), was missing a front tooth and took notes from our talk on his hands while eating a carrot (with his back teeth). 'Women are going to change this world,' he told me, punching me on the arm.

After the Sunday-hiking teachers had left, I read some more Junger while I drank my camp coffee and then took my time packing up. I followed the trail through the Blue Gum Forest. It's a glorious winding trail that's not heavily trodden. As the sun reached the valley, the eucalypt oil released and the late-season blossoms drenched the air with honey. A few hours passed and it occurred to me that I should have intersected with another river by now. I was shoe-horning my way into a dense thicket of tea trees when, suddenly, a young guy appeared behind me. 'Are you lost?' He generously realised I was startled and added, 'I mean, I think I am too, and I live nearby and…I'm only eighteen.'

And for good measure, 'My mum reads your books.'

He explained — that he recgnised me from the green shorts I was wearing.

The young guy, whose name I never got, was dear, dear company as we spent 45 minutes trying to find our way back to the trail. We trundled along, him a metre or two behind asking me questions. He'd finished school a few months earlier and was trying to decide what to do with his life. 'I mean, how did you choose a meaningful career?'

'Well,' I replied, 'I didn't.' I told him that I kind of flopped around, switching degrees and industries. But I kept putting my hand up for the extra role, volunteering, running various community groups, offering to redesign the food and wine pages of the magazine I'd just done work experience for (I was offered the job of editing the section afterward), writing lefty op-eds on social issues and sending them to the opinion editor at News Corp's *Herald Sun* (I was a little relentless; they eventually gave me a weekly, paid column in the paper). And so and on.

I just made myself necessary. Or at least annoyingly present. I cared. I fired up. I saw voids and lunged at them.

I told him I was aware how horribly unfair it is that we impose the idea of having an uber-meaningful life on young people. It's not enough to have a good job, it must be a meaningful career. And yet where are you meant to derive a sense of what's meaningful, what's right, when we don't have discussions around such things, and we don't value them in our own lives (and instead laud money and 'things')? The unfairness has amplified post-corona virus as young people face a future of very limited career prospects.

'It's tricky to just go find meaning,' I said. 'But you can always find a way to help out, to fill a void. Being necessary can just be ordinary, or it can even just be 'for now'. You don't have to have a grand whiteboard plan. But, you see, just doing something necessary, in a curious way where you follow what you care about, becomes meaningful in the doing of it.'

He said he found this idea a relief 'How about becoming a teacher?' I suggested. We finally reached Acacia Flat. I think the guy was keen to park his hammock near my tent and continue chatting. But I said I was going to go further upstream. I needed to think out my own necessariness.

The next day, with another nine hours of sleep under my belt and a sense that I could do anything because, really, with nine hours' sleep I can't see how there can be any problems left in life, I climbed out of the valley via a series of waterfalls and found my way back to my friend's car.

I'd made my decision.

78 A few years earlier I'd appointed Harry and Brett as my accountants. I'd just published my first book, *I Quit Sugar*, initially as an eBook. Shortly after, it came out as a print book in Australia and the United States, where it was a *New York Times* bestseller then fairly quickly appeared in forty-plus countries around the world. At the time I was living out of two suitcases in an army shed in the forest but had to get a bit more grown-up with where my career was suddenly heading.

One afternoon Harry and Brett sat down with me in their Sydney office. Brett had a whiteboard.

'What are your financial goals?' he asked, his marker poised.

'I don't do them,' I said. 'I'm not motivated by that kind of thing.'

'Well, we can make something up,' Brett said hopefully. 'What would you like your life to look like in five years?'

I paused and really thought about his question. I've written before about a particularly dark night of the soul episode when I got unwell in my mid-thirties. Wrestling with existence, having had no sleep for three days, I descended so low I was ready to die. It felt like an inevitable conclusion as there seemed nowhere else for me to head. I was calm and resolved.

But in that calm nihilistic cul-de-sac, I was able to see I had one last choice left. I could die...or − and it was a radical idea − I could choose to live but do things completely differently. As in, do life on my own radical terms, stripped of everything that had entrapped me, and with just the clothes on my back. If I was prepared to toss in the whole lot, why not try this one last wild option?

I chose to live. It was a big, true, blood-pumping choice. And it meant making a commitment to myself: to never get caught up again. If I was to ask life to have me back, I had to get real. I would have to watch myself carefully, be my own moral vanguard, and when I got sucked into the more-more-more trap, to back away.

'Okay, guys, my financial goal is to not become a sad sack.' Harry asked me to explain this in financial terms. 'I don't want to become one of those people who finally earned enough to buy the Toyota hatch they'd always dreamed of only to feel they then needed an Audi and then a Range Rover and so on and so on until suddenly they're the old person with creaky hips and no friends and an oversized car wishing they'd learned to play bowls earlier. Then they die.'

'Right,' said Harry.

I continued. 'In five years, I'd like to have made enough money to live on the minimum wage CPI'd until I'm, say, ninety-four,' I said. 'I'd then just do stuff that mattered, where money doesn't have to be in the equation.'

This seemed like a nice age to — live to.

Brett wrote all this up on his whiteboard.

Five years later, to the very week, Harry, Brett and I reconvened. The digital platform I'd built had grown year after year, and the business was in the BRW list of fastest growing start-ups. Me, I'd forgotten about my financial goal. But my accountants had quietly been working to it behind the scenes. 'We reached your goal,' they announced. 'So, what shall we do now?'

'Sell.'

I'd made a commitment to life, I had to stick to it. The movement I'd built had become a business and while it was wonderful to employ a bunch of bright young people and I'd enjoyed the sport of growing something, marketing it, playing with P&L charts, I felt it was time to pass the baton and start contributing in other realms (at this point I was just finishing *The Beast*.)

So I spent the next eleven months working with my board on various deals with media companies. I'd met Alister, a venture capitalist, in a café. He overheard me getting frustrated with some new widget on LinkedIn. He showed me a few tips and we got talking. He emailed me afterward and offered to help me with my business. He introduced me to Billy who offered to step into the business between gigs setting up digital businesses and support things from the front line. These four generous men – Harry, Brett, Billy and Alister – along with I Quit Sugar's GM Jorge and some of the senior staff worked with me on my 'sell' plan. We schlepped around town with a presentation and got the wind kicked out of our proverbial tyres by various executives who dealt only in numbers.

The business had been valued at some ludicrous amount. Selling was appealing. But it entailed being 'golden handcuffed' to the business, my noggin all over the brand, as a multinational company scaled and pillaged the life out of what I'd built. Nothing I wanted in life required money. What would I buy? And everything that I valued, that I knew to be good, would be compromised, including the actual values behind the I Quit Sugar message.

Money does this.

There's an experiment that was done with a bunch of Israeli childcare centres. Parents kept showing up late to pick up their kids, so fines were introduced for late pickups. You know what happened? The number of late pickups doubled. The observation was made that when money is introduced into the equation, we drop our sense of moral obligation. Hmph. Parents suddenly cared less about it being unfair to the childcare workers when they could just pay their way out.

Yep, money does this.

As each company put forward terms and conditions, my spirit desiccated. During this period, *First, We Make the Beast Beautiful* was published, and I'd begun asking the questions that led me to step out on this current jaunt. Discussing anxiety in a deeply and necessary way made this next step in business growth seem life-sappingly *un*necessary.

79 I got back from my Blue Mountains hike and two weeks later, on the first working day of the New Year and almost six years to the day after sitting down and nutting out my financial goals, I called Harry and Brett.

'We're not going to sell; we're going to shut everything down,' I said. 'And give the lot to charity.'

The letter I wrote to the community in the wake of my decision described my thinking best. I've cut out the waffly bits:

As many of you know, the I Quit Sugar journey started at a time in my life that had given me cause to re-evaluate what mattered in life. From this place I decided to (re)build my life according to certain values. These values went on to steer the business.

The big commitment I made to myself back then was to not get caught up in the cycle. This meant doing things differently. It meant not taking on advertising. It meant starting small and growing at the same pace as the community was able to manage the messaging, and at a pace at which I could feel (dare I say it) authentic. It meant sticking to seemingly non-commercial principles. It meant 'giving first', aiming only to educate…and then seeing where it would all go.

Recently I've realised that to remain true to my original commitment, I must pivot course.

I explained that continuing with the business would mean focusing wholly on growth, scaling and money (getting caught up in the cycle) and that selling the business was equally untenable as I'd have to stay on while a new owner steered my name and brand and values in directions I didn't wholly agree with.

And so, after twelve months of a protracted set of discussions with various parties I have had to make what I believe is the best entrepreneurial decision I can: I'm closing, not selling.

Yes, admittedly, my health – mental and physical – and my belief in living a life motivated by moral values were considerations. They always are. But, again, a hypocrisy seeps in if I remain someone who sacrifices my own well-being and values for money and success. This is the ultimate disservice to the message I've peddled for years. I have to walk my talk, otherwise, what the hell is it all about?

I announced I was selling off the assets of the business – the recipes, the images, the furniture and equipment, the tech platform – at fixed prices, with fixed due diligence periods and with this rider: everything would be going to charity projects that I would build with good people and that would do expansive stuff for the good of the community (ergo, don't try to bargain or tyre-kick me). I immediately felt lighter and connected. I had acted. I had done something. I'd also been a bit deviant.

I could've sat back and let the commercial imperative drag me down a path that was not right. And then, dot dot dot, I'm old and I die. Or I could mix things up, not play by the rules, be true to what my soul was crying out for me to do and...just do it.

And see what happens. The sport of watching what happened next was worth more than any wad of cash. The media mostly didn't get it. They wrote up a few click-baity conclusions, leaving out the giving-all-my-money-away bit. You know those experiments where they get you to watch a basketball game and to count the number of times the blue team passes the ball? And because you're watching what you want to see, you miss the whopping great gorilla running across the court? I think it was like that.

Things got perfectly ironic, too. I turned to corporate speaking to pay my living expenses. Almost immediately I was booked out by – wait for it – banks and other financial institutions to do keynote talks on – hang on to your hats – how to have a meaningful career not based on money. And I don't think anyone found it overly incongruent. Because that's where we're at. Our group soul is being called to this bigger, more necessary appointment.

I continue to build these projects – every six months I launch a different one – and any profits from the IQS enterprise (such as my ebooks) continue to fund them.

They ran stories reporting that I'd 'gone broke.' I'd stopped believing in my own 'dangerous diet' that made money out of people's weaknesses. Blah, blah…

248

start

where

you

are

80 I speak to a stack of great humans desperate to do something, to act to save what matters, and they ask, 'But how and where do I start? How do I know what is necessary, how can I be most necessary, most of service?' I hand the podium once again to my favourite Buddhist nun, Pema Chödrön. She runs a thread through her books to the following beat:

Wherever you are in your life right in this moment is your vehicle for waking up.

Could there be more elegant, sigh-of-relief-inducing words of wisdom?

'If you're a mother raising your children, that's the vehicle for waking up. If you're an actress, that's the vehicle for waking up.' She goes on. 'If you're a construction worker… if you're a retired person facing old age…if you're alone and you feel lonely and you wish you had a mate, that's the vehicle for waking up. If you have a huge family around you and wish you had a little more free time, that's the vehicle for waking up.' That is, start where you are, because that is the best situation for showing you where you're stuck, where you need to go. There is no need to hover around the edge, waiting for a perfect moment, because when you simply step into the breach – hot mess or otherwise – you become necessary. And thus you come alive.

'Start now. Start where you are. Start with fear. Start with pain. Start with doubt. Start with hands shaking. Start with voice trembling but start. Start and don't stop. Start where you are, with what you have. Just… Start.'

At times, many times, I've wanted to shout this from a megaphone and rooftops.

I've also found it a useful mantra for guiding my own necessariness. In that period as I wrestled with what to do with my business, I had been stuck in a vortex of material temptation while questioning my values and fighting the tug of being 'caught up'. That's where I was. It was dead uncomfortable. I felt alone in the decision, alone in the responsibility. But that was my vehicle for waking up. This almost panicked discomfort took me to this place where I was ready to draw the bold line in the sand. That's what our life situations do – take us to the edge where we can choose to see pain and loss as a necessary and noble thing.

81　But the act, the something that you do, need not be so bold. It might be quite ordinary. Ordinary can be very necessary. In fact, when we step aside from the neo–liberal model that tells kids they can (and must) be everything they dreamed of and insists we all become the most productive economic units we can, ordinary is refreshingly and disarmingly effective. Being necessary might be helping the homeless, volunteering in a soup kitchen, taking time to chat with your elderly neighbour. It can be the simple act of sitting alone outside parliament as a 15–year–old girl with a sign that reads 'School Strike for Climate'.

My friend Lucy had been feeling powerless in the face of the climate emergency. In fact, and I don't think she'll mind my sharing this, she'd been feeling stuck and unable to engage or start on a bunch of things, feeling her life as a mum with two wild boys at home was not impactful or 'necessary enough'. Ahead of one of the big school strikes for climate, Lucy despaired that no one would do anything. The parents were claiming it was too hard to get into the city on the day.

So, she stepped forward and booked a minibus. She then set up a booking document on Eventbrite. She'd never done this before. Within an hour the bus booked out with parents and kids now able to join the rally. She upgraded to a coach. And then to two coaches. Within 48 hours she'd gotten 130 people to sign up to the strike. I then shared the story on my social media, and it prompted other people to copy what Lucy had done. It started out a little bit ordinary (although I'd argue it was nattily brave), but the fact that Lucy stepped up and did something enlivened many others to step up, too.

I'm guessing Lucy got several hundred parents and kids to

SARAH WILSON

that pivotal international strike.

Through my work in the climate movement I've been asked to advise companies on 'what they can do'. I was brought into a brainstorm session with a bunch of leading tech CEOs and venture capitalists. They wanted to create a new! big! climate charity that would fix things! After some whiteboard scribbles and passing of snacks, I was asked my thoughts. 'Can I be brutal?' I asked, and didn't wait for a response from the room of mostly men. 'You guys are not climate experts and the world doesn't need another charity to split off in another direction. But the people who've been working in this space for decades, who do know the science and the politics, they need apps and tech help and investment. Go to them. Offer your help.

'Start where you are, where you can be of service, not a hero.'

I added that the climate movement also needs a bunch of white, rich, middle-aged businessmen to come out publicly and back them as often and as loudly as possible.

As Sister Joan would say, we have to follow (and bankroll) the prophets.

82 You start. Then it spreads. Action begets action. Care begets care.

Studies show that we tend to give when we're around other people who give. And that any kind of giving brings joy, better health and meaning to the giver. Americans who were regularly generous with their neighbours were twice as likely to agree that they have a purpose than those who were less generous to neighbours.

You see, once you just start – wherever you are – things become. The starting is the thing. I turn to various writers and artists to remind myself of this:

Picasso: 'To know what you're going to draw, you have to begin drawing.'

Chuck Close: 'Inspiration is for amateurs – the rest of us just show up and get to work.'

Isabel Allende: 'Show up, show up, show up.'

And, because there's a Rumi quote for every occasion: 'As you start to walk on the way, the way appears.'

83 I'm going to emphasise something to bear in mind when starting out where you are. Important change, and being necessary, requires sacrifice. We are not a generation used to such a notion. Our currency is merit, being deserving of something, having the right to something. Having it all.

But let's ponder this. We tear muscle fibre to get abs.

We have to let a psychological story in our heads die for a new one to be born. We have to let go of childhood to become an adult. We sacrifice a trifle comfort today (staying on the couch, scrolling) for a more meaningful life for the future. And when we know it's time to act and be necessary, to save this life we love more than anything, we do have to give something up. We do have to experience some pain. That's just the deal. But I pause here to ask, is that so bad? So onerous? Or is it a relief? Or some emotional response not dissimilar to what the Brits felt during the London Blitz, when hanging in a grim bunker with neighbours they'd perhaps never spoken to before, delivered a sense of belonging to something bigger than themselves. And pretty much what I'm guessing Americans felt in the 1940s when they halved their meat consumption, turned off lights, stopped driving and 15 million relocated to find a war job, often across state lines, to be of service to the war effort.

We've forgotten that we humans actually love an opportunity to suck it up and go without. We've been denied the wisdoms that remind us of the blessings that sacrifice brings forth. To take the World War II example again, the sacrifice led to progressive change for women – five million women joined the US workforce for the first time and daycare centres were built in factories to support them.

I knew I had to keep sacrificing. I set up a work structure (guardrails) where half my week is now spent making money that I give away. It comes in, and it goes out. Sometimes I get windfalls (Lithuania buys the rights to one of my books or I get a speaking gig that pays me more than I anticipated) and I'll hand a wad to a man cleaning windows in the belting sun at the traffic lights. I don't have a car window to clean. I stop on my bike, hand over some notes and leave before too much privileged self-congratulation can go down. There is about 30 seconds, though, where the two of us can just see each other in our shared humanity before the lights go green.

And I knew it would take more and more (blessed and marvellous) sacrifice on this road ahead if I genuinely wanted to save this one wild precious life and arrive at the connection we all long for.

#buylesslivemore

84 If you're serious about starting where you are, and with being necessary and sacrificing, consume less. Of everything. Immediately. And keep going. Go further.

At a minimum we all need to halve our consumption should we wish to continue living on this planet. But global consumption is rising as developing economies expand. By 2030, the consumer class is expected to reach almost 5 billion people. This means 1.3 billion more people with increased purchasing power than today. This terrifies me. If we're to be fair to our brethren, given we've consumed so much for so long in the West, we should probably be compensating for these nations, who not only consume a fraction of what we do, but will be most impacted by the destruction caused by our hedonistic grande bouffe of the past 100 years or so. And, let's be real. It's not about buying the 'right' or righteous things and throwing out the wrong. It's about buying less.

And less.

And, as often as possible, buying nothing at all.

85 This part of my journey began in my childhood. I started out in a position of less, and over several decades, the less I consumed the more I realised I needed – and wanted – less. About twenty-three years ago I'd reduced everything down to two bags. As things wore out or got used up, I simply didn't buy more. A few years back I got down to one bag; everything I needed in my life amounted to 15 kilograms.

Of course, I live in a privileged world, where consuming less is a choice I can make. But I argue – and without apologising for the 'should' that's about to follow – that we-the-privileged *should* all be making this choice. There is enough food on the planet to feed the world (we currently produce enough to feed 10 billion!) if the privileged ate (and wasted) less, to use one tangible example.

Refer back to that factlet on the CO_2 impact of food waste, on page 113, if you like.

I will try not to come across as judgey, however. Instead I'll aim to sell in the untold joy and charm of less, keeping things somewhat relevant to the context of reconnecting a despairing soul back to life. For, ultimately, this is the marketing angle I've always tried to take: you buy less, you become more.

I think it's often thought that consuming less takes hard slog (and much humble-bragging and virtue-signalling on the socials to counter the misery of eating boiled bones and an old cabbage for dinner). I've had people feel sorry for me, others tell me I need to practise more self-love when they learn how I choose to live.

Consuming less is also super-confronting for anyone who grew up in the current system. My neighbour made this really great point when we shared a glass of wine a few days after she lost her mother to a long battle with Alzheimer's. 'Most of us confuse capitalism with love. We buy too much equipment for our small babies; we buy the expensive coffin for a parent; we set the table lavishly to show our friends we care.' I hadn't thought about it that way. We want to care – and connect – and it's totally understandable that we buy our way to love-giving. That's the dominant language. Likewise, our self-worth is tied up in rewarding ourselves with things. As my neighbour said very helpfully, 'When we realise that our desire to spend comes from a good (if somewhat confused) place, it is easier to forgive ourselves – to feel less guilty.'

Yep, and when not burdened by guilt, a human can then get on with making this life better.

But honestly, whenever I'm faced with choosing between 'less' or 'more', consuming less always presents as the more alive and vibrant option. It's light. It flows. 'More', by contrast, feels boggy and suffocating, like a sad wet day. As I dug deeper in my pursuit of connection, I realised living without stuff cluttering my vision, I was better able to see what mattered to me. I was also more agile – both physically and psychologically – and could then reconnect more readily with what mattered and to arrive at a spot where I only bought what I needed. I grant this: It's hard to know what we need in a world that dictates the terms of 'need' to us. And so you might find my approach – to focus on the joy first and let the awareness follow – helpful.

Aim for less–less–less

Let's flesh this out, working to the joyful reconnection sell-in...

One, don't go to the shops. When I am asked how I live minimally, I mostly say, 'I don't go to the shops.' It's a silver bullet to the heart of the issue. However, I will break things down a bit here.

Where I grew up there were no shops nearby; my parents couldn't afford the petrol to drive repeatedly into town to the shops. So we didn't – or couldn't – buy shit we didn't need. Simple.

Also, there was no rubbish service. So anything that came into the house had to be re-purposed. Which got us all very mindful about, yep, shit we didn't need. Old car tyre inner tubes became the new inner seals for the drum in the 20-year-old washing machine. Dad had two versions of the same 1969 Peugeot 404 he'd bought years before he married which remained our family car until I was in my late teens. One sat up on blocks in the 'junkyard'. As a fuel gauge or a clutch broke, he'd cherry pick the best part from the spare.

Those of us who grow up with a 'there's a patch of dirt, now go play' childhood either become the worst kind of consumers, on an aggressive mission to make up for the lack of Cabbage Patch Kids and Transformers in our formative years, or we forge a (possibly) equally reactionary path of succeeding without things. I'm of the latter camp. So are my younger brothers and sister.

We've talked about it, my family and me. There's a sort of laziness that drives our thriftiness. We literally can't be bothered doing the schlep to the shops. We observe our friends pack into the car on a Saturday, wrestling a spiralling car park and trolleys and ticket machines. 'The Shops' generally takes up most of their day (for shopping begets shopping). You go for kids' school shoes and you 'might as well, while you're there' come back with a waffle maker and new towels.

My siblings and I agreed a long time ago to never buy each other presents. At Christmas, we all – including Mum and Dad – chip in and hire a house down the coast instead and my nieces and nephews re-gift their old toys to each other.

Once you get the lazy hang of not going to the shops, things start to flow in a lovely begetting way. You become protected from marketing and advertising onslaughts. Plus, you can shield yourself from unnecessary anxiety.

As I explained in *The Beast*, the bit of our brain that controls decision-making also modulates anxiety. When you overtax it by making a whole stack of decisions it triggers anxiety (and when your anxiety is triggered, you can't make decisions). Shopping is one big onslaught of decisions. Crimson or chartreuse? What does this romper suit say about

You tend to shop online? I don't, but I found two tips that might help if you've gotten sucked in to spending, especially via Instagram. One, remove all payment methods from your phone. Manually typing in your card number each time is painful and acts as a deterrent. Two, use the Freedom app to disable your Instagram account on payday or at other times you tend to 'impulse shop' online.

my entire identity? Don't shop and you save yourself and your kids from the anxiety and the onslaught of manipulative messaging.

Plus, you're spared the packaging and wrapping and foam beads that you have to cart to the bins. Plus, you don't have to spend your Sunday having clean-outs and organising storage solutions. And hiring storage sheds. And so on and so on.

Nope. Instead you can spend your weekend lying in a park staring at the sky, or going for a hike with friends or family. See how it just keeps begetting and flowing?

Two, ditch your car. As I got older, I found my less-less-less resolve tested. It was comical how it played out at times. At sixteen, while robustly campaigning against corporations and embracing grunge anti-fashion, I accidentally became a model. I was approached in a shopping mall (perfectly) and a contract with an agency followed. And off I went and paraded a whole heap of shit that no one needed.

When I landed a contract with a London modelling agency at eighteen, the grunge era's consumerist expression back then was the waif look. The agent told me they'd crop my hair into a pixie cut and help me lose a kilo or two (I never asked how). They'd then fly me to Japan to earn some quick coin. 'Come back after Christmas and we'll get started,' they said. I felt squirmy. I wasn't sure why. I've since learned that when I squirm, something is erupting in me. Erupt it did. On Christmas Eve I went to the north of England and drank pints and ate chip butties for a month, putting on 8 kilograms. Quite an achievement. I then took off travelling on my own around Europe for a year and put on another 5 kilograms for good measure. Consumerist vortex averted!

In my early twenties, I became a journalist, working for multinational media companies, and at twenty-nine became the editor of *Cosmopolitan Australia*, a veritable catalogue of shit no one needs. A stint in television followed and I was festooned with a whole heap more shit that I quickly worked out no one needed (booster bras, clitoral stimulation gel, monogrammed cupcakes). Again, I managed to sidestep – or sabotage – the tempting material suck-hole of more-more-more. At *Cosmo*, I managed to not own a handbag. Or a straightening iron. Or a hairdryer, for that matter.

And I ditched my car. Most days I ran or rode a bike the 10 kilometres to work (and to after-work red-carpet events and the rest), which was categorically not a done thing in mag land.

It was about 'flow' for me. You know, living in such a way that you are not held back by dumb, clunky life-clogging stuff and moving effortlessly around the joint, reconnecting with what matters. It took 20 minutes to ride up and over the hill from my apartment at Bondi Beach to the city. Driving took 40 minutes in peak hour. Riding is a door-to-door affair. There's no driving in circles to find a parking spot. And you can drop in and pick up your mail or groceries on your way home, without having to find another spot and risking fines. For any trip under 10 kilometres in a large city, riding is the faster, easier option. Of course, it's also cheaper. It costs

I have never owned a handbag, let alone a designer one, despite being 'offered' several as an editor. I see owning a toting vessel that costs up to half a years' rent merely because it's been slapped with a fancy logo as the final frontier of consumer sucked-in-ness.

Dad and I did the calculations together over email some time back.

about $10,000 a year just to keep your own car on the road (registration, insurance, servicing, fuel etc). My bike cost me $1,200 to build using second-hand components fifteen years ago. I've replaced the tyres twice. And have it serviced every two years or so. Oh yeah, and it goes without saying, riding provides oodles of eco karma, too.

Of course, not everyone can get rid of their car (we do everything we can…whatever that looks like). At times I have had to have one. But there are great car share schemes now. And bike share set-ups. And public transport options that can be factored in to reduce car kilometres. And a lot of joyous flow to be had.

I was invited as a panellist at a food festival some time back. The theme was, wonderfully, 'flow'. I shared with the audience how insane it was to drive to a gym to work out on a stationary bike then drive home, change and drive to work (an example I referred to earlier). 'I mean, why not just ride to work and be done with it in a quarter of the time,' I asked. The moderator raised her hand and said, 'I've never in seven years of doing exactly what you've just described thought about it that way.' When I emailed her to check if I could use her anecdote, she told me she now walks to the gym (to sit on a stationary bike).

Three, live out of one bag. Okay, this, too, isn't for everyone. But you might find the psychology instructive; cherry-pick as necessary.

I left my career in magazines and TV in my mid-thirties

after developing that gnarly autoimmune disease. What followed was a fairly swift slide from the social matrix. I was unable to walk or work for almost a year and in some weird planetary lesson-bludgeoning, I was stripped of most of my possessions – I was robbed several times, tax bills rolled in, contracts fell through.

Eventually, with the help of Mum and Dad, I was able to pack up what remained of my belongings into one small storage cage and a couple of suitcases and hit the road. I first made my way to that army shed I mentioned earlier, in the forest outside Byron Bay on Australia's subtropical coast, staying there until I healed. After that, I moved from city to city, country to country for a total of eight years, gradually letting go of most of even this stuff as I realised I could do without it. I finally got down to that single 15-kilogram backpack, which I found I could live from for five to six months at a time when I was on the road.

I ran my I Quit Sugar business while living this way, did regular TV appearances, had meetings with publishers in different cities, went on dates around the world. I had two to three capsule outfits that could be rolled up compactly. I had one bra and three pairs of undies. Seriously, you don't need more. I'd rinse them in the shower with me each night (this also sees clothing last longer).

I didn't have stuff that doubled up on other stuff. Like, I've never owned an iPad, not when my laptop and phone can cover the job. I use jojoba oil for cleansing and moisturising and for thinning out my mascara, which itself is made of almond oil and charcoal and which I also use for covering my grey hair regrowth. I had that one pair of green workout shorts. I gave away books as I read them. I found I only needed three items of kitchen equipment – a slow cooker, a stick blender and a good knife. Which, admittedly, didn't come with me when I travelled.

I found it fun to see how agile and free my life could become. I could arrive in a city with my backpack, skip baggage collection and head down the stairs (avoiding the slow lift) to the train (which I could navigate with ease). I could jump on a share-scheme bike or scooter straight from the station, my bag on my back, and head to my accommodation or straight to a meeting.

Oh, the flow.

86 I'm now going to break up this long, numbered list with a small tale about 'fending'.

I've told this — story a few times over the years because it was so formative. It wasn't the first time I'd been forced to go without. But it was the first time I'd appreciated the full worth of fending.

When I was nineteen, I was mugged in Nice. One minute two men were yelling at me in a language I didn't recognise as I crouched at a train station locker struggling with a combination lock. The next they'd disappeared with my passport, money, all my clothes, my 1988 issue of *Let's Go Europe* with half of Italy and all of Scandinavia torn out, plus my notebook with the details of the family I was to start working with as an au pair in a few weeks' time, and the orange canvas backpack with the external metal frame that my Uncle Tim had hitchhiked around the world with. In a blink, I became an unidentifiable woman of non-provable age who was the sum total of the clothes on her back and the French she'd learned from a textbook in the public library next to the London pub where she'd worked and lived up until a few months ago.

This was pre-Internet and pre-parents helicoptering in to save your not-quite-adult hide. A British couple in the station gave me their phone card, a waiter in a nearby café threw a wine cork at my head to get me to move on.

I walked down to the beach and jumped in the Mediterranean in my underwear. Some US Marines bought me McDonald's. It was the first time I'd tasted the sugary premasticated culinary symbol of all things American. The taste of freedom! Abundant, yet deeply unsatiating. I remember clocking the semiotics as I faced a baggage-free future.

In the late afternoon I boarded a train to Paris. I figured if I was going to jump a train I may as well do it first-class; I settled into a bunk bed and slept. When the conductor came around to check tickets he smiled as I explained my predicament in rudimentary French. I gave him a pretend name and address. And he gave me a pretend fine.

For almost three weeks, as I tried to sort passports and money wires, I wandered the streets and gardens of Paris. I couldn't buy my way out of my predicament. The Australian Embassy demanded $200 for a new passport; the banks demanded a passport before they'd give me $200. There were no online complaint departments, no digital ID options, no social media on which I could vent this admin insanity, tagging all parties involved. Nope. I had to wait it out. And fend.

I was reduced to primitive creative skills to meet my basic survival needs. I jumped the metro and snuck into hostels. Each night I'd hover around a backpacker hostel on Rue de Vaugirard and wait for travellers to enter; I'd casually follow them in and find a spare bunk bed.

I took the baguette offcuts from the hostel in the morning before slipping out unnoticed and then visited the street markets as they opened and scooped up the bruised tomatoes and cucumbers they tossed into boxes in the gutter. Stallholders might hand me a fig or a chunk of cheese. I approached picnickers in Jardin de Luxembourg to borrow their Swiss Army knives to cut my tomatoes. We'd chat. They'd give me a swig of their wine.

I used the word fending back then to describe getting by moment to moment and using all my faculties to do so. Of course, even at the time I was aware this stint living on the streets would probably be short-lived. I had no debts, no dependents. I would not wind up destitute or trapped because I am systemically privileged (white, raised in a country with access to great education and healthcare and messaging that I'm entitled to fight for things). And so I was able to find the experience liberating – not entirely terrifying.

I remember it felt like a dance. It was expressive, my blood pumped vibrantly, and I moved in time with the rhythm of life, improvising the hell out of the situation. I always say of this experience that I've never felt so free in all my life.

We are in our element fending. We evolved fending. We have keen senses of smell and hearing, amazing problem-solving skills and bodies that can flex and bend and manoeuvre our way out of danger. We also developed an ability to cooperate while fending, to call on strangers to help when we need it.

Some posit that our greatest moments as humans–including happiness–are spawned from creative fending, from making something from nothing. Researchers at Harvard Business School coined the term the 'IKEA effect'. When we make stuff with our own hands, we like it more than the purchased version – even if you 'built' it from a flatpack and it's called Fartfull (IKEA once stocked a children's desk by such a name, seriously). Philosopher-turned-motorbike mechanic Matthew Crawford argues in *The Case for Working with Your Hands* that we're most satisfied when we're getting our hands dirty. His research shows tinkerers with sheds are happier than the rest of the population. Our innate desire to fend also explains why cake mixes didn't take off in the 1950s until the formula was changed to require 'cooks' to add their own eggs.

The sad, small-human opposite of fending, of course, is to stay stuck on the couch and to buy our way through our day, ordering in our food and entertainment online, delegating this life-sparking fending to others.

But back to the numbered list…

Four, buy nothing for, say, 13 months (other than loo paper and groceries). Again, not (possible) for everyone. But perhaps you'd like to do a modified version thereof.

My experiments in not buying stuff stepped up a gear a bunch of years ago when I went 379 days without shopping for anything but food and basics like toilet paper. I know this because my accountant called to ask me, 'Why do you have no receipts? How are you actually living?'

This wasn't about me making a statement or setting out to create some highly marketable blogging concept (a few years later, a mushroom of social media enthusiasts emerged with a business model whereby they'd blog about wearing one dress for a month, or living in a tiny house for a year and seal a book deal off the back of it). No, I was just still being lazy and flowy.

I kept doing long stints like this – 9 months, 13 months, 15 months at a time – at the end of which I would head to a mall and stock up on a new bra, running shoes, a good quality jumper or pants, and perhaps a new vegetable knife, all in about 90 minutes. On two occasions I got calls from the credit-card fraud squad as I left the mall. 'Madam, we are detecting unusual spending activity on your card.' I had to confirm my identity and that I'd indeed been shopping.

I'll get even more granular now, because I know many are not satisfied by my 'just don't go to the shops' refrain. Let's say I get the urge to buy a new pair of undies. It's time. I'm down to three pairs, all jowly in the gusset. New knickers would be nice. I map out a day to head to the shops. But then I get a bit lazy. I can't be stuffed doing the schlep. At this point I gameify. I put off going to the shops a week, then another week. It becomes fun to see how long I can delay the gratification of shiny new knickers.

The Stoics practised this as a form of character training. I remember reading about it at university. Seneca would set aside a certain number of days, 'during which you shall be content with the scantiest and cheapest fare, with coarse and rough dress, saying to yourself the while: "Is this the condition that I feared?" It is precisely in times of immunity from care that the soul should toughen itself beforehand for occasions of greater stress.'

I do the same. I check in repeatedly on how I feel when I go without. I generally feel free, like I'm not being sold the more-more-more imperative, and I quite like the feeling of strength this elicits. The fact that I've suddenly given myself an excuse to dodge a trip to the shops opens up a slot in my weekend and it's like I've lucked into some amazing time-saving hack that no one has discovered yet. I find I get very clear about what matters to me, too. There's an oxytocin gap left that my fabulous new knickers were going to fill. And so I have to fill it with something else which, no doubt, will matter more, if only as a result of the conscious pause I've allowed myself.

Prolonging the buying of something also gets me creatively fending. Undies are a bad example to explain this bit. So let's switch to, say, a new fashion item. The idea occurs to me: I'd like to wear something 'of the current decade'. I might have noticed millennials wearing cool sneakers with skirts or love-heart sunnies and felt the tug to buy myself some social currency. I delay it a week, then another and so on. And soon the desire dissipates and seems a bit silly. And I notice what I thought was a cool trend has become ubiquitous.

And so instead I wear a red floral dress I bought when I was eighteen, a pair of black wool gaberdine stirrup pants I bought twenty years ago, jeans I've inherited, cowboy boots I found on a street in Brooklyn... I keep them all and they come in and out of fashion every few years. I have dress-up dresses from my teens that I will wear to black-tie events. When a T-shirt goes totally grungy under the arms, I cut off the arms.

Living this way necessitates buying only high-quality, sustainably made garments, looking after things (I take my good clothes off as soon as I get home) and not washing clothes unnecessarily (I'll wear a shirt four days in a row before putting it in the laundry basket, airing it out on a hanger between wears). Which is time-saving and makes sense and is flowy, too.

Again, I say this knowing that there are people all around us who don't have the luxury of choosing what they need or don't need. For them, frugality is a necessity, not a game. But, again, to a large extent the inequality in the world is a direct result of over-consumption by people like me and anyone with the time and ability to be reading this. And I'm going to throw this in here: passing on our sloppy seconds to the needy when we've over-consumed is not the fix. The fix is to consume less. And to perhaps spend all that extra, flowy time you have on your hands advocating for systemic change. But I digress...

Five, buy second-hand or find it on the street. More recently, after eight years on the move, I finally decided to settle in one spot for a bit. I rented an apartment in Sydney's Bondi Beach and unpacked my one bag (and storage cage). It was an experiment, to see if I could 'do what I'm not doing'.

I set about furnishing my place. I did so without buying anything new, apart from a bed, built locally. I also had a couch that had taken me three years to research and have built from sustainable and recycled materials. I'd never owned my own large household appliances. Or a table.

I've made do in all kinds of ways over the years, including living with more than thirty different housemates and/ or partners who brought such things to the equation. For my new home, household goods were bought on eBay and Facebook Marketplace, including rugs, my washing machine and fridge. Various plants, bookshelves, lamps and a side table were picked up off the street.

There are attendant benefits to this, apart from the obvious saving of resources. Like, you're not exposed to the chemicals and flame retardants sprayed on new furniture. And you become quite unbothered by the idea of being burgled.

Plus...you don't have to go to the shops.

— Don't laugh; Steve Jobs took ten years to do the same – his wife told his biographer Walter Isaacson that he didn't want to buy something he wouldn't like, or that wasn't fit for purpose in 20 years.

Six, start a love affair with leftovers. History is filled with instances where an idea starts to take off and some enthusiast has to go jump the shark. Fluoro and 'Don't Worry Be Happy' motifs were fantastic fun. Then some ebullient individual comes out with hypercolour tees!

Some of my friends think I'm this enthusiast in the campaign against waste.

I have ranted about food waste for decades and wrote the first ever completely zero-waste cookbook (348 recipes, no food wasted in the making of the book). Forget vegan vs meat inclusive vs organic to-ing and fro-ing. The most impactful thing you can do to combat the various environmental and ethical debates around what to eat is to not waste any of it.

If wasted food was a country, it would be the third largest producer of CO_2 in the world, after the United States and China. Just one-third of the food we waste could feed all the starving people in the world.

And as I explained back in the climate change chapter: *the biggest contributors to the food waste disaster aren't the supermarkets, the farmers, or the restaurant owners. It's us. Everyday consumers.*

But there are things we can do:

After washing, wrap in an old tea towel or pillowcase. Never store in plastic bags!! For more, see my book *Simplicious Flow.*

- Dish up only as much food as people want.
- Enforce not leaving the table until everything is eaten.
- Cook up uneaten food into bubble-and-squeak.
- Learn how to store fruit and vegetables so they last in the crisper for two weeks.
- Buy discounted meat that's almost past its use-by date

and would otherwise be tossed by the supermarket in a few hours (and put it in the freezer immediately).

And you can go a step further if you eat out from time to time. A few years back I started collecting butter scraps at cafes. Cafés and restaurants always give you too much butter and it just gets tossed if you don't finish it. It kills me. So, I wrap leftover butter in my dining partner's napkin (I refuse napkins), fold it and place it in my bag. 'Doesn't it melt?' people ask. Oddly, not so much. I put the bundle in the fridge as soon as I get home and the butter can be lifted off cleanly, even when it's melted a little. The buttered napkin is then stored ready to use for greasing pans, in lieu of baking paper.

— I invite anyone who never eats butter to tell the waiter to not bring any before it's too late (ie. it hits the table and is deemed 'contaminated'). Ditto if you don't want your side of toast or bread.

I've not had to buy butter in years.

I do a similar thing with bones and fish carcasses. I collect them from all the plates of people I'm eating with (at home, at friends' houses, and out at cafés). And I make bone broth. I've also been known to take bones from surrounding tables. Some have asked, 'Surely people freak when you ask for their bones?' Well, maybe they're a little surprised. But most also listen to my explanation and then gush something about how we all need to do more to save the planet and on two occasions strangers have accepted my offer to meet them in a few days so that I can give them a jar of the broth that I make from their bones. Which is always a nice rounding out of things. It generally gets them on board with making their own broth (I point them to the recipe on my blog).

— I do the same with strangers' butter. I always ask first.

— I invite you to carry a small container or bag at all times for this activity.

People also ask, 'Don't you worry about germs?' Well, no.

I'm about to boil the living daylights out of the things for several days. This never fails to stop people in their tracks. Of course!

I also collect uneaten bread, avocado slices and the dregs of meals, which I re-purpose into savoury bakes, French toast, etc. (Again, I reheat at high temperatures; leftovers always should be – yours or those of strangers.)

I appreciate not everyone wishes to be so...enthused. But. Gosh. I dunno. I oscillate between wanting to scream into a megaphone, 'This-is-the-only-way-we-should-rightfully-be-living-and-come-on-everyone-let's-do-it-for-the-kids,' and focusing on making the enthused route so charming that it's irresistible. I've ultimately opted to try the latter approach.

I shared a quote on Instagram from African American activist Toni Cade Bambara: 'The role of the artist is to make the revolution irresistible.' My caption pointed out everyone is an artist (we create our days, our interactions, our legacy). We can change the story with what we lend charm to. Even eating other people's bones.

Seven. Just. Don't. Chuck. Stuff. Out. 'Have you seen *Minimalism*? You know, the documentary on Netflix? You're just like those guys.'

I get this often. I have a response: 'Yep, watched it. Nope, I'm not like them.'

I politely point out that the two dudes from Ohio who made and star in the documentary are declutterers. They chuck stuff out for what I gather are aesthetic and psychological reasons. Me, I try to chuck nothing out. My aim is to not buy stuff in the first place and instead use up and re-purpose everything I already have or have inherited. Or that I take from strangers' plates. The point isn't clean surfaces, it's to minimise resources, to have a lighter, more flowing footprint on the planet.

Besides, there are at least two scenes in the documentary where the two ex-corporates are hurtling down a freeway with disposable takeaway coffee cups on the dashboard. I mean...

Japanese author of *The Life-Changing Magic of Tidying Up* Marie Kondo fuelled this confused approach to minimalism. She demonstrates that 'less' is achieved by dumping anything that doesn't bring joy into plastic bags and donating it to thrift stores. It's spawned a whole (consumable) industry. In Australia there is an actual Institute of Professional Organisers with more than a hundred 'qualified' members. The nuanced truth here, however, is that we are chucking out so much stuff (and buying so much stuff to start with), thrift stores are only able to take 5 per cent of clothing donated. The rest is dumped in landfill. The other nuanced truth here is that fewer and fewer people actually shop at thrift stores. I mean, do you? As often as you donate? Do your friends? Who do we think is buying all our unwanted stuff?

It's a shame, really. In her books, Kondo does discuss the far more alive and connected Japanese concept of *mottainai*, a Buddhist term for the need to respect and feel gratitude for

— After the series first screened, Kondo (emoticon eye-roll) launched an online homewares store full of stuff no one really needs, like a $96 soup ladle.

the resources around you, and is used to suggest regret when something is wasted. But this bit of the minimalist equation was disregarded in the Netflix series. Saving and mending and reusing clearly doesn't make for sexy television.

Equally, 'sustainable consumption' or 'conscious consumerism' are neither minimalist nor sustainable. One study compared footprints of 'green' consumers to regular 'non-conscious' consumers – they found no difference between them. Because buying anything – compostable, ethical or otherwise – uses resources.

To work with a tangible, let's take my hoary old obsession – takeaway coffee cups. Disposables are a travesty, but buying a reusable cup comes with a price, too. It takes twenty uses for it to come up 'cleaner' from an emissions point of view than a single-use one (the glass or metal is more resource heavy than paper and plastic). Which becomes problematic when people break or lose them before using them twenty times. The truly sustainable solution is to use a mug you already own, or to make your own portable version. I take an old glass jar (with a lid) and wrap it in a dozen or so of those rubber bands that your tenderstem broccoli or kale come tied in to provide the insulated 'silicon' grip. I use a bottle opener to whack a small ventilation hole in the lid.

I guess my concerned point is that it is impossible to buy our way to 'less'. The only action that will make a difference is not buying as much stuff and throwing less of that stuff out.

An idea: what if, to be able to dump our unwanted goods at charity stores we had to actually purchase from the store first? An item bought (and therefore not bought new from a store) earns us the ability to donate one item. Would we view things differently? In Slovenia, they apply this scheme to rubbish collection. Residents have a swipe card that earns them credits for every carefully sorted load placed in the five recycling bins. Only when you've got enough credits can you access the bins for rubbish that goes to landfill.

87 Consuming less isn't just about buying or wasting fewer things. The approach flows into all aspects of life. It's doing fewer activities, signing the kids up to less extracurricular guff that winds up making them stressed and less resilient. It's expecting less from each other, and it's travelling less on holidays, so that we can connect more, be more present. It's only boiling as much water as you need in a kettle, because an electric kettle is the most energy-zapping small appliance in a kitchen (notice how it's always the kettle that blows the fuse?). It's adding fewer flavours to food (too many flavourings overtax our digestion). It's putting fewer items on a meeting agenda (so what matters can be discussed mindfully). It's washing our clothes less and using less washing powder — I often cite a *Choice* study from several years ago that found half a scoop will clean clothes just as effectively as the full recommended scoop. when we do. It's living life consciously and truthfully. In many ways it's constantly asking yourself, at the deepest level, 'What truly matters?'

Real minimalism sees us engage with things as they are. With less noise in our heads, our souls can hear the call to join life. And if we put down some baggage, we can be ready to be wildly, joyously necessary.

88 Now, some of you might have been busting to ask this from the beginning: What about all the flying you did to write this book? Yes, let's talk about my flight shame or, in Swedish, *Flygskam* as it's being called around the world. I hiked around the world to tell a tale of consuming less. Hypocritical, much?

Very possibly, but I thought it would be helpful to show

how I wrestled with this eco quandary myself (and how I wrestle with all of them).

First, many interviews and hikes were actually done within a bike or train ride from where I was living or visiting for work, sometimes for up to six months at a time during my nomadic period.

Aside from the — Jordanian one coming up, a holiday side trip.

That said, my nomadic period did see me catch several long-haul planes in a year and aviation contributes about 2 per cent of the world's global carbon emissions, which some might say is not humungous, but at the individual consumer level, a plane trip is up there as one of the most polluting things we can do.

From here things get very nuanced. For instance, flying produces fewer emissions than driving in the bulk of instances. If you are in a car with fewer than three people (the average occupancy rate for cars in America was 1.6 people per vehicle in 2017), flying tends to be more sustainable per person per kilometre. Especially if you drive with the air-con on, or if there's a traffic jam. If you're travelling long distance, flying weighs up as the far better option (a plane's CO_2 emissions are higher during take-off and landing). There are other detailed factors: the way jet fuel both cools and warms when it interacts with other gases in the air, the impact of contrails, whether you travel economy or business (on long-haul flights, carbon emissions per passenger per kilometre are about three times higher in business class), and so on. Plus, there's this consideration: when you live in a massive, isolated country like Australia lacking in other transport infrastructure (such as high-speed trains), flying is often the only option.

As with many of the world's complexities, there is often a more elegant truth to be found. In this case, it is to travel less. At the end of that eight-year stint of living on the road I committed to staying put for four years. I rode my bike, walked, or caught public transport everywhere (I've not owned a car in almost a decade), and travelled interstate rarely (the pandemic assisted me in this somewhat!). I've now committed to living in Paris so I can be a mere train ride away from the work I do in Europe. Trains cut your carbon emissions seven-fold, enabling you to – in Swedish again – *Tågskryt* ('train brag').

Not perfect. And I wrestle with my choices often, while having to also accept that I live in the world (as it currently exists). And as I wrote this spiel I truly had to ask if I was seductively justifying myself to myself. And whether I am in fact doing everything *I* can? I'm sure this is a real-time tussle for you, too. It's an important one. I'll keep tussling over here until a clear fix becomes apparent, if ever.

SARAH WILSON

ST IVES TO PENZANCE HIKE, ENGLAND

I had been in the United Kingdom for book promotion obligations and figured I'd take the opportunity to hike the historic pirate route around the southwest coast of England. It's a wild and woolly single trail that hugs the Cornish coastline, with pubs conveniently located every 20-odd kilometres, which is very pirate-friendly.

I arrived in St Ives by train from London with my small travel bag – the 15-kilo one I'd reduced everything down into – and stayed in a loft in a pub. I always try to stay in lofts.

There is so much to learn from a town's roof line. Plus, vibrations from the street are dulled by the indented roof line aspect. In the morning I headed downstairs and ate an egg and wilted spinach with white toast and a mug of milky tea. I smiled at an older couple with pillowy cheeks sitting next to the breakfast buffet. They told me they were from two towns up the train line and about their bad night's sleep and asked where I was off to. All jolly and pillowy. 'I'm hiking to Penzance,' I told them.

'I wish I could do that,' the husband said.

His wife stared at her eggs.

'Well, why don't you?' I asked.

'Ooooh, I'd never go without Sue,' he replied with a sigh,

and patted Sue's shoulder.

After breakfast, I set off into the British summer elements. On that day it was a 20-kilometre route through rain and wind – a balmy 14°C before you factor wind chill and wet underlayers.

Sometime after lunch, after meandering along cliffs and through prehistoric-looking fern scrub, I passed an old man in a tweed cap and army-issue anorak. He was sitting against a wooden post, cradling a sheep dog against the wind. They were both staring out to sea. 'Is she keeping you warm?' I asked.

The old man looked up. 'It's her last visit to the ocean,' he said. 'She's being put down this afternoon.' Tears rolled down his face.

I started crying too. 'I'm so sorry... She loved this beach?'

The old man nodded like a small boy, wordless, and started sobbing. I gave him an awkward hug, the only kind you can give an elderly, sobbing Englishman. And walked on.

I passed through Zennor around lunchtime and sat in the Tinners Arms pub to dry out my socks and drink an apple cider. DH Lawrence lived here at one point. My friend Angela texted me one of his poems later when I told her where I'd been:

When we get out of the glass bottles of our ego,
when we escape like squirrels turning in the cages of our personality
and get into the forests again,
we shall shiver with cold and fright

but things will happen to us so that we don't know ourselves.
Cool, unlying life will rush in…

Cool, unlying life will rush in… I dig it.

That evening I arrived at Gurnard's Head, a pub that sits in a paddock facing a dramatic headland. I read *The Rules Do Not Apply* by Ariel Levy over a plate of pork with local asparagus and a glass of claret at dinner in the front bar. Levy, a feminist journalist who has led a life in defiance of restrictions, gets pregnant with her wife using donor sperm in her late thirties, but miscarries traumatically at nineteen weeks. She blames herself but her doctor blames her age – he tells her that she thought the rules did not apply to her and left it 'too late'. Levy's life then implodes post-miscarriage. Her pain was very familiar to me. By this stage I'd had one miscarriage and I was actually doing this hike to kill a bit of time before I set off to Crete to go through sperm insemination myself, using the generous Danish poet's contribution, at the age of forty-four. There are no user manuals, and no insurance schemes, for those of us who have not played by the rules. I reflected on this as I watched a couple in their sixties on the other side of the dining room do the silent halfway-through-the-meal plate swap. They nodded approvingly at each other's fair splitting down the middle. Freedom has its price, I thought.

By day three I was on to Jean-Paul Sartre's *Nausea*, which I'd swapped in the pub after finishing Ariel Levy. It was still raining. I passed a coast-watch tower where the volunteer waved madly at me from his foggy window. I walked through a tiny little hamlet of stone cottages at Porthgwarra, England's most beautiful beach, according to brochures. There was a little boat shack serving tea and pasties. I jumped in the icy ocean naked and then sat and read a bit of *Nausea*. The sun had come out.

The dread that the main character Antoine Roquentin felt when he observed the pointless absurdity of life had previously gotten me too depressed to finish the book. I appreciated Roquentin's despair. This dread is so very visible when you don't play by the rules, and you hover on the outskirts. But lying in the sun with a body and mind soothed by the days' ambling, I was able to read through to the bit where the former adventurer sat under a chestnut tree and finally 'got it'. He realised that meaninglessness was the very path to our freedom. In the face of absurd meaninglessness, we have no choice but to create meaning in our own lives. Discovering that we are all one, that we are consciousness that can witness the roots of the chestnut tree, often becomes the meaning we choose to create, Roquentin finds.

— Not at all unlike Albert Camus' exploration in *The Plague* (I mentioned this on page 177), written a decade later.

I arrived at Sennen that evening after wading my way through sand dunes for a good hour. I booked into the pub right on the water. The ocean was thrashing the levy across the road and families were determinedly eating ice cream huddled in a little parlour, the windows steamed up. I sat downstairs in the pub and chatted to the manager while I waited to check in. She was a young woman who'd just left her fiancé and moved to this small town only a week before. My 15-kilogram bag became the focus of our chat.

'Oh goodness, I wish I could do that,' she said with a sigh, pointing to my bag.

'Why can't you?' I asked.

'Oh, I couldn't afford it.'

'But it doesn't cost anything to have less,' I explained, a bit baffled. 'My living costs are way less than those with a mortgage and a car and all the other trappings of a life spent ensconced in "things". Plus, walking is free.'

She looked at me, also baffled. I realised she was convinced that I had some special privilege that enabled me to make this choice. Otherwise, why couldn't she just do it? Admittedly I'd taken three days 'leave', and the train ticket south was not cheap, plus I didn't have kids. But neither did she.

I remember being in her situation. And how the excuses I made always seemed so seductive.

In a world where we buy our way to solutions, we assume there is a price for this kind of freedom. There is, but it's not a pecuniary one. It's having to stand as yourself without your things, and then to walk your own path.

Is this what we feel we can't afford?

A lot of humans have known for a long time that less makes us happier and freer and better humans. I've derived solace and conviction from this over the years.

'The things you own, end up owning you,' says Chuck Palahniuk via the character Tyler in *Fight Club*. Socrates wrote that happiness is not found in seeking more, but in developing the capacity to enjoy less, and F Scott Fitzgerald wrote in a letter to his daughter in 1940, 'Once one is caught up into the material world no one person in ten thousand finds the time…to examine the validity of philosophic concepts for himself.' And for good measure, Bertrand Russell famously penned this: 'It is preoccupation with possession more than anything else that prevents men from living freely and nobly.'

The next day, the sun came out again and I moved onward, setting off early. After a full day of blissful strolling with a soft, meadowy breeze and Mediterranean-like views, I reached Porthcurno, passing the Minack Theatre, an outdoor amphitheatre built into the cliff by one woman with her bare hands over the course of decades. She died at eighty-nine a few years back. The big stone theatre overlooks the beach. I learned from a fellow rambler that the theatre reviewer for the *Guardian* had travelled all the way from London to see the performance that night of *The Third Policeman*. As I walked past, I bought the very last ticket. I was told I was 'ludicrously lucky' to have secured one. I ate fish pie and peas at, yes, another pub and then returned for the performance at dusk. The play was not great, but there were dolphins and seals cavorting in the water in the background as the sun set.

After six days on the coastal path I eventually made it to Penzance. I stayed in another loft and rinsed out my muddy gear in the handbasin, ready to head to Crete the next day. I watched seagulls circle above the skylight and tried to recall a Margaret Atwood poem… Something-something about the moment when you finally own a bunch of things but then the trees and the waves and the birds all pull back from you and you hear a whisper…that you own nothing.

— I later Googled it. It's called 'The Moment.' Do look it up.

pay

attention

!   think

!

Between stimulus and response there is a space. In that space is our power to choose our response. In our response lies our growth and our freedom.
—**Viktor Frankl, Man's Search for Meaning**

89 Viktor Frankl penned this line after being released from Nazi concentration camps where he'd endured three years of hard labour. Some of you might know he wrote the book *Man's Search for Meaning* in just nine days after being released. He argued that he'd survived, while hundreds of thousands of fellow prisoners perished, because of his ability to not be distracted by others' impositions on his thinking. He made the conscious and deliberate choice to own that space between what was happening around him and how he was going to live.

Today, though, we live in an 'attention economy'. The more-more-more system tosses us bread and circuses and it's bought our ability to think clearly. A bunch of super smart people working in behemoth tech companies design products to drag our attention away from true connecting by keeping us on an addictive, hedonistic treadmill of human smallness, buying their products. Over 90 per cent of the data in the world today was generated in just the previous two years. We are inundated with the equivalent of 34 gigabytes of information a day, enough to crash a laptop in a week. YouTube and Netflix autoplay videos and next episodes; Facebook and Instagram manipulate when people receive feedback for their posts, ensuring they arrive when we feel vulnerable and will thus stay in the platform's vortex. This handful of information companies now steer most of our consumption and information-sourcing choices.

They also control truth. A fake news story paid for, or planted by, dodgy interests can spread around the globe in seconds, duping us into believing something (usually) highly divisive. The platforms encourage sharing and prioritise scandalous news. And because we've forgotten the art of reading deeply and carefully, we are likely to accept it unquestioningly. And spread it.

I've done it. I shared a news story that claimed our (then) prime minister had flown his family to the other side of the country to avoid the bushfire smoke in Sydney during the Black Summer fires I keep referencing. It was right in the middle of his atrocious handling of the fires (he'd just returned from Hawaii, where he'd decided to take a holiday, as several fire fighters were killed and millions of animals perished). It had been shared countless times, and was entirely plausible, so I assumed it was legit. But it turned out a satirical newspaper had written the original story. I, embarrassingly, had not paid attention. We have lost our cognitive resilience, along with the other resiliences required to navigate life with our eyes and hearts wide open.

Little wonder politicians speak in riddles, journalists get facts wrong, complex moral issues are reduced to facile economic equations or some other form of black vs white reductionism, when we all get our news from social media tiles. Little wonder we are failing miserably to get on the same page about the very real threats to our existence.

I get it. I get you, fellow tossed 'n' turned humans.

90 We are also living in a state that psychologists call 'continual partial attention'. So, while we have more interactions with other humans, they are partial connections – connection-lite. So parents, for example, have more contact time with their kids today – but it's partial and distracted, predominantly due to the tug of technology.

We tend to focus a lot of our concerns about kids' anxiety and welfare on their screen time. But the impact of parents' screen addictions has been shown to be far more damaging to their kids. A lot of parents today (and I seriously have sympathy) exist in this state of continuous partial attention, constantly checking their devices as they spend time with their kids, and this is interrupting an ancient emotional cueing system between parents and kids, whereby responsive communication is required for learning, according to tech-industry veteran and researcher Linda Stone. Kids learn to speak, and to develop their social skills and moral framework, via their caregivers' very present mirroring, their signals, nods and cooing, or stern correction. Studies at Temple and Harvard universities have shown that without this parental presence, kids suffer significant developmental injuries.

Which I know will sting many truly earnest parents reading this who are − let's face it − equally injured by the imperative to be always 'on', always working, always parenting, always available. It should sting all of us. But I also find myself feeling some softening and connecting compassion when I learn such truths. We are all in this. No one is to blame. This collective distraction is messing up all of our relationships: with other people, with animals and trees, with the democratic process, with the truth and with the Earth itself.

It becomes a noble, 'Big Human' responsibility, then, to wrestle our attention back.

91 Oh, and there's this. We live in a society that seriously disses on considered thinking. We tell someone, 'You think too much.' I've been told this since I was a kid. I live in a country where putting your hand up and saying, 'I've thought about this deeply, done my research, and something is not right

here. Couldn't we be doing things differently?' is seen as anti-the-tough-it-out-battler identity we insist on hanging on to even though it's no longer 1880 and we don't ride off sheeps' backs any more. 'C'mon, Sarah. You're being un-Australian. She'll (better) be right.'

Unsurprisingly, we began disparaging thinkers as the 'intellectual elite' and the 'chattering classes'…ooooh, whaddya know…at around the time neo-liberalism kicked in in the early '80s. Thinking-lite tends to emerge in times of economic opulence. We sink into that comfortable couch, numb out and dumb down. A cult works best when its members stop thinking.

But not thinking is neither benign, nor merely ignoble. Not thinking is also dangerous. As Hannah Arendt demonstrated, it was the non-thinking, or thoughtlessness of Nazi officers that enabled them to commit mass murders. I was in Europe when the results of the Brexit referendum came through in 2016. I remember watching the news reports showing stunned Brits telling the camera that they hadn't really thought through what was at stake. They realised they were pro-EU but hadn't voted, and now it was too late. Similarly, as I wrote this chapter, I watched Australians rush out and buy toilet paper in response to the COVID-19 outbreak, causing violence and panic and distraction from the critical precautions people needed to learn about.

The RAND Corporation, a centre-right US think tank (the irony does not escape!), published a report warning of 'truth decay' – the phenomenon whereby a world is so flooded with spin that it becomes bamboozled as to what's actually real...and so descends into further non-thinking.

This truth decay is happening on all sides of politics, in business, media and on the streets, right at a time when we need truth and refined, considered ideas and direction. Pizzagate; Boris Johnson's Partygate; David Icke and his lizard theories, and a former president advocating bleach cures all spring to mind.

— Pizzagate: A false child sex ring conspiracy tracked to a pizza shop via a hacked email that emerged from Hillary Clinton's office. A gunman believed the story and travelled across the country to fire a rifle in the restaurant.

I get it. I get you, fellow bamboozled humans. The issues that plague us and threaten to destroy us – social injustice, the state of the planet, crises of human despair– are incredibly convoluted, intertwined and systemic. Their causes wind down thousands of sedimentary layers below the surface, and to discuss them meaningfully, to *fix* them requires winding down those layers, mindfully, patiently, lovingly.

But precisely because everything around us is so complex and deeply systemic, we have become a species that exists in a permanent state of shell-shock. We would like everything reduced to simple black and white equations, thank you very much. We don't have the time or bandwidth to do the work required to dig ourselves out of our predicament. Instead, we tune out, eye roll, throw our hands up and resort to blanket absolutism or distraction. There, sorted, gone! Now, let's go shopping.

Again, I get it. But we have to think deeper. It's non-negotiable. Because this shit matters. Yep, it's hard, but we must do it anyway. Because hard work results in the good stuff. I do not know of a single game changer throughout history whose modus operandi, was, 'It'll be alright' or 'I just like to take it easy.'

92 You could put your cynical pants on for this one. In Silicon Valley, among the very same white-sneakered tech CEO crew who have taken control of our attention via their gadgets and widgets and algorithms, the very latest craze is Stoicism. Back in 300 BC Greece, the Stoics preached a life dedicated to vigilance, minimalism, perseverance, political engagement, duty, a lot of asking of nuanced moral questions…and the paying of mindful attention.

Ex–American Apparel executive turned philosophical life-hacker Ryan Holiday leads the movement. His Daily Stoic site and bestselling books have gained him acolytes including entrepreneur and author Tim Ferriss, Twitter CEO Jack Dorsey, and Digg founder Kevin Rose, along with Tiger Woods, LL Cool J and Gwyneth Paltrow. They are all quoting Seneca, Marcus Aurelius and Epictetus across their social feeds.

Epictetus: 'The more we value things outside our control, the less control we have.'

Seneca: 'It is not the man who has too little, but the man who craves more, that is poor.'

Marcus Aurelius: 'Concentrate every minute like a Roman – on doing what's in front of you with precise and genuine seriousness, tenderly. And on freeing yourself from all other distractions.'

But rather than be cynical I prefer to see the phenomenon

as an example of just how much our souls crave mindful, present connection. And besides, it's spawning some helpful solutions, too. Check this out...

Do a dopamine fast

Also hailing from Silicon Valley is the vigilant practice of abstaining from the kind of stimulation and distraction that triggers the highly addictive dopamine hormone. The tech community are all into writing long LinkedIn posts about their exploits. (I'm still resisting pulling on those cynical pants!) It essentially entails starving yourself of all the stuff the neo-liberal system chucks at us and that eventually numbs the reward receptors in the brain, meaning we need more stimulation to get the same hit.

— Vigilance, I enjoyed learning, derives from the Latin root *vigilia*, which means wakefulness.

More stimulation numbs us further and around and around we go. A dopamine fast sees you quit all the breads and circuses: junk food, TV series, porn, shopping, and of course devices. Interestingly, the Chinese government has imposed this kind of fasting schedule on gaming for kids as of 2020. New laws place blocks on night-time use, and also daily time limits (1.5 hours during the week; 3 hours on weekends).

I've been playing with it a bit. I'm not one for bio-hacks. But I found it helpful to frame the exercise as an act of defiance (I will not have my attention bought!). I supply a bit of detail here because I know many of you are probably craving some straightforward instruction on the matter.

First, choose what you want to abstain from. **Perhaps start with three distractions at a time:** choosing from Facebook, Instagram, Twitter, WhatsApp, sugar, junk food, phone calls, texting, taking photos, emailing, TV, Netflix, gaming, gambling, recreational drugs, shopping (some fans go as far as cutting out sex, eating and eye contact).

Second, set up an abstinence schedule. For example:

- 2 hours before bed
- 1 day of the weekend. Essentially, bring back the Sabbath!
- 1 week per year. Go on a tech-free holiday. Do a silent retreat. Vipassana retreats are available around the world (10 days of meditation, no talking, minimal eating, minimal eye contact and obviously no technology).

My friend Dan Buettner, author of *Blue Zones* (places in the world where people live the longest), identifies observing a Sabbath as one of nine lifestyle habits that contribute to longevity and happiness.

Third, try some of these tech hacks:

- Download an app like Freedom or Cold Turkey that blocks distracting websites and social media while you work on your computer.
- Turn off all alerts and badge app icons on your phone.
- Disable 'see online' functions on your social apps. I need to stop feeling the particular pressure that comes from others knowing I'm online and therefore should be responding to their messages outside of the time frame that suits my priorities.
- Change your lock screen. I learned this technique from Catherine Price, described as the Marie Kondo of our

brain's attention. She advises changing your lock screen to one that shows three questions: 'What for? Why now? What else?' I tried it with the (beautiful) question: 'What are you yearning for?' It gets me to stop and pay attention when I go in for a diversionary dopamine hit on my phone.

- Change your home screen. When I met with life coach, author and entrepreneur Marie Forleo during her Australian tour she showed me her phone's home screen: photos of Sicily…on her opening home screen and on the screen after that. And on another two after that. She must flick several screens before she gets to the one with apps on it. 'It creates a gap,' she says. 'While I scroll across, it's a trigger to tell me to get a grip.'

- Use Boomerang to ensure emails can't reach co-workers' inboxes until business hours. (Look, it might suit you to write emails out of hours, but if we're going to shift the culture, we have to protect each other's attention, too.)

Finally, just go old school. If I'm driving, I put my phone in the boot. When I'm working, I leave my phone three rooms away. In a drawer.

And I play with leaving the house without my phone.

I started out small. I'd leave it behind when I went across the road to pick up mail. Then I graduated to going out to dinner without it. I'll text my dining mate to tell them I'm not taking my phone. This creates an imperative for both of us to be on time. We can't send a breezy, semi-avoidant text en route, working on the assumption that the other will be sorting through work emails anyway (which is our rationalisation process). It lifts us all.

THE CRADLE MOUNTAIN HIKE, TASMANIA

After finishing a major project a little while back I needed to connect with nature…and humanity. I signed up to a group hike along the Overland Track in Tasmania, a rugged and remote six-day walk traversing glacial mountains, rainforests and alpine plains through World Heritage-listed wilderness in the middle of the island. I normally prefer to hike solo. But sometimes you must shake up the snow globe a little.

When hiking solo you pay attention to your surrounds which brings you in nice and close to life. You also pay attention to the ugliness deep in your psyche that can bubble to the surface, which you can sort and soften using the aforementioned calm. Hiking with others, on the other hand, means you must pay attention to the conversation and to the particularities of each human. Both are primordial. We evolved walking solo with only nature to keep us company, and with others in long perambulating conversation. We yearn for both types of connection.

The hike sets off from Cradle Mountain and you cover

about 85 kilometres, including side-trips, arriving at Lake St Clair on the final afternoon where you can stay in the historic Pumphouse Point lodge, positioned out in the lake at the end of a long boardwalk.

This walk is one of the most famous in the world, and it would have to be in part for its pristineness. The air in this part of Tasmania is said to be the purest in the world (Chinese companies, literally, bottle it) and the region is one of only two national parks on the World Heritage List to tick off all the heritage criteria. The region has eons of undisturbed quietness that bestows a calm energy. I could feel it in my mitochondria when I arrived.

There's certainly a distinct vibrancy in our group as we set off across marshland on a narrow boardwalk on the first day. We are a group of eight hikers (and two young guides); there's one other single woman, a few years younger than me. It takes a while for us all to find our group rhythm, but soon we're heading up into a volcanic rockscape.

It's late summer; the air is cool, but the sun piercing. Soon things mist over. Whenever I come to Tasmania and enter its largely unspoiled wilderness, I immediately lose sense of where in the world I am. It's such an original land with the most uninterrupted human history on the planet—that is until white people removed or massacred all but a handful of the First Nations peoples. It can feel like you're on the Italian coast one minute, in the Canadian Rockies the next. The weather will shift, and I can confuse the spookiness and moss with Iceland.

SARAH WILSON

Where we are hiking there is one road between us and Antarctica. We are quite literally at the bottom of the Earth.

When the misty rain sets in, the group settles into clusters of three to four. Hiking conversations gurgle along. They froth and turn as they need to but invariably flow their way into a steady stream of common human sharing, of love and loss and childhood moments. All the good, reflective, mindful stuff. Rarely do we discuss our jobs or status.

Every topic gets to unfurl completely, never forced or rushed. Sometimes I like to sit back in the group and observe the magic of The Group Hiking Conversation. No matter what the mix of ages, sex or backgrounds, everyone in a walking conversation eventually arrives together in the one lovely pool of mutualism. Or perhaps a field, the one beyond right and wrong, is a better metaphor. It generally only takes about an hour or so.

If you're sensitive and self-conscious, it can be exhausting work at first, being so aware of the subtleties of each person. My mind can jump all over the place trying to navigate motives and needs. But after that initial hour you do adjust to the primitive rhythm, like you're dialled into our ancestral way of keeping company and bearing mindful witness to each other. It feels like home.

In West Bengal, they hold *adda* – intellectual, meandering conversations, often in public spaces and with lots of tea. *Adda* is always done in a group and is always free-form. Politics, philosophy, life and death are debated – generally for hours. It's considered a vital leisure activity. I'm not sure where I first heard about *adda*. But it would have to be one of the few remaining traditions that sanctifies deep, considered, thoughtful talk. It stands in the tradition of the French salons during the Enlightenment and the Greek symposium. I know some people like to talk about the era they most wish they'd lived in. Me, I've always dreamed of being dumped into Parisian salon society in the early 18th century where I could freely slay a robust debate with ideas I'd craft and hone as an artist does a lump of clay. We would solve problems. Lofty, life-raising ideas that would stand the test of time would spread and shift the world onward. We'd think, talk and do something.

The closest I've come to such a forum today is hiking in a group.

By late afternoon each day we'd arrive at our cabin, hidden 100 metres or so off the trail in the forest. We'd shower and then congregate to drink wine and continue the *adda*. I'd join the group after everyone had settled into couches and beanbags and then sidle up to someone, like a cat. I found myself aching to collapse intimately on the people I'd meaningfully conversed with all day.

A day of walking will dislodge all kinds of deep truths. They will surface through the fatigue as you sink into the couch; after a day of walking off our barky layers, we reveal the trauma rings in our trunks. Among my hiking crew were a dairy farming couple who told me about their daughter's challenges with coming out as a lesbian as a young teen. Their truly liberal compassion didn't line up with some of

299

their otherwise conservative political thinking. My black and white assumptions were thrown. It was sublime. I got to see the childlike vulnerability of the 65-year-old tough-nut former school principal in our group who missed his wife, to the point of sentimental tears most evenings. He said he never cries and never talks about crying. And we talked about that.

Yet another — teacher who hikes!

Home, this was home. And amid strangers, too. It was also so extraordinarily clarifying. When we talk through things deeply, and connect in *adda*, all the complexities of life, including the moral quagmires, somehow become manageable. Our brains can sift through them and comprehend from a place of calm perspective where the priorities line up in an orderly fashion and we can put up the right guardrails and see our north stars.

When we got to Lake St Clair and caught the wooden ferry over the water to the information centre, we all went our separate ways. After a week of more meaningful chat than any of us are likely to have for a while, none of us felt sad to part. Everything was in perspective, everything was manageable.

93 At several points in this journey I held a number of discussion groups. You could call them *addas*. I'd organise these *addas* when I got to a particularly stuck point, when I didn't know where I was heading. I asked strangers who'd approached me in the street, who had told me about their overwhelm, to join. I invited bankers who'd raised their hands at some corporate events I'd spoken at. I have a climate-change-denying neighbour – he came along to one of them, too, with a friend.

We'd meet up at a local wine bar and I'd open the conversation by asking everyone to turn off their phones then I'd lead with some loose questions. For 90 minutes things would meander passionately around various themes – the climate emergency, not being able to connect with family members on tricky issues, our guilt, our stuckness. I always left feeling enlivened by the shared considered thinking.

After one such *adda* (with about thirty people), I didn't sleep, nor did four others (they told me the next day via email). It was a particularly animated discussion; I wrote back and apologised for overstimulating, and perhaps further overwhelming everyone. Margot, a manager high up in one of the national banks, wrote back, 'No, no. Don't apologise. We never get to talk about this stuff. We're worrying about it, but where do we ever get to talk it out? It was fine to be overwhelmed because we felt it together.' The others asked if I could organise another such group.

During the corona virus isolation period I looked into the benefits of the *adda* a little more (I had the mindful, attentive time!). Crisis spreads an existential feeling of unsafety in the neurons around our heart, lungs, through our nervous system and viscera. As we discussed earlier, it makes us seek out other humans so that we can down-regulate the paralysing fear.

What psychologists call 'disconfirming experiences' work

best. These are activities where we consciously and mindfully attune to each other (group soul!), convincing us we're safe enough to settle down in our nervous system to then do something to save our lives and life generally.

Engaging in deep intentional and vulnerable conversations, and keeping eye contact as much as possible, whether it be in person or online, is deemed most effective. One psychologist advised pausing – for as long as 90 seconds – after something important has been said. The point was made that this style of fully undistracted and attentive communicating could actually see us disconfirm better than most IRL interactions we have in non-crisis times.

Join an *adda*
I highly recommend joining or creating a deep thinking and talking group (with or without tea or wine) as you navigate your way on this journey.

Go to Facebook Groups and click on the Discover button. It lists events and meetups in your area – literary salons, poetry readings, philosophy and cheese nights. You can fine-tune your search by topic. Join some of the groups so you can keep an eye on upcoming events. You'll then be sent invites to join similar groups and events.

Or start your own group. Perhaps you're working on a creative project and would love to get feedback from strangers. Post it, offer to buy a round of drinks or a cheese board and see what happens.

Join a book club. Discussing a deep read can be a great forum for a deep conversation. Bookshops and galleries often hold them. You can also start your own virtual book club on Google Hangouts. I have a book club study sheet for both *The Beast* and this book on my website that you can download if you'd like to use my books as your pivot point.

A pain needs to be shared for us to pass through it. Let's keep thinking and talking. Let's connect by conversing as often and as widely as we can. This journey here is a conversation.

get
antifragile

94
Philosopher and former financial risk analyst Nassim Nicholas Taleb invented the word 'antifragile' to describe how most aspects of the human condition – and life broadly – require repeated exposure to shocks, random volatility and hardship to survive and thrive. Our bones, our immune system and our muscles all have to be put through antifragile experiences to perform best. So too our financial markets, ecosystems and our emotional grit.

Most cultures had rituals and practices that taught antifragile practices. And for good reason. They prepared us for real life. Kids were put through initiation ceremonies that entailed enduring pain or being removed from the tribe and left to fend, alone, for weeks at a time in the wilderness. We knelt on stone in prayer. We were taught to appreciate the role of suffering rather than being told to run from it. We fasted. We trained. 'What doesn't kill you will make you

Isn't it fascinating – and perfect – how many experts in this new field of waking up were formerly economists or financial traders. I refer to quite a few in this book.

stronger,' our grandmothers used to say. 'Patience is a virtue,' my mother would say in her calm way when my A-type impatience saw me shove and slam things to finish-lines. 'Things happen all in the fullness of time,' was another of her steady wisdoms.

Taleb is one of many voices calling for our culture to (re-) cultivate some of these old-school traits, should we want to continue an awake, humanised and whole life on this planet. The suppression of volatility, disorder and uncertainty – via helicopter parenting, eliminating triggers or businesses assessing risk to the point of complete inaction, for instance – sees everything become fragile. 'Complex systems are weakened, even killed, when deprived of stressors.' They don't get to correct themselves, which itself strengthens a system, he argues.

Ah, yes, we don't get to correct ourselves! We don't get to do that long walk down the hall of mirrors and come out the other end somewhat flummoxed but entirely fired up to become bigger, better humans.

95 We've already covered the importance of a bunch of antifragile stuff: going to your edge, getting 'spiritually heavy', pushing through the fear-guilt-anger-despair-overwhelm cycle, practicing resilience, paying attention, thinking deep and sacrificing. They're all needed in a more – not less – unpredictable, chaotic, volatile world. They all help us to reconnect.

SARAH WILSON

But as I ventured further along this wild and bumpy road, I knew I, too, had to go further. I'll be specific. I knew I had to get more *morally* antifragile.

The existential threats were coming thick and fast. Some of the concerns I was exploring just two years ago almost seemed a trifle indulgent. The beautiful questions and moral quandaries had become far more challenging. As I mentioned in an earlier chapter, we now had to consider questions that are almost God level, such as who should get access to ventilators and who must die. We have to face our own participation in the widening gap between haves and have-nots, and a bunch of other gluggy moral batters that have largely been left unstirred until now.

Psychologists call it 'moral injury', where violating your own conscience around one issue to prioritise another causes trauma. I was feeling this moral injury profoundly as I was forced to think and feel through some very ugly stuff in my head. Like, whether corona virus was a blessed 'correction' for the planet, forcing privileged folk like me to wake up to the death and destruction caused by endless growth, while at the same time being aware underprivileged lives were being lost. Like, whether it was a good thing the crisis was sweeping aside redundancies, like businesses producing unsustainable products and marriages that were precariously balanced on unhealthy co-dependency, while being aware I had friends who owned said businesses and were struggling in said marriages. I wrestled with whether the cost of measures to control the virus, such as mobile phone surveillance and

I very quickly unsubscribed from the argument that corona virus was a wonderful 'equaliser'; I'm not sure where such a notion will be sitting by the time you read this. Entirely dismissed, I hope.

306

the emergency powers being rolled out, were too expensive, ethically speaking, to justify the lives they might save.

I was doing moral calisthenics with my personal choices, too. What mattered more, given the escalating urgency and terror – getting cranky about takeaway coffee cups, or putting my time, care and money to projects that might stave off mass suicides and potential civil unrest as the world's vulnerable and growing have-nots fight to save their lives? What mattered more, my personal happiness or Big Life?

To attend to what life was asking of me, I had to fortify my moral character further. My tendency is to flee into mania, get wild with ideas and action plans and then collapse in a (numb) heap soon after. I knew I would have to sit and endure the moral struggle, nobly, warrior-like. The Stoics say much on this. Excellence is not an action, it's a habit. Tenacity is not inherent, it's cultivated. 'Be like the rocky headland on which the waves constantly break.' Fully warrior!

— From Marcus Aurelius in *Meditations* which, by the way, saw an uptick in ebook sales of 356 per cent in early 2020.

96 So 'force majeure' is a legal term that refers to something super bad and big that prevents someone from acting responsibly (or acting at all). It's also the title of a movie on Netflix I watched when I was travelling in California some time back. Basically, an avalanche strikes a French ski resort where Tomas and his wife and kids are having lunch on a terrace. They all survive (I'm not ruining anything). The drama lies in the fact that when disaster struck, Tomas bolted to safety leaving his wife and kids to fend for themselves, *yet* *he still managed to grab his phone.* It's a thoroughly modern existential tale that taps into how men are grappling with masculinity, or at least that's the gist of most of the online commentary around the film that I read. I'd argue it taps into how we're all struggling with what life is asking of us — morally — right now.

Tomas' behaviour could be excused as force majeure. But the point we (and Tomas) must face is that it's often in disaster that our true character is revealed. We don't get time to think. But if you're someone who's cultivated noble, antifragile character traits then you do the right thing by impulse right at the critical juncture. Stoic pin-up kid Aristotle said much on this. He argued goodness took committed cultivation. Then you find yourself doing the right thing automatically, without having to think, because it's in your bones. You practise putting your family before your phone in everyday life, then when an avalanche strikes, you save the right thing. Metaphorically speaking.

Or as Tim, my meditation teacher, often says, 'You water the root so you can enjoy the fruit.'

THE KUMANO KODO PILGRIMAGE WALK, JAPAN

I had to pass through Osaka on my way to Europe in the middle of writing this book and figured I could squeeze a hike in. I'd read the region was known for its Shinrin-yoku or forest bathing. I researched a dozen or so associations and emailed a spiderweb of inquiries around the globe and was eventually steered to a Yamabushi monk who lived in the mountains on the Kii Peninsula south of Kyoto. Kitsumi was his name. Three different sources said he'd be able to give me an 'authentic' experience.

— I go into this in more detail on pages 311-312.

The peninsula is crisscrossed with Shinto pilgrimage routes. Emperors and their families and pretty much everyone else from Kyoto walked these trails in the 11th century. I worked out I could meet with my monk by walking the most famous of the trails, Kumano Kodo, staying in small inns along the way. Hiking logic perfection!

When I landed, I headed to an old schoolhouse on a farm about 20 kilometres from the start of the trail, a train and bus ride from Osaka. I was meant to catch another bus to the trailhead the next day, but at the farm gate I noticed a large map with cute motifs of chipmunks wearing hiking packs denoting pilgrimage paths and worked out there was in fact a path that meandered through citrus orchards to where the

309

Kumano Kodo kicks off, adding an extra 5 kilometres, but saving an annoying bus ride. The next day I grabbed some rice balls and picked an orange from a nearby tree and set off directly from the farm. Hike flow!

For the whole day I saw a grand total of…no one. A large snake visited me twice while I meditated on the steps of a shrine around lunchtime. It came and went, pausing about a metre in front of me for a while. I asked social media that night what snake encounters signified. Transformation, apparently.

It was 4pm when I hit the main trail. I stared at the big map pinned to the all-weather shelter for a bit. And then off I set.

For the next three days I climbed upward, navigating large mossy steps through sun-dappled birch and cypress forest.

The steps don't abate. A 12th-century poet wrote that words don't exist to describe how tough they are. The Japanese inscription of this is engraved into a plaque at the top. I stayed in small villages in the spare bedrooms of lovely Japanese families who didn't speak English. I slept on tatami and sipped a lot of miso and failed to work out the whole slipper etiquette deal wherever I went. This part of Japan is still stirring itself into the modern age; farmers in their eighties till fields by hand and the houses and village infrastructure remains very pared back and utilitarian.

On day four I finally met my monk. Kitsumi walked up to me on the main street of his town wearing the traditional Yamabushi mountain climbing get-up – white stockings, little webbed white slippers and a bunch of colourful pompoms denoting the different qualities a monk must master wrapped over his torso. And a conch. I wore trail running shoes and my green shorts. It was a hot, sweaty day and we set off up the mountain at a rhythmic pace, his pompoms and bells jingling.

I explained to Kitsumi that I'd travelled all this way to learn about forest bathing.

He turned around. 'What?'

'You know. Shinrin-yoku.'

'Never heard of it,' he replied.

'You're kidding!' I exclaimed then explained that the world's extended forest bathing community heralded him as the guru.

'Ha! I'll Google it later,' he replied. I later realised journalists and active-wear brands had come to visit him on his isolated mountain, quoted his wisdoms, but had never explained to him the context. Shinrin-yoku was a Japanese practice, but a relatively modern one. And Kitsumi was a monk who was simply living out the old traditions that forest bathing was no doubt drawing on.

We both laughed then I asked him if he could put his bells in his pocket because the jingling was really annoying me.

As we climbed up the pine needle-cushioned path, Kitsumi decided to talk to me about endurance.

I learned that this peninsula and its pilgrimage trails are sacred in the Shugendo tradition, a religion of sorts that blends Shinto (nature worship) and Buddhism. Shugendo literally means 'path of training to achieve spiritual powers' and the Kumano Kodo was used by its followers to develop tolerance of hardship, or endurance, the key 'supernatural power' required for spiritual enlightenment and moral wrestling. From what I can gather, the pilgrimage was often done by those facing death. They came here to either die on the route, and have the opportunity to be rebirthed properly, or, I guess, to be reborn in this lifetime by actually making it out the other end alive. What doesn't kill you makes you live longer!

'You suffer to live,' he tells me. 'You practise endurance to know life.'

'Oh, yeah. I totally agree.'

We talk about going to our edge, that sensation of pushing so hard and then…something happens. You are not 'you' any more. You have to get over 'yourself'. And become morally brave and alive to what life is asking of you.

To be at the pointy end of your abilities and gumption, you have to leave your head behind and become part of everything else. You have to draw on the energy of the trees and the mountain to keep going. I was tired on this particular day. My thyroid was playing up, leaving me weak in my knees and slightly dizzy. But I kept putting one foot in front of the other, drawing up energy from the earth through my feet, breathing in air that creates a cool, vibrant rhythm inside me until it becomes trance-like. Mountains take you to this point very effectively.

There is no sense of when the pain will end when climbing

a mountain – you can't see your destination. And you should never look up! It's the number one tip I give novice hikers. On steep grades, keep your gaze to about two metres in front and you'll be fooled into thinking it's less steep than it is. Mountain climbing also takes heavy glute work. A Pilates instructor once said unlike other muscles, your glutes will always hurt when you activate them, no matter how often you work out. Glute endurance has no end point!

Kitsumi told me he isn't one to pull things apart too deeply. He just knew that when he started practising endurance, he became a nicer person. This is central to the Shugendo practice – you don't endure just to reach enlightenment. You also endure to be of radical service.

At the top of the hill, Kitsumi blew his conch into the valley and we meditated for a bit. Afterward, we climbed down and had a cup of tea together. I then continued my hike.

I got asked by a few tourists if I was doing the hike as a pilgrimage. Some people do the Kumano Kodo like they do other spiritual routes by collecting stamps at shrines and, I guess, absorbing the legacy of those who sacrificed and endured before them. But I treat every hike as a pilgrimage. For me, every hike gets me touching that spot in myself where I must draw on my inner strength and my inner desire to be fully alive and awake and morally brave. You start, there's no turning back and nature takes over.

I hiked for another two days. At the final village there is a natural *onsen* in the river. In the late afternoon I sat on a hot patch in the shallows of the river, my head resting back on a rock, and watched a hawk circle as the moon came up.

97 There are a few other simple things that we can do to cultivate the endurance we need to stick to this journey we've been called to...

We can delay gratification

Most of us today would probably fail the marshmallow test. You may have heard of this 1972 Stanford experiment. A marshmallow is plonked in front of a kid who's told she can have a second one if she can wait 15 minutes without eating the first. Fifty years later, experimenters followed up kids who'd 'passed' the test and found that an ability to delay gratification (at least among the WASPY children participating in the study) positively correlated with future success and lower incidences of obesity and other diseases, as well as happiness.

I used to get training in delaying gratification just being a kid. Me and my siblings saved up for things, we had to wait for stuff for, like, 364 days. It was uncomfortable having to go without and wait. But in the process we were suspended in a place of reflective pause. We made very conscious, mindful consumption choices. We thought about what mattered to us. Sometimes we'd work out we didn't really want the thing we'd craved in that pause. It operated as a moral guardrail, curbing individualism, greed, consumption.

My brother Ben took *five years* to research and save up for his first BMX. We were all part of his journey; we all knew the details of this damn bike ('black Apollo with chromoly frame and gold Araya alloy rims'). I don't think a kid loved a bike more when he finally got it.

Today, in our instant-gratification world, we can 'manually' delay gratification to realise these benefits and to practise enduring. Save a treat for after dinner, change your credit card to a debit card, quit Afterpay and do layby (or just keep a penny jar), put off going to the mall for knickers for a week, then another, have your kids wait until their birthday to get their BMX. TBH, I could get all life-hacky here, but it's not my style. I think it's more fruitful – and antifragile – to let you get creative with ideas that might extend you into antifragility.

— As per pages 293-295.

We can meditate. Badly.

Meditation is a perfect exercise in antifragility. It is physical discomfort, boredom, coping with failure (part of meditation is overcoming the belief you're doing it wrong) and often involves some serious moral wrangling, all in one intimate package. It's even more bountiful when you're crap at it.

I went on Tom Bilyeu's podcast a little while back and explained this to his audience of 1.5 million subscribers. 'We all try to flee from the discomfort while meditating,' I told Tom. Me, I start thinking of what I want to eat for breakfast, I'm irritated by the barking dog outside, I want to cheat and do 15 minutes instead of 20. When this happens, we are instructed to come back to our mantra (or our breath or whatever), gently and effortlessly. Now here's the boon bit: if you're a great meditator, you might do this a few times in a session. But if you're crap you have to gently bring your attention back every few seconds. Which means you build a bigger 'coming back gently' muscle. Which in turn means that when you go back out into your real life, you have a greater ability to stay in crappy discomfort and keep going. To feel the shittiness but do whatever life is calling you to do anyway.

My challenge to you is to take up meditation (if you've been avoiding it because it seems too loose and unguaranteed as a life-bettering technique) and to meditate even (especially) on the days where you're too frazzled, you're too busy, you've taken sleeping tablets and you'll probably be crap at it.

We can be bored

Around the time — capitalism also reared its head. Just saying…

Check this: bored, as in the word, wasn't invented until 1760. Before that I guess we just sat in tedium and sucked it up and benefited from the antifragile effects parlayed.

Researchers have found that boredom leads to more creativity – it promotes daydreaming which sees the brain create new innovative connections. Newton was purportedly just sitting under an apple tree staring into space when he discovered gravity. The theory of relativity struck Albert Einstein as he rode aimlessly on his bike. Subsequently, I read another study that showed innovation among young people is at its lowest in history, with scores decreasing each year

316

since 1990 (even while IQ increases). I wonder if not being able to stay in boredom has led to this uncolourful outcome for young people?

I read Bertrand Russell's *Has Man a Future?* while contemplating this chapter. The dude was well ahead of his time. He wrote the book in 1961 aged eighty-nine and launched a campaign of civil disobedience off the back of it, such was his concern for the future of the human race. I like this line: 'A generation that cannot endure boredom will be a generation…in whom every vital impulse slowly withers, as though they were cut flowers in a vase.'

And then we can 'stay longer'

I now have a phrase that I work to when meditating, or I'm on a call with a chronic repeater of stories, or I'm listless, or I want to flee from a moral injury: 'Stay longer.'

Sometimes I repeat it over and over. When I do, I can feel into the idea that sitting through the discomfort is actually not so bad. In fact, over time I've come to find it far more charming than the tiring, 'small human' process of fleeing.

You know what's made it fun? Recasting the experience as special. Common to all antifragile practices is getting cool with the pause between where you've just been and where you desire to be. It's an important pause we've been gifted, is how I choose to see it. It's a quiet, very intimate space. We usually fill it with fretting and fleeing and hating the situation and trying to fix it. When we simply stay, we suddenly have bonus minutes – sometimes hours – in our day to simply be with ourselves and to notice how peaceful it is to be okay where we are.

I apply 'stay longer' to all kinds of ordinary lowlands. I use things like bus stops as a trigger to practise staying bored. When I reach for my phone waiting for the bus (or a cab or the pedestrian light to go green) I put it back and just stand there and be bored. I watch myself being bored – the precise way I flee, the way my head jerks to the right when this particular discomfort sets in. Which is not that boring, as it happens.

Ditto Sunday lulls. If I find myself between chores or commitments on a Sunday afternoon, I own the nothingness of it and lie on the floor and stare at the ceiling and ride out my boredom. I might get the gut-sinks thinking everyone else is having more fun, being more productive, or being less lonely. I may want to grab my phone and see who has commented on my last post so that I can get a 0.4 second hit of something happening-ness. And then I watch all this going on in my body and this, too, is quietly fascinating.

I practised this a bit during corona virus isolation.

It also helps to know that we actually perform better when we stay in discomfort. A study has shown students whose assigned reading is typed in an ugly, difficult-to-read font remember more of what they read in the short-term and score higher on exams in the longer term than those whose materials are more legible. A noticeable, annoying buzz of background noise can increase a person's creativity, shows another study.

318

98 The American Catholic monk (with distinct stoic leanings) Thomas Merton once said, 'One of the strange laws of the contemplative life is that in it you do not sit down and solve problems: you bear with them until they somehow solve themselves. Or until life solves them for you.'

Stay longer and then things solve themselves. What sweet words to an over-earnest A-type mind!

American writer and activist Glennon Doyle has a similar shtick she works to: 'You go into pain, you stay and wait, then you rise. Pain, stay, rise – they follow each other always,' she says. 'If we don't stay we deny ourselves the opportunity to rise.'

be comfortable

not

knowing

99 Now here's a funny story.

I'm a terrible gripper, especially when confronted with uncertainty.

I'd been sitting at my desk gripping at life, trying to control the uncertain flow of things, to force things to happen with my white-knuckled hold.

I'd been hustling like a mofo, trying to line up a bunch of interviews for this book. But I had been getting no email replies, no certainty, for weeks. You might know the scenario. This kind of all-encompassing stuckness comes in big, unexplainable waves, when you're a gripper like me. Like, in one week, three projects you're working on, a party you organised and a hiking trip are cancelled or grind to a halt and suddenly your entire life is superglued to the pavement.

So I hustled and gripped harder, looking for certainty amid all the unanswered emails and rejections. Of course, hustling and gripping are just as avoidant of life and true connection as going numb and acedic.

I was about to implode. But I can now see the signs before I do (from years of my own self-help work and therapy, TBH); I could see I had to circuit-break. I had to shake things up and...'do what I'm not doing'. So I got a (non)grip, shut down my computer and committed to no more emails for 48 hours.

I rode to a café at the other end of the beach promenade with my notebook. As I sat down, I saw an email come in on my phone from Stacy, my book agent in New York. I only read the first line. 'Maria Shriver declined. She's travelling.' I'd been hustling to interview the NBC journalist and author on her spiritual approach to uncertainty, funnily enough. I sighed and put my phone in my bag.

In these moments I remind myself to, again, 'do what I'm not doing' and ride the 'is-ness' of life. I chatted to two women in their seventies who were doing a cryptic crossword together after going to the gym across the road. I sprung them cheating; they were flicking to the answers at the back. We laughed and talked for 15 minutes about getting old (the freedom of it!). Then an ex-employee sat down and told me about her recent relationship break-up. And. Anyway. I was there longer than I expected.

I got up to pay.

And. I. Kid. You. Not.

Maria Shriver walked in.

I couldn't quite believe it myself so I quickly cross-referenced the distinctive rings on her fingers with shots on her Instagram feed where you could see her hands. Yep, it was Maria.

What are the chances, you might ask. How does such serendipity work? I doubt we will ever know. We can only know that life is bigger and more mysterious than we can ever imagine. And somehow, for reasons and forces beyond our knowing, when we release our grip and join life's mysterious stream of is-ness this kind of crazy shit happens.

I approached Maria and vomited out all of the above very excitedly, although I tried to tone it down given that she'd just come off a long-haul flight an hour ago. She was delighted. I didn't ask to interview her. I'd already got everything I needed from my interaction with Maria Shriver.

100 We hate uncertainty. It's always existed (I mean, the only certainty is uncertainty), but we used to be far more antifragile with it.

You might be as old as me and remember as a kid making plans to catch up with your mates in the holidays. I'd arrange on the Friday at recess to meet under the clock at the bus interchange at 10am on the second Tuesday of the school holidays. There I was the following fortnight right on time. Sometimes my mates would not be there. It would be 10.45am and still no sign. I'm trying to recall what I did. Yeah, I felt rejection. As an undersized kid with an eyepatch, I didn't have a stack of friends at school, so I'd probably figured I'd been stitched up. We couldn't really contact anyone to see if they'd missed a bus or broken a leg. We didn't have Instagram to scroll through. We couldn't message to say, 'I'm heading to the park, meet me there' to save time.

And, yes, the not-knowingness was shitty and uncomfortable. Sometimes our friend would rock up an hour late. Or not at all and – do you remember? – we'd just have to cope. That was life and it was shitty at times. But we learned to suck it up because that was the way it was.

In that hour of non-distracted killing of time at the bus interchange, I suppose we were gifted the opportunity to mentally and emotionally resolve things for ourselves and – importantly – get over ourselves. Parents didn't do interventions. We couldn't bludgeon a friend with a tirade of abusive texts. We endured. And we joined life in its 'it is what it is'-ness.

Yet what do I tend to do today? I rail, I blame, I fix things in a huff. All that formative antifragile training has completely unravelled. There are few guardrails, or rituals, that force me to sit with myself and suck it up. When someone is late, I can send a passive-aggressive '?'. If I'm a bit unwell with my autoimmune disease–related inflammation, I cancel a meeting last minute rather than showing up and smiling through my brain fog (and surprising myself with how a human can actually rise when put through some paces). And so my suck-it-up muscle has become entirely feeble and my character has become so entitled that when a call centre keeps me waiting 15 minutes, I'm outraged and am unable to curtail my rudeness when they finally pick up.

It's so crook.

Have you noticed we're using the word 'unprecedented' to describe just about everything now? Weather patterns are 'unprecedented', politics is becoming increasingly disunified, voting and economics are no longer following the usual patterns and we are facing viruses we can't track or predict or respond to with an immediate vaccine. More Black Swans are headed our way, more butterfly effects, more chaos, more pandemics.

Which can make us cling to quick fixes and anything that feels like sturdy ground (despotic leaders) more than ever. Oh the death spiral of it all!

101 Worryingly, we are the least cool with uncertainty we've ever been…just as the world gets crazy uncertain and requires crazy-arse fixes. From us. I mentioned earlier that innovation among young people is at its lowest in history. A Queensland University of Technology study published in 2019 found that young people also have the lowest ability to deal with ambiguity and risk in the workplace…and at a time when a Foundation for Young Australians report revealed that the jobs of the future will demand 260 per cent more creativity (and risk taking) than jobs of the past. Another study found that investment in innovation around the world has declined sharply as Western nations in particular shun risk. American entrepreneurship has been declining since the 1970s.

102 Virginia Woolf's famously challenging line has come to mind often on this journey: *'The future is dark, which is the best thing the future can be, I think.'*

By dark, Woolf is said to have been referring to the 'unknown' and 'inexplicable'. And she made the observation in the context of a world that was six months into a world war, arguing the unknown was an opportunity to create a better future than the one humanity was cruising toward. Her caveat at the end of the line – 'I think' – anchors her point potently.

You might agree that darkness is being felt acutely around the world. Our future on this planet and all the wild non-normalness has been brought right forward. We have had to step into this dark chasm and it feels like we're free-falling, with nothing to grip on to. I always think of Coyote chasing Roadrunner and plunging over the ravine, frantically trying to grasp at something solid on the way down. I think this is what many of us are struggling with most – this not-knowingness. It can feel frantic. I got frantic. Then I'd do what I was not doing and shut down my computer and go and join the great unknown.

I have a little mindset switch when I do. I say, 'Sarah, let's just run the experiment. Let's step into the unknown and see what happens. Nothing more.' The pressure to know is instantly removed. A lightness comes over me, things become playful.

I generally find that when I just let myself run the experiment I'm suddenly free to see a whole stack of openness and freedom ahead. No one knows, no one has answers, let's get creative and loose and alive. And then it becomes the most fun ever to just sit, calmly and lightly and playfully, and see what happens next. Does Maria Shriver walk in? Does a more beautiful question arise? Do you feel differently? Do you, strangely, feel like you might have arrived in some flow?

103 Your doubt can become a good quality if you train it.

Not my words; Rainer Maria Rilke's.

As I say, my fear of not knowing is particularly gnarly. It kept tipping me into that overwhelm cycle and holding me back. So I took myself off to therapy. I needed to train my doubt. I found Natalie, a psychotherapist. I told her I was sick of talking about my issues. I wanted to get radical and step up into the next phase of my maturing. I'd been pissing around my edges. Like a cocky teen who doesn't know what she doesn't know. I wasn't in the arena, as Theodore Roosevelt (and Brené Brown) put it.

I've gone to a plethora of shrinks and coaches over the years. The most fruitful interactions have occurred when I've needed to evolve, not just when I've collapsed in psychic exhaustion. We need help evolving, too, you know. I can't recommend this enough: paying someone to slingshot you over the moat of your own seductive making and out into the world of your next heroic adventure.

Natalie and I set out on an awkward journey together using my body, instead of my intellect, to work through my calcified grasping at the known. Somatic therapy, as it's called, or embodied or nervous system work, is having its moment in the therapy limelight. Michael Singer, Ken Wilber, Gabor Maté and Philip Shepherd are at the forefront of the approach. I won't flesh out the full specifics of the discipline. But I will share two techniques that have got me cooler with my not knowing.

Sit in your pelvic bowl

I rang Philip Shepherd in Toronto to get him to talk me through this fabulous hack, which Natalie had initially introduced me to. Shepherd's work is about bringing our awareness down into our bodies so that we can experience a wholeness that allows us to be in unknowingness.

He argues we have gone so far into our heads, into rigid abstraction, that we've lost touch with our true awareness, or awakeness. Our head-centric approach sees us operate like a lighthouse – the coned beam can only spotlight bits of life at a time, it can never capture the 'whole' in the darkness, and so it leaves us fragmented and adrift (and scared of what exists in the dark unknowing). The antidote is to go in the opposite direction, and to practise resting your awareness in the pelvic bowl, the area in your abdomen that scoops from your two hipbones back around to your pelvic bone, which is at the opposite end of your noggin, in energy-center terms.

You could be skeptical of such un-headish language. I almost was, until I got out of my head and tried it.

You can do this as a breath meditation. Or make it less

formal. Philip talked me through it on the phone. It goes a little something like this: with each breath, bring your attention to the base of the pelvic bowl, to your perineum. Clock this area, feel into it. Got it?

Now imagine a spacious corridor from your perineum all the way up to the top of your head. Turn your awareness to the top of this corridor, at the top of your head.

Then allow this awareness to slide slowly through the corridor down to the perineum. If you stall, if you feel resistance, that's cool. Philip explained this simply means you've encountered some kind of emotional block and need to see it as an orphan. 'Give it love,' he explained. It's an odd notion, but it worked as I tried it. Soon the resistance dispersed. But you check in. Is it still there? You keep doing this until you arrive at the bottom like a stone landing in a pool, gently but firmly.

Okay, now notice the stillness down here. Notice the emptiness.

When I do this exercise, I feel like my pelvis has no boundaries, no bones, and the awareness extends outward, on and on. At the same time, there's a heaviness that makes me feel connected into the earth beneath me. I relax into this solid and slightly paradoxical vastness.

My stomach gurgles loudly as my parasympathetic nervous system comes online. Stuff is going on down there at a tangible level. I'm not sure what, but I can feel my body expanding into wholeness, which feels remarkably like a knowingness. A knowingness of the wholeness. And somehow everything makes fulsome sense in the unbounded uncertainty of it all.

John Coates (a former derivatives trader turned neuroscientist) used a similar technique to show how sitting in and listening to their gut saw traders become better risk takers who could beat trading algorithms. I use the technique now to access my gut feeling, which in turn has seen me get less grippy, but ultimately truer, with my decisions. For years I've tried with my head to comprehend what people meant when they said, 'listen to your gut'. I'd wind up panicking. You too? I know now you just have to go and sit in it, swirl around in the vastness, and then a radical okayness comes over you. That's gut feeling.

Do a koan

Natalie also introduced me to this koan exercise by Jun Po Kelly Roshi. It's a pearler. Perhaps see if someone can read this bit out to you. With koans, which are Zen anecdotes or riddles that use paradox to take you straight to 'the great doubt', you kind of have to hear it and be surprised by it (so don't read further if you're going to try it this way).

Right, so sit comfortably. Go into silence – vast and expansive. Listen to the silence. Listen more deeply than you've ever listened. With each in-breath, draw deeper into pure silence. With each out-breath, bring this consciousness forward.

Listen without an opinion.

[Listen for 2 minutes like this.]

Now, I ask you to answer the following: who are you,

who am I, who are we, within this deep, heartfelt listening?

[Pause here.] What's your answer?

[Struggle and squirm as long as you need to answer this.]

When Natalie ran me through the exercise I sat on the couch and tried to feel it in my pelvic bowl. I felt the vast silence, the wholeness, but as soon as I tried to answer 'Who am I?' I kept trying to think of the 'right' answer. My 'good girl' reflex, which kicks in when a problem requires a solution, grappled and grappled, trying to get it right and feeling terrible about the prolonged silence. Good girls don't keep people waiting. The pelvic bowl focus soon crackled out of reception.

Natalie just smiled at me patiently. 'I know what the answer is meant to be,' I said, exasperated. 'I know I'm meant to say...'

Natalie raised her eyebrows, 'Yes?'

'Love,' I said with a humph.

This is the problem with doing a lot of 'work on yourself'.

You're too readily versed in the language. But a koan's job is to cut through this.

Natalie laughs at me. 'But...?'

I'm getting shitty now. I do a sort of tuck in of the chin and jerk my head to the left with a shrug of my shoulder.

'What was that?' Natalie asks, pointing at me.

I throw my hands in the air. 'Oh, I don't know!'

Natalie claps. 'That's it!'

I smile, embarrassed. 'Oh, yeah...I don't know.'

My 'I' doesn't know. Koan perfection.

In the vast silence of the wholeness of life, my head-centric, rigid, top-down self doesn't know, and doesn't have to know and is better off not knowing.

As Jun Po himself says, 'Finally we are getting nowhere.'

FOREST BATHING HIKE, TOPANGA CANYON, LOS ANGELES, CALIFORNIA, USA

In the final months of writing this book, I was in LA and figured I'd try forest bathing or Shinrin-yoku again. There's an association that issues accreditation to guides and also trails around the world, with several in Los Angeles.

— After my quasi go at it in Japan (pages 309–313).

Shinrin-yoku is integrated into the medical system in Japan and is covered by health insurance in both Japan and Korea. Since the Japanese government formally introduced forest bathing in 1982, studies have rolled in to show the healing effect of trees for both emotional and physical health. One study showed that a mere 20-minute walk among trees lowered levels of salivary cortisol (the stress hormone) by 53 per cent. Even just living close to parkland with trees has been shown to reduce our chances of developing mental health issues (adjusting for things like age, income and relationship status). A bunch of studies put the effects down to phytoncides, the antibacterial oils that trees release.

In addition to boosting immune system function, reducing blood pressure and heart rate, improving sleep and creativity, and fighting cancer (a number of cancer and health clinics in the United States now incorporate forest walking into their treatment plans), these compounds (along with the experience of being outdoors and exercising) also affect mood, stress, anxiety and 'confusion'.

In 2015, a team of researchers in the United States, Canada, and Australia was able to put a very neo-liberal dollar value to the whole well-being value of forest bathing. The researchers found that an additional ten trees in a given area corresponded to a 1 per cent increase in nearby residents' well-being. To get an equivalent well-being improvement using money, you'd have to give each household in that neighbourhood $10,000. Want a peaceful 'hood? Plant trees.

I've always immersed myself in the nature around LA. When I travel there for work, I land at 6am and head straight to one of the canyons and tear up the dusty trails that wind above the city. I like to sweat out the plane grime. Sometimes the heat of the desert behind the canyons drags the ocean air over the city like a thick blanket, and a hike up Griffith Park or Runyon Canyon or Topanga or Escondido can be most surreal. Everything – the gritty flight, the hectic, spaghetti freeways – is fogged out. And it's just you and the sharp, pure light that I (and generations of Hollywood directors) have always loved about LA.

I met with Debra, an accredited guide with the Association of Nature and Forest Therapy who used to work in movies

THIS ONE WILD AND PRECIOUS LIFE

until it became empty for her. She'd chosen a tucked-away route on the way to Eagle Rock, a wonderful climb I'd done on a previous trip.

Debra explained what my Yamabushi monk mate in Japan was unable to. Bathing in a forest doesn't require getting naked in leaves and sticks. It's about submerging in nature by just existing in it as mindfully as possible and allowing it to teach you some good shit that your head can't sort on its own.

Debra led me in exercises to connect me into the experience. One entailed spending 5-10 minutes with three 'bits' of nature – a tree trunk, a flower, a vista, whatever – as though they were strangers at a party toward whom I was gravitating. And to have a chat with them. I've never been great with these kinds of performative, 'intuitive' activities; I simply couldn't access my gut feeling most of my life. But the more I've hiked in nature, the more I've been able to attune to this feeling side of myself. I'm thinking it's because hiking takes us to our original way of being from which these soulful faculties emanated.

I wandered along the trail and found myself drawn to a bend in the path. The trail followed an old wooden fence line around the lip of a canyon and then veered off through a thatch of trees. I looked at it and I immediately knew why it appealed, why I'd want to connect with it at a party. It headed into the setting sun and I couldn't quite make out where it cut through the trees. As I stared at it, and absorbed the symbolism, I realised it all elicited a lightness in my heart space. The unknown endpoint was exciting. Unlike my usual anxious response to the 'unknown', having a chat with it in a party-like setting was…enlivening. It made me smile. I'd written about this in my anxiety book – that anxiety and excitement trigger the same response in the brain, and it's an option to simply recast the feeling we get ahead of an exam – or the unknown – as the far more productive 'excitement' rather than the paralysing anxiety. I then conversed with a split tree trunk. In any another setting, in any other book, this would be way too much for many of you, I imagine. (And me!) But, hey, we've been on this journey together for a while now. I studied the long, sinewy lines of the wood on the outer part of a kink, and the bubbled, constricted texture – like elephant skin – where it bent inward. Where the trunk split open, you could see all the distress lines, the history of the tree as it adapted to changes in the environment. And what came over me was an incredible okayness with the anxiety I had been feeling for months – the vast, unfathomable unknowingness of where we were all heading collectively amid warnings of mass extinctions and pandemics, as well as not knowing where this book would wind up. This trunk had grown as it needed to, and the elephant skin bumps and kinks became a necessary part of its story. So, too, everything in life.

The journey behind this book had become a metaphor for so much more by now.

As I say, when I'm in nature I can go to this place of intense attentiveness and I can gravitate toward and intuit and feel things I can't in the rest of my life. But why? And why does it feel so attuned and 'arrived'? It's partly the lack of dumb-arse distractions that assault us in life beyond the nature park. When we're not being pinged, and sold to and honked and bumped, we can hear the whispers of our souls.

I looked into it further. It's also about fractals.

Fractals! It's about fractals! Nature's patterns – tidal pools, rings in trunks, flower petal formations – are organised as complex configurations, each part of which has the same statistical characteristic as the whole. The human retina also moves in a fractal pattern while taking in a view. This congruence, then, creates alpha waves in the brain, which is the neural resonance of relaxation. In other less technical words, looking at natural phenomena makes us feel like we're part of it, part of the natural order. You know, that we belong.

As I drove back down the valley to the plant-based cafés and Aperol-spritzed bars of Venice Beach, the heat was dragging the blanket of fog up through the valley. By the time I returned the sun was obscured and the traffic was in gridlock. All of which I found to be fractally apt.

A FLÂNEUR IN PARIS
(IN WHICH HISTORY REPEATS ITSELF)

Another way to get far cooler with not knowing is to walk aimlessly through a big city.

I was in Paris for some publisher meetings and decided to

stay a little longer to write. I feel held in Paris; I always have. Paris is a city where, gloriously, the café chairs face out to the world. For me, this shows a deep curiosity, an unapologetic need to observe life as it plays out on the street and, despite its inhabitants' reputation for aloofness, a palpable ache to connect. Indeed, I have experienced more wild interludes with strangers in Paris than I have in any other city.

Paris is also a city where you walk. It's always been a city for walking. It is perfectly right – and defiant! – to walk aimlessly and detached, for the sake of observing.

Which is exactly what a flâneur does.

Around the same time Nietzsche was hiking in Switzerland, Wordsworth wandered the Lake District, and Whitman, Thoreau and Muir ambled around America, the flâneur became popular among artists and thinkers in Paris who, too, strove to live beyond the strictures and alienation of the emerging consumer era. To be on the street, among the people was counter to bourgeois pretensions. Ever since, nomads and writers have come to Paris to be held in their itinerant uncertainty, famously wandering about and sitting in cafés and other public places 'alone together'. Ray Bradbury once said, 'there's nothing better than to walk around Paris and not know where the hell you are.'

Now, the funny full-circle, serendipitous thing is that when I arrived in Paris this time, my two credit cards and my two travel cards were cancelled. Yep, four cards from three different banking institutions. My direct debits were barred, and with them Uber, PayPal, my phone, etc. Twenty-five years after the mugging that left me to fend creatively, here I was again. With no Uber, no cash for cabs, I was also jumping trains to get across town and relying on the kindness of strangers. Uncanny, right?

— Flick back to page 264 for reference.

'But how on earth did that happen? Didn't you call the banks? Could they not do anything? It's not 1992, FFS!'

When friends and family asked these and other bleedingly obvious questions I had to say, 'I don't know.' Naturally I fought. I gripped. I blasted the banks. But they couldn't work it out either. It was a clusterfuck of loopholes and admin dead zones,..or something like that.

I went to my edge. I had to release my grip. And join life in all my not-knowingness.

And then – once again – magic happened.

A truly beautiful and generous man I met on a dating app reached out (having seen I was in Paris) and offered me his city apartment – totally unaware of my situation. He let me rifle through his drawers, use his toilet paper and towels in full trust for over a week before he could confirm I was who my profile said I was (we finally met on my last night in Paris).

— I didn't, but the point is I could have.

Then I got an email from the CEO of an e-scooter company I'd sat with on a speaking panel a year earlier. I was able to ask him, while he was there, for access to his international service using straight-up bank details, bypassing my credit cards. I had transport!

That said, in keeping with the unknown-ness and the untold freedom that comes with such free-fall, I mostly flâneured.

One lonely Sunday, totally stuck with my writing, I set out west. To be able to sink into the wonderfully free *je ne sais quoi*-ness of not knowing where you end up, you have to let go of anything that can distract you into distress. Shopping will do exactly this. It instils both an imperative (to achieve a result) and a FOMO vibe (when you don't). Which is why Paris is a perfect flâneur city. It remains relatively resistant to crass consumerism. Half the shops remain shut, even in Paris, on Sundays.

A flâneur's journey should also be kept close and small, a whimsical exploration of what's just outside your door. Ambition, you see, gets in the way of being lost. It should also be very very ordinary. Which makes it a great thing to do on a lonely Sunday, especially for anyone who gets Weekend Panic (that existential fretting that occurs in the unknown-ness that two days without purposeful and distracting work presents and that sees you doubting whether you are doing it 'right').

I wound my way through pedestrian streets and arcades in the 7th arrondissement and found myself in the Galeries du Palais-Royal. I had a coffee at Café Kitsuné. My friend Anthia had mentioned it. And here I was! Ha! Opposite my little metal table out in the gravel galleries, a man in his sixties lay on a park bench reading, his bag under his head. A quote was inscribed into the bench above him: *Je m'écorche aux cristaux qui dansent dans mon corps.* (I go crazy, crystals dancing in my body.) I had no idea what this meant, which

Although locals talk despairingly of the 'H&M' effect' gripping young people.

was fitting.

As I sat, I got an Instagram message from my friend and musician Clare Bowditch. It was a photo of an exquisite Parisian business card pinned to her office wall alongside a photo of her and Leonard Cohen during a tour they did together. Clare wrote that she couldn't remember where the business card was from, but she was obsessed with it. 'In case you happen to be in a neighbouring arrondissement, could you find out?' It was a brilliantly Clare thing to do – to sense my ennui and issue me with an adventure because she knew that this would buck me into gear. I set off to find this mystery business, asking strangers for directions and not looking at a map.

— Clare later told me that she could have looked it up on the Internet, but that would have been no fun. Having me do the adventure in situ, 'that would be fun.'

It turns out the business card was from a pottery atelier in the 2nd arrondissement where the light streamed in through medieval windows, giving the porcelain a pillowy luminosity. There was a small collection of super-fine mugs on one shelf featuring line drawings of angular, tortured hands by artist, actress, model and singer Lou Doillon, daughter of Jane Birkin who, for full-circle effect, had famously covered Leonard Cohen's song 'Famous Blue Raincoat'.

Fully flâneur-ish, non-knowing, whimsical perfection.

I had to buy one of these mugs. My bank had managed to get one card to work with tap only, enabling purchases under 30 euro. The assistant split payment into three taps.

— I also bought a pencil in the shape of a cigarette for Clare. And told the kooky sales assistants the whole story in my cracked French.

I then crossed the river with my mug and my story and meandered to Jardin de Luxembourg. I passed a gallery featuring Japanese prints of octopuses, which was cool, given

The Beast had one on the cover.

I'm a child of the — I found a pencil shop. I needed leads for my Pacer. It was
eighties and still a cash-only store. The lady told me to take them, as a gift,
have my Pacer
from this era. pushing them into the palm of my hand. I accepted. (And
(It's a brand of went back the following day with a bunch of flowers, which
mechanical pencil I was able to buy with tap.)
that takes super-
fine refillable And so on and so forth. It's how a flâneur goes. You get
leads made of loose and alive with not knowing and then magical shit
graphite.) happens.

104 I'm a massive fan of this form of walking. It opens me up
in a similar way to walking in nature. It gets me to a space
where I feel free in the uncertainty, rather than uncertain
in the freedom. Virginia Woolf flâneured (in London) to be
'right in the centre and swim of things'. In the essay 'Street
Haunting: A London Adventure', she writes of heading out
to buy a pencil (funnily enough) in London's winter dusk.
It's an ode to getting lost. That is, lost in the sense of being
deliberately open to the unknown, to consciously join a
society of strangers. 'We shed the self our friends know us by
and become part of that vast republican army of anonymous
trampers.' I, too, love the centre and swim of things. You don't
know where the flow you enter at street level in a big city
will carry you. But something always happens.

get
wild

We must become ignorant of what we have been taught and be instead bewildered. Run from what is profitable and comfortable. Distrust anyone who praises you.

Give your investment money, and the interest on the capital, to those who are actually destitute. Forget safety. Live where you fear to live. Destroy your reputation. Be notorious.
— Rumi

105 I'm sitting on my balcony watching a wild tropical storm roll in. The night sky is lit with violent veins of lightning. There's an eerie silence. The birds have retreated, breath is held. And then suddenly the earth exhales. The magnolias and murraya dump their waxy scent into the night and as the barometric pressure drops, the earth seems to open up, ready to receive the rain. The smell of its organic underbelly is the smell I associate with rain – peaty and sweaty. Excitement builds and builds, the lightning is now frantic and then, finally – crack! – violent tropical thunder erupts. She's here. A few heavy drops of rain fall. The pressure is too much and – voom! – down she comes. Within seconds the winds arrive, ripping roofs off houses. The next morning there are trees washed up on the beach.

I run inside, shut down all the windows and watch the carnage from my lounge. It's been a summer of wild weather. A summer trapped indoors. This was the summer of the hottest days on record, the worst drought in 800 years, bushfires that left the air quality 26 times above levels considered hazardous to human health, equivalent to smoking over a packet of cigarettes in a day. The rest of the world looked on and saw my country as a portent.

The way I saw it? Nature is angry. She's royally pissed off. Not that I need to anthropomorphise the weather to make this point. As economist and former senior scientist at the US Natural Resources Defense Council Rob Watson says: 'Mother Nature is just chemistry, biology and physics.' The wildness and destruction we're seeing is the chemistry, biology and physics out of whack. The intricately interconnected equilibrium of everything has been thrown and it's expressing outward, wildly. And as per the planet, and life on it, the equilibrium of our human interconnection is also thrown.

We can't forget we are nature (the sum result of chemistry, biology and physics). Timothy Morton, he who brought us the term 'hyperobjects', argues the unwieldy enormity of the climate crisis has made humans realise this. All the human mastery of science won't tame it, fix it, keep it separate from us. The reality of the Anthropocene period is that it has forced us to wake up to the fact we have never stood apart from nature – we are of it, we are it and we can't throw out, say, a disposable coffee cup without it coming back to us and biting us in the arse (washing up on the beach while we sunbake). And so it is entirely fitting, I think, that we join nature…and get wholly wild, too.

WADI RUM HIKE, JORDAN

One of my most recent hikes was through Wadi Rum, a massive valley cut into the sandstone and granite running through the middle of Jordan. The valley is still home to the nomadic Bedouin people and has been used for Mars scenes in a bunch of movies, including *Red Planet* and *The Martian*. My friend Kersti and I had promised each other this adventure for years and it just happened to fit into a convoluted work trip that combined six commitments in the northern hemisphere.

We hunted around for a local Bedouin guide. Of course, as flow – or speech recognition algorithms – would have it, some guy (the younger brother of a girl I waitressed with in my late teens) posted some climbing pictures shot against the distinctive bright red space-scape of the Wadi Rum valley and they popped up at the top of my Facebook feed. I reached out and asked if he knew a local guide. He introduced me to Oadh, who has nine kids and whose family have lived in the valley for many generations.

And so it was Oadh who led us through the desert on a five-day adventure.

Each day Kersti and I wound scarves around our heads and set out behind our spindly shepherd as he snaked his way along pathways that only he seemed to see in the hot red sand. Desert walking very quickly becomes mesmerising. It's not unlike walking in snowshoes. You have to shuffle out and over, rather than try to dig your feet in too determinedly. And you have to get into a relaxed rhythm, cool with the resistance the sand presents. Otherwise a bad case of the frustrated despairs can sink in.

Oadh had a vague destination each day, mostly based around finding patches of shade. Over the five days, we worked our way down the panoramic valley and back up the other side. This was landscape that left us mute. Kersti and I ran out of paltry, hyperbolic exclamations and eventually had to stop marveling at how every vista looked like the one Lawrence of Arabia came galloping through. It was vast. We were small. End of story.

We saw camels and stopped in on some of Oadh's family, living in nomadic lean-tos with goats and kids running around, and drank tea so sweet you could stand a spoon in it. We squatted on a carpet with them, swatting flies and watching the shenanigans.

We'd find shade around lunchtime, eat and then Oadh would disappear to pray to Mecca and come back singing. Then we'd siesta together for a few hours, continue on for a bit and set up camp under the stars. We'd eat chicken, tomatoes and potatoes (in various combinations) over a fire.

I'd catch Oadh staring off into the nothingness on a few occasions.

'What are you doing?' I'd ask.

'Enjoying,' he'd say.

I woke one morning and said I'd had crazy dreams.

'Me too,' he announced from his squat over the fire where he was boiling up water for coffee.

'What about?' I asked.

'Camels,' he said.

Kersti and I noticed that Oadh never bitched, never complained, and didn't need to know any details about what we did back home, what our opinions were. We asked if he and his relatives were okay with us not covering up fully.

'Of course! Wear shorts! You are not our culture. Just enjoy!' he replied.

On several occasions, stretched out by the fire and humming out of key, Oadh would spontaneously declare how happy he was. 'Ah, I'm happy,' he'd say. Sometimes he'd sing it.

We asked him what makes him happy. 'Spending time in the desert with people.' Spending time. It occurred to me that being a nomad in a desert is not a restless 'looking for something'. It's a very arrived belonging. Even modern nomads, the various roamers I've met living in vans in dry expanses around the world, possess a certain 'arrived vibe'. Permanent exposure to a sky of shooting stars at night, sunsets that take over the whole screen at day's end, and that stillness and quietness a person can disappear into, renders you not wanting for anything more. 'More' is superfluous in a desert where the heat and the harshness strip you of accoutrements and artifice. Make-up melts, crisp clothing or long-winded excuses just don't survive. You get over yourself. And arrive.

Thoreau wrote of desert walking for a magazine article in 1862: 'Your morale improves; you become frank and cordial, hospitable and single-minded... There is a keen enjoyment in a mere animal existence.'

I'd brought along James Hollis' *Living an Examined Life* and read snatches of it during our siestas. One afternoon Kersti and I lay in a rock formation up high, under an overhang, eating oranges while Oadh snored in the shade on the ground below. I got to the bit where Hollis asked, by way of a technique for living a true life: 'Does this choice enlarge or diminish?'

Now *that* is a beautiful question.

Hollis added that in most circumstances, when we ask this question, we should know the answer immediately. We do, don't we, when we're brave enough to put things through this simple lens.

Does this choice enlarge or diminish life?

I started applying the question to all the dilemmas plaguing me. Do I stick with a company I'd partnered with on a project who'd dropped the ball three times recently due to internal and morally void politics, despite being prestigious and powerful? No. Do I say yes to an invite from a wild Irish cookbook author who offered to host me in Dublin should I wish to visit while I was nearby in London (and she'd make CBD oil brownies and take me swimming in the Irish Sea if I did)? Yes! Do I continue writing a book that argues a case against the only system we've known, based on a visceral, heartfelt belief that our desire to reconnect is fundamental, and in full awareness I may cop it bad from trolls and media bullies when it's published? Hmmmm...Yes!

— We'd never met before; we are now friends for life.

When I interviewed Hollis on FaceTime a few months later I told him this singular wisdom had changed my life. It gave me the permission I needed to get unapologetically big, expansive and wildly activated. And to ask others if they could possibly join me.

It was perfect that I read it while hiking in a desert.

106 I reckon we're scared of choosing the enlarging, rightfully wild option. We're simply not used to standing up and saying, 'No! Enough is enough!' I mean, we bitch and moan about things on Twitter. And ask, 'Why isn't anyone doing something?' But we haven't tended to sacrifice, run from comfort, destroy our reputation, as per Rumi, and fight for the connected life we love. Not for some time. Nope, we've been choosing the diminishing options. *Urgh.*

I've covered the reasons why several times already but please bear with me while I corral it all together here.

We've denied our outrage and let our wildness be concreted over. Technology has kept us small. We don't trust our bewilderment; we've been busy being 'good' little citizens and obeying 'rules'. Oh boy. And, understandably, we believed the rules were good, that they'd grant us freedom and preserve our individual rights. We even self-regulated the rules with #virtuesignaling, #humblebragging, competitive parenting and the micro-management of young people (such that they had no time to question the patriarchy or to express the frustrations of their generation through song or art, besides it would interfere with their grades!). 'Yeah, and all that getting ahead business,' said my brother Pete during a visit with my nephew and niece. 'You don't have time to question anything if you're flat out getting ahead.' Pete has always had a knack for seeing things from steep slants. Then he added, 'Sarah, what a horrible concept – getting ahead. What are you getting ahead of? It's the people around you, neighbours and friends, and at their expense.' My goodness, yes.

107 But our wildness is not lost. No! It's not such a distant memory for some of us reading this, either.

I was a teen in the grunge era – the late '80s and early '90s – where we quick-unpicked the Nike logos off our thrift store sweaters, studied gender politics and did sit-ins and strikes on issues that affected us and – more often – others. Some cultural commentators claim wildness died out around this time. In 1993 the United Kingdom clamped down on large-scale outdoor raves, which some commentators say spelled the end of revolutionary culture in Britain. Kurt Cobain suicided in 1994, allegedly 'tortured by success' – the fame and materialism clashed with his grunge, anti-establishment roots. This was also the era of political hip-hop.

By the early '90s it had morphed into commercially oriented rap. And we all went shopping instead. *Clueless* came out in 1995 and Paul Rudd's character Josh's pious activist efforts were the subject of comedic mockery: 'I'm going to a Tree People meeting. We might get Marky Mark to plant a celebrity tree.' We pitied (poor) Lisa Simpson's relentless fight. Feminist character Wendy Testaburger in South Park is outcast by her girlfriends for refusing to dress like Paris Hilton. Me, I was teased for continuing to speak out on feminist and other political issues well after it was cool, nicknamed 'Saffy' in reference to the dowdy daughter in *Absolutely Fabulous* who fruitlessly challenges Patsy and Eddy's vulgar consumer excesses.

Of course, many continued to laud the words and fight of Dr Martin Luther King Jr, Nelson Mandela, Mary Wollstonecraft, the Suffragettes and the Freedom Riders, but figured it was all of another era (while admonishing the Occupy Movement and the work of Black Lives Matter even when they spoke the same messages, continuing the unfinished fight). They wore Ramones T-shirts and declared 'Smells Like Teen Spirit' the greatest rock anthem of all time, but for the past three decades largely kept quiet and economically productive, convincing themselves we earn our way to freedom, and that wildness was owning an SUV and taking it off-road in a dream sequence.

108 But I began to feel a swing back to wild – and to making choices that enlarge not diminish life – when I saw quarterback Colin Kaepernick kneel during the Super Bowl national anthem in protest against racial injustice and police brutality. His football contract was not renewed. Trump went feral, but Nike swooped in and featured Kaepernick in a massive billboard campaign: 'Believe in something. Even if it means sacrificing everything.' Bam! Kaepernick's career didn't pick up, and the fiasco has not abated, but the gesture signalled to me that the world might just be ready to awaken from its acedia.

To my earlier point, 30 per cent of Americans opposed Kaepernick, the same percentage that opposed Dr Martin Luther King Jr when he protested. However, 90 per cent approve of Dr King *now*.

Soon after that, #metoo erupted. Then Greta protested her country's climate policies and within a year millions had joined her rally and she'd become 2019 *TIME* Person of the Year. Dave Navarro vocally endorsed for US president Marianne Williamson, who called for a moral uprising in American politics and a Department of Peace (and got through to the second round of debates, becoming famous for the memes created around her activism-preaching speeches). A tiny Dutch NGO sued its government for not

Williamson has announced she's running again in 2024 btw.

protecting citizens against climate change and won. Amy Schumer deliberately got arrested to draw attention to the Kavanaugh protests. Jane Fonda got arrested four weeks in a row to draw attention to the climate emergency, and Joaquin Phoenix made an Oscar speech that stole the headlines:

— In December 2019 the Dutch government was ordered to reduce CO_2 emissions by 25 per cent by the end of 2020.

> I think we've become very disconnected from the natural world. Many of us are guilty of an egocentric world view, and we believe that we're the centre of the universe. We go into the natural world and we plunder it for its resources… We fear the idea of personal change, because we think we need to sacrifice something; to give something up. But human beings at our best are so creative and inventive, and we can create, develop and implement systems of change that are beneficial to all sentient beings and the environment.

109 Overall, protests globally tripled between 2006 and 2020 and have spiked in the past three years. The Greeks have another ripper word, with no English equivalent, to describe this wild, bold, true person that is emerging. The *parrhesiastes* is someone who speaks truth to power. They step forward to talk straight to the fundamental principles of our universal moral code. The *parrhesiastes* of the world have tended, from as far back as ancient Greece, to lead us during times of rupture.

110 For me, I'd been getting progressively wilder since I closed down my business and donated the proceeds (or was it since I left the corporate world in my mid-thirties and started living minimally? Or since I was a teen?). The climate crisis, however, saw me step fully into the bewildered space, where redundancies and non-essentials increasingly struck me as absurd, making the precious stuff stand out in stark contrast. The Lemming-like way we were living our lives, wedded to a market-driven cult, appeared so vividly *insane*. If I'm to be honest, becoming a woman in her forties with diminishing patience for the dumb 'n' numb shit also contributed to my be-wild-ering.

I felt into my bewilderment and got more and more comfortable with destroying my good little (female) citizen reputation. Speaking up on social media, on inequalities, tax laws, coal industry politicking, letting go of my profits, calling out the gaslighters, culling my false prophets… It was enlarging life and it was about time. I stopped apologising, too. It all felt very right. I reckon some of you might have felt the same.

I started getting letters and private DMs about my posts where I spoke out on various issues. From teenage boys. And grandmothers. And farmers. Most weren't ready to write comments in the public scroll. They wanted to tell me, though, that they liked the messages. That they made sense. And to keep going. It felt wild.

111 Have you heard of Kali, the Hindu goddess of rage?

To cut a long and fun mythological story to a paragraph, once upon a time the god Shiva was being a lazy, flaccid bloke, spending all his time meditating and failing to protect Earth. So the other deities sent him the goddess Shakti (who takes the form of Kali, goddess of rage, when required) to coax him into waking the fuck up. Anyway, a bunch of things happened where some other deity dudes do the wrong thing by Shakti and put power in the way of good, which maddens Shakti, and then Shiva tells her unhelpfully to (eek) 'calm down' and then basically 'forbids' her from speaking up. At which point Shakti transforms into Kali, a formidable monster-thing with fangs and a necklace of severed male heads. And she rages. Shiva gets the point quite quickly, lifts his game and re-acknowledges the importance of the feminine.

— Goodness, there is so much in this!

In Hindu mythology, which dates back around 5,000 years, Kali is both the fundamental feminine energy that animates the world, and the righteous rage that keeps in check the masculine forces of greed, sloth, power and control. She would erupt in the goddesses when a man underestimated or blocked the feminine or refused to show up for life. Kali destroyed to allow new life to be created.

Most myths stand the test of time, in metaphor form. I find comfort in the universal truths they spell out, and, in this case, the most bodacious acknowledgement that rage – and, yes, female rage – is often entirely appropriate and purposeful. There's not a woman – or man, actually – who hasn't smiled, air-punched or nodded wildly upon hearing the Kali story.

112 Which brings me conveniently back to activism again. I've already flagged that activism works. Remember that 3.5 per cent figure? If you can get 3.5 per cent of a population to participate in sustained, non-violent protest, change happens. In Australia, protests saw the Franklin River in Tasmania's pristine south-west wilderness saved from damming. In the United States, on the first-ever Earth Day in 1970, 20 million people demonstrated nationwide, which led to Congress – led by staunch Republican President Nixon – passing the *Clean Air Act*, the *Clean Water Act* and the *Endangered Species Act*, and creating the Environmental Protection Agency.

The Berlin Wall came down just two months after public protests occurred throughout Germany. Black Monday protests reversed a proposed ban on abortions in Poland. Extinction Rebellion protests in the UK saw the government declare a climate emergency. In early 2020 plans to expand Bristol Airport were rejected after climate protests, and indigenous activists in Indonesian Borneo won a court battle to stop their land from being coal-mined. History, including recent history, is full of these examples.

However, there's also this: *nothing but* activism will work. Bill McKibben has been a leading climate activist for thirty years and is possibly the most influential leader in the movement. He's a practising Christian and has been arrested nine times. We emailed a few times and chatted on the phone during this journey. 'Back when I started I assumed we were in a sensible argument. I thought facts could get us through. But we have to accept this argument is not about facts and science. It's only about money.'

I asked, 'So what do we do?'

'Bottom line, no one has the money to match the oil companies. We never will. The only way humanity will win is with passion and spirit.' Activism.

McKibben also pointed out that it's a straight-up mathematical problem. We can spend energy converting 3.5 per cent of people to reusable coffee cups and solar panels, or we can spend that same energy inspiring 3.5 per cent to join a protest to block the fossil fuel companies. He flags the infamous Keystone Pipeline protests in 2011. It was the first major oil infrastructure fight. Everyone at the time said the protests would go nowhere. Yet, 50,000 people circled the White House and soon enough the whole thing was blocked. 'Since then there's not been a pipeline that's not been fought, aside from in a few despotic nations. And we've won most of the fights, or at least slowed down the building.'

McKibben more recently, along with Naomi Klein and the Sunrise Project, argued the most hopeful path lies in activating the big funding institutions– insurers, super funds and banks – to divest from oil. If the funding to the fossil fuel companies is whipped away and turned to clean energy investment, the fossil fuel companies would literally run out of gas. Shortly before we went to print oil prices had tanked

A simple start: immediately switch your — insurance and superannuation to ESG funds.

to below zero due to global shutdowns; watch this space with much hope and get prepared to get activist when the prophets ask us to join them.

I recommend — following Bill's 350.org updates, Emily Atkin's HEATED newsletter and Australia's The Climate Council on this. See my resources sheet at sarahwilson.com for more.

As McKibben told me this, Margaret Mead's famous quote came to mind: 'Never doubt that a small group of thoughtful, committed citizens can change the world; indeed, it's the only thing that ever has.'

Emma Marris in her book *Rambunctious Garden: Saving Nature in a Post-Wild World* spells out the maths super well. Emma, along with 42,000 others, is fighting a gas pipeline in Oregon that would create 36.8 million metric tons of CO_2. She makes the point: 'If we manage to stop construction, each of those people could claim credit for preventing 1/42,000th of those emissions – some 876 metric tons per person!' Now, for contrast, the average individual American emits 16 metric tons a year. Did you get that? 876 versus 16 metric tons. It would take 54 years of individual zero–carbon living to make the same dent that activism can.

Climate scientist Joëlle Gergis is a lead author of the IPCC report and author of *Sunburnt Country: The History and Future of Climate Change in Australia*. She said to me in an interview, not in a despairing way, that science has done everything it can. 'All the science is in. Now we need the influencers, the teachers, the business owners to take the baton.' She adds: 'It's community action that has brought us the most measurable and hopeful solutions so far.'

A number of scientists are imploring us to come out and act, be necessary, choose the enlarging option. There was a meme floating around that quoted presidential environmental advisor Gus Speth (*TIME* magazine has called him the 'ultimate insider'): 'I used to think the top environmental problems were biodiversity loss, ecosystem collapse and climate change… But I was wrong. The top environmental problems are selfishness, greed and apathy…and to deal with those we need a spiritual and cultural transformation – and we scientists don't know how to do that.'

You and I do, though!

How you can get activist

I'm asked how to go about this all the time. I'm going to be a bit abrupt here, OK? I generally answer by going back to what I've said many times – just start where you are, doing everything you can and go further and further. It's like any hobby or passion. Keep it ordinary and humble, then enjoy getting wilder as you learn more. Start consuming less, reading the news, attend your first protest, commit to signing a petition every day (learning about the cause first), switch your feed to inspiring prophets and share their messages boldly, then ask the more inspiring question of yourself, 'What can I do next?' The answer comes, because you're already in the fray and, as I say, action begets action and it's a beautiful question to ask your soul. You meet new people, — find new links down the rabbit holes and soon enough you're off and running wildly. And it all just falls into place.

That said, I have a big resource list of places for you to start at sarahwilson.com that I will update over the coming years.

113 Possibly one of the most beautiful moments on my journey occurred during those global strikes in September 2019. I'd agitated for weeks on the importance of attending. I'd had to push through my own resistance – I'm not a fan of public displays of anything. But I was rising to the enlarging option (and the cries of the scientists and kids to help them). I posted and tweeted and called the relevant organisers to get the best information to share. There were seven people in my travels to rev up engagement, however, who were resistant – they were either oblivious about it or claimed to be worried for their safety. By the morning of the strike I was despondent. I sat at home on the floor of my study and wept, partly from exhaustion. The Resistant Seven were playing on my mind. I couldn't believe my fellow humans were not firing up at such a critical opportunity to be heard (and contribute to that 3.5 per cent figure). My bigger self knew I should be more compassionate – other people had the right to their own opinions – and that going in too hard could be counterproductive. But my gripping self just wanted to inspire, to rally, to embrace these people in an enlarged group soul.

I got to the rally in Sydney's Domain, however, and my spirits lifted. As I walked down Oxford Street, I joined streams of kids and adults carrying placards, already singing and chanting. Close to 100,000 people descended on the park. The two young girls in fully norm-core glasses who led the event beamed life and enthusiasm with their speeches and rally calling. Tough–nut union leaders covered in tattoos bear-hugged them and thanked them for doing this work and talking in reasonable terms about a just transition. Around me I saw grandparents in sensible sunhats with their backpacks and non-disposable water bottles and groups of men in suits who'd walked up from the city wiping tears from under their sunglasses. It was jubilant.

But this is the magical bit. Over the course of the next 24 hours, I somehow – and really rather beautifully – ran into each of the (formerly) Resistant Seven. They not only attended the strike, but also brought along a friend or their kids. And you know what else? All seven made a point of saying that they were glad they were pushed because their minds and hearts were officially blown. One couple said they couldn't believe how many of their friends on Facebook, after they posted some shots from the day, gave them grief. 'They just needed to be there to get it,' the husband said. Yes! Yes!

A young guy who'd not known about the strikes until I gave him my elevator pitch in the street a few days earlier took his girlfriend and I ran into them having a drink that evening. 'We're weirdly celebrating,' they said. 'The whole day felt like a celebration.'

That *is* the weird thing. To protest, I found, is exhilarating and exultant for it connects us to what does in fact really matter – the planet, each other, life, caring, loving, our true nature. It also gets us awake to the nuanced, difficult realities that have itched at us too long, and reminds us of how good it feels to be awake. These strikes and protests, like *adda* and the ordinary connecting efforts of everyday people during isolation, also bring us together to attend to something bigger than our small selves. We get teary because we recognise ourselves, and life, in the passion of everyone around us. It brings us home after so many years of being homesick. And this, too, we realise, really matters.

Perhaps I shouldn't be so surprised that standing up to the system that fragmented us into a globe of isolates, should bring us back together and back to the life that we cherish so much. But I am.

114 I've thought about this deeply. I think some of our reluctance to get fully wild stems from a desire to maintain faith in our governments and corporations. I have this desire. I mean, I belong to a progressive, liberal society for goodness sake. This is not how things are meant to go! I think – and correct me if I'm wrong – many of us can't quite believe things are bad enough to warrant getting wild and deviant. I mean, there we were, taking out a mortgage, planning our university majors or a trip to Bali with the kids next year, and then…how could we suddenly be talking about boycotts and impeachment and government overthrow? We shouldn't have to protest in this day and age. We shouldn't have to fight for our rights. How did we arrive at the pinnacle of human evolution in such a ruptured society with our very existence in peril? As one *New Yorker* article asked as the US healthcare system crumbled from the corona virus toll, how did the 'greatest nation on earth' end up with nurses wearing garbage bags?

I stayed in the home of Krishnamurti in Ojai during my trip to California, and found this quote in one of his books:

'It is no measure of health to be well adjusted to a profoundly sick society.'

115 A while ago I wrote about how the former Australian prime minister had failed us as a leader over that summer of being trapped indoors and why we'd landed in such a dire environmental, social and political situation:

> *Over several decades we have become politically disengaged, lulled into a false and constructed belief that 'those in charge' will do the right thing, and that 'someone else' will hold them accountable if they don't. Like the media. Or other politicians. But those in charge haven't been doing the right thing. They've ruined our water supply, our reefs, they've sold off chunks of our land, they've allowed thousands of animals to become extinct. And they've got away with it because we've not been paying attention and we've half-bought their non-truths and distractions (while the media's impartiality has been eroded).*

Yes, we haven't been paying attention. The corona virus exposed this further. I mean, the whole superstructure failed us so spectacularly, we couldn't help but pay attention.

First it created the perfect storm for the crisis – a pillaged — As I've touched on already.

planet, a people that had forgotten how to cooperate, polluted air and marginalised populations (prisons, ghettos etc.) that made controlling the spread impossible. Disaster struck and decentralised governments suddenly waved their hands helplessly. They couldn't feed people, get money to them, save their jobs or make protective equipment. Ergo, nurses wearing garbage bags. The more-more-more mentality had led to hundreds of millions of people living beyond their means, leveraged in blind faith to the economy. But right when it was needed, the economy collapsed, taking their insurances and superannuation with it. Planes grounded and oil prices dropped below zero. In a matter of only weeks the entire house of cards came apart. I'd rallied against capitalism for decades, arguing it had no future, but I'd never imagined it was *that* fragile!

So, what came along to save us? Good old-fashioned umpires, such as unions, experts, and the community. In just one week, a group of UK doctors designed a crowdfunded ventilator that could be produced from widely available parts for under $US1,300, while in Boston unions mobilised workers at General Electric to demand that instead of laying them off, the company re-purpose their workplace to produce respiratory gear that the government was failing to provide.

Mutual aid organisations stepped in, too. Prison abolitionists bought soap and sent it to prisons, relief funds were set up to support artists and sex workers (who miss out on any kind of government entitlements) and activists rallied to feed poorly paid healthcare workers at the front line. Mutual aid is a form of activism – it ignites from the grassroots and mostly operates to expose and educate the world about inequalities, often leading to radical change. Tenant advocacy groups that provided mutual aid in Mexico City following the 1985 earthquake played a pivotal role in the city's transition to a democratic government.

The 'welfare state' also stepped in. Childcare in Australia was made free to all, so too emergency health measures, like virus testing while job seeker payments were increased to a humane amount. In the UK and the US, moratoriums were put on evictions and foreclosures. No market was doing the corrections or leading us to salvation. Indeed, some commentators found themselves awkwardly arguing the unfolding scene looked not just a little bit socialist.

The fragility of the system – and the ultimate supremacy of Mother Nature – was made particularly apparent when we started seeing wild boar roaming deserted Italian towns, deer walking the streets of Nara in Japan and kangaroos skipping through Australian CBDs, and we learned that in China, measures to contain the virus in February alone caused a drop in carbon emissions equivalent to New York's *annual* emissions. The more-more-more system was *that* tenuous! And nature was that tenacious! As Rob Watson also said, 'Mother Nature always bats last. And she always bats 1,000.'

This is the perfect batting average in baseball (for those short on sports lingo).

Many of us, of course, thought the pandemic would be the jolt we all needed to wake us up. How could we go back to such an unfair system or let greedy governments lead us so astray again? How could we not bow to nature and not join its flow, after everything that had been unmasked? We hoped we would emerge boldly imagining better. Alas, we reverted back to form – and then some – right? Sadly, or perhaps wonderfully, I feel there will be more opportunities to learn our lesson approaching very soon.

116 It's not a bad spot to quote Dr Martin Luther King Jr from his 'Remaining Awake Through a Great Revolution' speech:

And one of the great liabilities of life is that all too many people find themselves living amid a great period of social change, and yet they fail to develop the new attitudes, the new mental responses, that the new situation demands. They end up sleeping through a revolution.

We are probably only just entering a great period of social change that demands a new consciousness. For all of us here engaged at the soulful level I ask, 'Would you want to sleep through it? Do we want to look back and be the ones who stayed numb, inactive, and let things slide back to the old, fragile, ineffectual, frighteningly unfair normal?

become
adult

If you're dedicated to change, let it cost you something.
— Viola Davis

117 I'd have to say that everything I've been fleshing out here looks a hell of a lot like growing up.

In developmental terms, the process of moving from adolescence to adulthood is one of taking on responsibility for your life, and life on this planet, beyond your own selfish pleasure and fears and discomfort. It's a stepping up into what nature is asking of us. As kids we are largely motivated by selfishness, and we must be taught about consequences. By our teens we understand consequences and have a pretty good feel for values and moral codes, but we live on conditional terms, doing stuff if and as it benefits us as individuals. And when it doesn't, we blame, avoid, hold back love, get outraged

and look for excuses, all of which we need to do while we're sorting out life and our place in it.

Eventually, playing victim to our urges and impulses gets kind of cringey, and being so preoccupied with ourselves turns boring and really quite meaningless. 'Is this all there is?' we ask. Is this why I'm here, to push the case for this lumpen conglomeration of cells over and above all the other things life has to offer? Honestly, it's hard to remain so convinced.

I think we tire of chasing the false gods of pleasure and new shiny things. Plus, time is short, and we are no longer in the 'run-up' phase of our lives. This is the main event! So let's live it. Step up to it. Meet it. And stop all this numb, life-lite stuff. At which point we become an adult.

The problem, though, is that our culture fuels teen-like individualism and has trapped us in a suspended state of indulged adolescence.

Our current system needs us to stay preoccupied with ourselves – atomised competing consumers behaving like a bunch of mean girls at a nightclub bathroom mirror applying the latest lip gloss. We get caught up in embarrassing peer pressure traps. So much so that we fail to see that getting coloured terrazzo flooring because Melissa and Trevor from the kids' school have it is pretty juvenile. We forgive teens for this kind of blindness because it's part of finding their own identity.

But what excuse shall we give ourselves?

I mean, we can keep blaming and deflecting, claiming we're a product of the polarising media propaganda machine and tech companies. We can keep explaining things away and justifying our overwhelm and need to cocoon, bleating, 'Why should I have to do it?' and 'It's not my problem' and 'It's too hard.'

But to do so is so very, very adolescent.

I am entirely guilty of having seductively made such excuses for myself, and all of us here. My aim was to have a productive, true conversation that was also compassionate about where we were at and how we got here. But I myself eventually arrived at a point where I had to stop the rationalising. And take responsibility.

Being an adult means quitting the excuses and owning the situation even when it's not your fault. It's doing what needs to be done precisely because no one else is doing it; it's joining a rally when it's your day off, it's packing up leftovers at the restaurant even though it will be a bugger to cart them home on the bus; it's going over and checking on the young woman crying alone on a park bench; it's getting rid of your car; it's putting your phone in your bag when a kid chooses to ask you their important question.

The wonderful thing for all of us here, I think, is that nature is making it easy for us to step up. So too our souls. They're summoning us to bloody grow up and get morally mature. And here's the most glorious bit of all; isn't this exactly what we've been aching for all along? To step up so we can connect with life? To enlarge? To arrive?

Compared to chasing my own happiness (so fleeting) or pleasure (so flimsy), being able to say at the end of the day that it was an honour to do what's right is a beaming thing. A thing that fills a girl to the edges as she lies in bed staring at the fan above in the fading lume of a day.

118 Why are we not mobilising to fight the climate crisis?

This question has hovered from the outset of this journey. It's taken me until now to be able to answer it with the right consideration.

Perhaps you've also been stumped. Why are we not heeding the meticulously verified advice of the scientists who tell us what must be done (but do so when they diagnose us with a brain tumour, or when we want a vaccine for a global virus)? Why aren't we signing the petitions that take just a moment of our day? Why aren't we all doing everything we can to save life?

These questions are often framed against the famous mass mobilisation effort of civilians at the start of World War II, as mentioned earlier, when the entire economy and mindset of countries around the world, particularly in the US under President Roosevelt's leadership, switched from individualist consumerism to collective action. It's a good counter-example. The threat the climate crisis presents is far greater, far more existential than any war to date, yet the bulk of us can't manage a few simple lifestyle swaps, let alone consider a 94 per cent tax rate for our highest income earners and large-scale food rationing.

We can equally frame the question (why are we not

See World War II reference on p.115.

uniting against climate change?) against the mass mobilisation that took place with COVID-19 for instance. Why haven't governments ordered us to do the equivalent of coughing into our elbows, to close non-essential businesses, to stop consuming and flying to halt the climate crisis? Again, climate change is far deadlier than this virus.

There are a bunch of straightforward explainers, I guess. Mobilising requires sacrificing our own wants for the needs of the collective. Leaders can generally inspire such solidarity with war. The threat posed by war is very immediate and there is a common 'enemy' situated 'out there' that we have to fight. The same applied to corona virus; once it strikes, death can follow within days (cause, effect, lockdown; it's easy to process cognitively), and there was an identifiable enemy. We saw how governments used war language with corona virus from the outset, even tagging it as having an 'other' persona (Chinese or Asian). To this extent governments were also able to justify extraordinary control and emergency powers that would otherwise never pass through legislatures.

With the climate crisis, however, there is no external 'enemy' that the government can declare war against; the — enemy is the government, and the system, and, oh shit, *us*.

And this is the trickiest bit of the climate crisis. We are both victim and perpetrator. It's a devastatingly hard paradox to navigate and requires incredible moral maturity to sift through. An adolescent society, of course, will revert to all kinds of cognitive dissonance to avoid traversing the difficult paradox. 'System justification' theorists show that situations

It's the same with other social challenges we have struggled to 'fight', like inequality, hunger (which killed five million children last year) or suicide (kills over one million a year).

which represent a threat to established systems can trigger inflexible thinking and confirmation bias, where we will cherry-pick the science we want to hear, for example.

119 On the day the World Health Organisation declared COVID-19 a global pandemic, I rode across Sydney to hear Christiana Figueres, former Executive Secretary of the UN Framework Convention on Climate Change from 2010 to 2016 (which is to say, the chief architect of the Paris Agreement) speak at an 'ideas discussion' event. I was listening to the evening news in my earphones as I rode up the hill. The Prime Minister, it was announced, was getting advice on shutting down the country in response to the pandemic. The lights had gone down at two intersections, traffic was in disarray, and the world suddenly seemed a very surreal place.

And did so a few — days later.

That night, Figueres was asked on stage to describe the time she had to decide whether to disassemble the crucial meeting of world leaders as they were about to finalise the Paris Agreement due to a bomb threat. If she did, she risked the entire agreement. On the other hand, she had no idea if the threat was real and thousands of people were in her care, including her two daughters. She chose the climate agreement (and, yes, the threat was a hoax). 'The decision was between doing my best and doing what was necessary. Doing our best, doing our bit, is no longer enough,' she said.

Her final words: 'We must now do *only* what is necessary.'

This means not worrying whether so and so is doing 'their bit' and whether our (small) bit will count. My goodness, such language is so painfully...small. I notice many of us tend to phrase things like this (and mostly when trying to explain away our own remiss behaviour): 'People (out there) aren't changing their ways because they're too comfortable/ addicted to their phones' etc. Which is immaturely deflective. In Australia, we talk of not having to do more because we only contribute 1.3 per cent of global emissions and will do our bit when bigger nations do their bit. Which is pubescent, small-minded and ignoble. And as Figueres said so perfectly, it also reflects a scarcity mentality.

— In the same way parents despair of their kids' addiction to devices, ignoring their own.

— Which is a case in truth decay. The figure is much higher when our coal production and per capita calculations are factored, see page 113.

This, to answer the original question, is why we're not mobilising.

A mature abundance mentality, on the other hand, sees that the benefits of firing up and mobilising are not capped at 1.3 per cent. If we do what's necessary to save our one wild precious life, the entire world gets all the benefits. 'When we do what's necessary, we get 100 per cent of the upside.'

120 I posed this question on Instagram right now sitting in the dark in my study.

'What if we stop having to be at "war" to create change? Would loving the planet and humanity so much that nothing else can get in our way, like a parent who'd do anything for their kid, work better?'

As I near the end of this journey with you, I know the

only way we are going to mobilise is with love. Big, stubborn, unflinching, animated, activated, mature love.

121 I'd like to get grown up with another thoroughly un-adult phenomenon we've not yet covered. So many of the crap remiss things happening right now have been explained away as being due to our being time poor.

We don't cook because we are time poor. We can't or don't mend our clothes because we are time poor. We fail to show up to community clean-ups or stay on top of current affairs or get engaged in the political process because we are too exhausted at the end of the day and so horribly…time poor. Can we get real about this? Yes, there is absolutely legit stuff being foisted upon us that means many are struggling to keep up with the basics of living. But at the same time there is a lot of stuff we – in particular the upper middle classes – are choosing to be sucked into.

Am I allowed to actually say this? Bugger it, we're all adults here. And there's urgency. We are mostly time poor because we have been doing things to get richer – which is insanity because the point of money is to buy us more leisure, make life easier, no? And the richer we are, the more time poor we get. Apple chief Tim Cook is worth hundreds of millions yet wakes up at 3.45am; Elon Musk is worth some $23 billion but boasts how he works 120 hours a week. I watch celebrities like Lady Gaga and Drew Barrymore, who I'm guessing don't want for much, burn themselves out flogging cheap cosmetics brands in budget chain stores around the world and it strikes me as madness.

Yale law professor Daniel Markovits suggests this behaviour reflects the particular traits of the wealthy: competitiveness and comparison with others. They don't ask, 'Do I have enough?' They ask 'Do I have more than everyone else?' In *The Meritocracy Trap*, he highlights that children in upper middle class homes are being 'hot-housed' through childhood, stress-tested into elite schools and colleges, and pushed to the brink of suicide or breakdown. George Packer reports in *The Atlantic* that rich New Yorker parents sleep on the streets to be first in line to enroll their kids at the 'best' nursery schools.

But, really, there is no trap. No one is making us do these stressful, expensive things. Once our basic needs are met, it's a choice. In *Dream Hoarders,* academic Richard Reeves simply says to those who cry time poor: 'Just stop.' I love that he does.

We all need to just stop. And make a decision. Are we going to stay stuck or are we going to finally sacrifice money, time, stuff, expectations for what really matters? Of course, I wrote this rant before the global isolation experience forced many of us to just stop. But the fire of my rant remains. We are yet to choose to stop. We are yet to make such a bold decision for the sake of the collective, the planet, our kids.

— Although we did stop, we have since restarted in the same old vein, so we need to 'stop' again, without being driven by another pandemic...

122 I like this reminder. It's a nice, still, basic one. The best kind. Every summer *New York Times* columnist Frank Bruni and his family – twenty all up, including nieces and nephews

— descend on a beach house and 'fling' themselves at one another for seven days and seven nights. His friends all question why he stays a week. Families are hard. A week is a long time. His reply:

With a more expansive stretch, there's a better chance that I'll be around at the precise, random moment when one of my nephews drops his guard and solicits my advice about something private. Or when one of my nieces will need someone other than her parents to tell her that she's smart and beautiful.

His key point is that to be present, we need to just stop being time poor — just choose — so that we can be there, present and ready for when life calls us up.

123 Remember the Lady in Red in that café in Ljubljana? Sitting there in her own company, completely undistracted, calm and smiling? All lovely and light in her cool aloneness?

Being the adult is also about embodying cool aloneness. A wondrous thing. It's being able to accept the reality that we are born alone and die alone. Being comfortable with our aloneness means we are able to draw on our own inner strength rather than frantically grasping out to distractions and seeking confirmation and answers from others. We cut the umbilical cord on our dependence. And trust our own internal wisdom.

It's supremely adult.

Sometime after the Lady in Red episode I reread Pema Chödrön's *When Things Fall Apart* and realised that she'd referred to 'cool loneliness'. I'd unwittingly pilfered her phrase. Chödrön wrote that cool loneliness is the vigilant practice of 'less desire' and avoiding 'unnecessary activity'. And 'not seeking security from one's discursive thoughts.' It's spacious, it's not desperate, it's totally cool. And adult. 'Hot loneliness,' she writes, is the frenzied looking for a way out or a fix; it's blaming and using old patterns to distance ourselves from our loneliness.

Goddamn I'm sick of feeling so hot.

124 Okay. So since I reckon we must all be on the same page about being adult, I will share that as I approached the end of this journey, I fell pregnant again, aged forty-five. It was the regular way this time – a friend generously 'helped me out'. It was also a very strong pregnancy; I had morning sickness that left me confined to the bathroom. Then my bipolar flared, like really flared. I was dangerously manic and didn't sleep. My thyroid turned furious and my health spiraled. My endocrine system was fighting for its life in such a way that I knew it would take years and years to recover. I know the signs now; I have had to rebuild my health before. It took almost a decade last time.

I was also alone. I had hot loneliness coursing through me. And I was terrified.

I had fought to be a mother and had grieved three

miscarriages by this point. But every bit of me now told me, 'You cannot do this.' It was also very much a 'doing my best' versus 'doing what was necessary' forked-road moment. I knew, if I'm to be detailed with you, that I would not be able to be of service in any way during the pregnancy and for many years after, given the information I had in front of me about the state of my body and mind. I would be a drain on my own resources and those of the people in my orbit. More than this, I worried about the impact of this on a child in my care. I had come so far to give life to a soul, but I had to act on what I felt was right in my circumstances, regardless of what I wanted.

As Nietzsche would probably tell me, no one could build the bridge on which I, and only I, must cross the river of life. I cooled down and made a decision I never in my life thought I'd make and terminated my pregnancy. I made the decision on my own. I told two people only. With decisions of this magnitude and pain I'd normally reach outward to friends and family, get their take, their sympathy, have them indulge my poor-me-ness. But this time I kept quiet, raw, expanded and still.

I've not previously shared this full, deep and traumatic reasoning behind my decision. I hope you trust it was not made in any manner remotely resembling lightly, nor in a moment of defeatism. Nobel prize-winning poet Seamus Heaney, in his 1996 commencement speech at the University of North Carolina, told the assembled graduates:

The true and durable path into and through experience involves being true to the actual givens of your lives. True to your own solitude, true to your own secret knowledge. Because oddly enough, it is that intimate, deeply personal knowledge that links us most vitally and keeps us most reliably connected to one another.

Of course I struggled with whether to share this decision here; there was no obligation to 'round off' my parallel journey of trying to fall pregnant in a disconnected world that had become something of a metaphor for the whole trip. Indeed, it didn't make the first draft. Why did it make the final copy? I guess I felt this was the necessary thing to do, too. Humanity suffers from not having conversations about the hard things, the stuff that we despair about and takes us to our lonely edge and makes us feel existentially alone. And this gagged, disconnected silence has proven highly destructive in all kinds of ways, not least of all in denying us a moral fabric we can weave back into when making our own big, painful decisions.

We say things like, 'We should talk more about abortion and miscarriage' and 'We need to discuss our eco-shame and all our fundamental fears.' And people like me — with a platform, pages in a book — can do this in a way that might get a better, more moral conversation going. So when I thought about it this way, I couldn't remain silent (for all that my naturally reserved, individual preference was to do so), particularly when here I am preaching the need for us all to face elephants.

The other factor – but one still related to this journey – was that life was asking me to show up in all my messiness – fully human, failing and trying. The times are demanding different things from us. The old mores, the former rules, are becoming redundant as we navigate 'new normals' and critical edges of experience. Another way to put this: I had fewer fucks to give about feeling ashamed or about what trolls and anyone wanting to question my spiritual faith and morality might say, and a whole heap more fucks to give to being necessary, loving and of service.

Do I regret the decision to terminate? No, I rarely regret anything I have thought through fully, with my heart and my belief in The Oneness, with cool adult aloneness and with all the actual givens before me. Do I wish circumstances had been different? Yes. Oh, my sweet, wild, precious, life, yes. And so recently I became a foster parent. Which brings me much joy.

In many ways, making my decision to terminate the pregnancy, and then sharing it here, has seen me realise the richness of sitting cool and alone. I like this idea put forward by Olivia Laing in her lonely moments living in New York: 'Loneliness might be taking you toward an otherwise unreachable experience of reality.' Yep, it takes you down, or out, to the big stuff, the quandaries that can't be accessed in the presence of others' consensus-seeking influence. It's intimate. It's raw. It's the edge. It's life. All of it.

125 Loneliness, paradoxically, can see you cure yourself of loneliness by bringing you to the most secure company around: yourself. Which in turn, puts you in the best position to steer your little boat to what matters – to the whole.

— And don't you just love that the word 'alone' stems from a medieval root meaning 'all one'?

126 Being an adult is most certainly about engaging in moral struggle. It's watching the news, reflecting, asking the hard and the beautiful questions, choosing the right prophets to support, blocking the haters. It's doubting, but not shying away. David Brooks concludes in *The Second Mountain*:

> *It doesn't matter if you work on Wall Street or at a charity distributing medicine to the poor. The most important thing is whether you are willing to engage in moral struggle against yourself.*

And Brené Brown wrote on her Instagram several years back:

> *Our job is not to deny the story, but to defy the ending – to rise strong, recognise our story, and rumble with the truth until we get to a place where we think. Yes. This is what happened. This is my truth. And I will choose how this story ends.*

Adulthood is wrestling the truth of our story, steering it and heaving it, tirelessly, in more and more gallant directions – if we want the better ending. We don't want to accept an ending that misses the point of our existence.

As I reflect on this now, I realise it's pretty much the classic Hero's Journey that Joseph Campbell and many others argue every great hero story follows. It guided George Lucas, most famously and directly, with the *Star Wars* films. Heroes get a calling into the unknown, to leave the familiar and find out what they don't yet know they don't know. They question themselves, resist leaving the familiar shores, but then they get bizarre help along the way that keeps them going. At some point in the journey they confront their mirror (an authority figure, often), unconditional love, and other challenges and boons that demand they surrender. Eventually some sort of death happens (something they cling to drops away, perhaps an adolescent dependence) and through this death, knowledge is finally obtained. The hero determines their own ending.

THE JOHN MUIR TRAIL, SIERRA NEVADA, CALIFORNIA, USA

After the termination, I had the opportunity to travel to the High Sierras during a work trip to California and so I decided to visit the Mammoth Lakes region where the famous John Muir Trail intersects with the equally famed Pacific Crest Trail in some raw, high, bear country. It felt fitting to go into the wilderness at this time.

It was the busiest weekend of the season. I was going to wild camp, with a pack of gear, and a good dose of my pain to wrestle with. Campers must apply for a permit on the trails, and they generally get snapped up six months in advance. But I knew somehow that something would work out when I got up there. It had to. I'd come all this way.

It did. Someone did a no-show; there was one permit left when I arrived in the mid-afternoon. I hired a bear canister, bought supplies and a pair of men's ski pants and a beanie from the thrift store (I hadn't banked on it dropping to freezing overnight) and took off, overwhelmed and slightly under-prepared. But coolly alone.

I spent four days up there, hiking between lakes – Ediza, Shadow, Iceberg and Thousand Island – pitching my tent at the end of each day. I cooked my gruel in my little camp stove, placed my bear canister 100 metres away and attended to my neurotic bathing ritual in various lakes and streams before hopping into my tent. Where I lay listening out for bears and avalanches. But mostly just heard silence.

— My fear-ridden OCD means I must bathe before bed. No matter the circumstances. It's been this way since I was a kid.

I'd taken Joan Didion with me – her *Slouching Towards Bethlehem* collection of essays. Joan is good hiking company. She lays words down defiantly and from a place where she feels like an alien in a world of rules and yet finds her belonging. When you hike solo, this is a conducive headspace. You feel like a weirdo, but the sanest one around.

Lying in my tent on the second night, wearing two sets of thermals, the thrift store ski pants, possum fur socks I got in

New Zealand when I was twenty-one and the secondhand beanie with a head torch over the top, I read her essay 'Goodbye to All That' about loving but ultimately leaving New York: 'Everything that was said to me I seemed to have heard before, and I could no longer listen… It is distinctly possible to stay too long at the fair.'

I'm not sure what it was about that line, but it saw me give up. Not all of it. Just the dull rollercoaster stuff. The staid rules, the social contract. And the (false) idea that I was weird and wrong for feeling as I did. The traumatic decision I'd made a few weeks earlier was not only to terminate my pregnancy, but also to cut the social contract with motherhood.

When I got up to go to the loo in the middle of the night, stars were falling from the sky.

I realise it must seem to you that on every hiking trip I do I have some almighty, life-about-facing epiphany. I'm a bit self-conscious about the convenience of this as a literary device. Ditto the weird deus ex machina coincidences that often surround these trips. But the truth is, this stuff generally does happen on a hike in the wilderness. It just does. And pithy quotes appear. When I returned my bear canister to the parks office at the end of the hike I read a John Muir line on a writing journal for sale in the foyer:

Thousands of tired, nerve-shaken, over-civilised people are beginning to find out that going to the mountains is going home; that wildness is a necessity.

The next day I got in my hire car and headed back to LA. I lined up a few podcasts for the trip. In one of the podcasts I listened to Krista Tippett interview Teju Cole who took James Baldwin's famous 'woke' quote ('To be a Negro in this country and to be relatively conscious is to be in a rage almost all the time') and broadened it to apply to contemporary life. 'Let me revise that: to be relatively conscious [today] is to be in a constant state of rage.'

I know this rage. I've brought it up in a few contexts throughout this journey. It's the rage of not comprehending how people could not vote for leaders who prioritise the collective good. It's the rage of watching governments approve coal mines and abandon the needs of First Nations peoples, justifying it all in rigid and deflating 'economic growth'-speak. It's the rage of being split apart when what we want is to be joined back together.

Cole went on to say that to be conscious, even at a superficial Instagram meme level ('hashtag woke'), is 'also to be in a state of quiet sorrow and knowing there are things we cannot solve.' But, he adds, this sorrow, this uncertainty, this confusion could be the 'anteroom' to the solution.

Oh yes, the anteroom. A place, a point, we pass through before arriving at...at...well, home.

home

We are survivors of immeasurable events,
Flung upon some reach of land,
Small wet miracles without instructions,
Only the imperative of change.

127 So wrote Rebecca Elson, astronomer and poet, as she faced her death at the age of thirty-nine from cancer.

I've landed here after a series of the most monumental rabbit-hole dives, painful explorations and rolling, wild hikes of my life with a deep, aching understanding that we are all in fact more connected than we realise. We all feel stuck. And we are all struggling to cope. We have been split apart and it's time we're split back together again. We are ready.

I've come to understand that at our human core, we are not so different. Let's take Trump. Few humans have polarised the planet more. But Trump's popularity stems from the fact that he has spent both his campaign and his presidency touring and doing in-person gatherings around the country. He taps into a craving for connection and belonging in a highly fractured culture. Yes, he does it by fostering an 'us vs them' tribalism, appealing to our small selfish selves, waging a war on immigrants, media, liberals and anyone who questions him. We can point fingers and be baffled. But the more nuanced interpretation we can choose is that such is our moral aloneness, we'll take the fear-based 'lite' version of connection if we have to.

We've all contributed to where we are at. You might have seen that viral clip of analyst and Princeton professor Eddie S Glaude Jr explaining with breakfast-stopping cut-through on MSNBC about white America having to confront its assumed innocence. He explains that it's easy to place blame for mass shootings or the rise of white supremacy on Trump's shoulders, but he says 'this is us and if we're going to get past this, we can't blame him. He's a manifestation of the ugliness in us... Either we're going to change or we're going to do this again and again.' When he said, 'this is us', this realisation left me simultaneously sickened and inspired.

In a similar vein, there's the viral clip of Barack Obama at his foundation's summit in October 2019, telling his interviewer that anyone claiming to be always politically woke should get over that quickly. 'The world is messy, there are ambiguities. People who do really good stuff have flaws. People who you are fighting may love their kids and share certain things with you.'

That intertwined, despairing clusterfuck going on out there in the world is not the point. They're symptoms. Technology is an enabler. The erosion of democracy reflects our own separation. The climate crisis is an extension of our disconnect from life. And corona virus exposed it all.

So here's the upshot. Life has been fundamentally interrupted by a pandemic, by climate disasters, by AI, by all kinds of structural change, and all of us here have the most glorious opportunity to take an inventory of it. We now have a choice – collectively and individually. We can go back to our old ways. Or we can move forward into something wild, mature and humanised.

We now live in a world where this choice – back to our old ways or forward into wildness – will be part of our existence ongoing.

128 'Only a crisis – actual or perceived – produces real change. When that crisis occurs, the actions that are taken depend on the ideas that are lying around.'

It's one of the many wonderful ironies that such great wisdom was uttered by none other than neo-liberalism founding father Milton Friedman. It begs: which ideas lying around are we going to focus on and bring to life as we journey forward?

So what would it look like to go back to the old normal? We'd go back to consuming, hating, disconnecting, blaming.

We would accelerate the destruction of the planet and humanity, perpetuating the ugly inequalities and wars. Things could easily head this way if we let it. A number of leaders used the state of emergency the corona virus presented to pass autocratic legislation (such as anti-protest laws aimed at climate activism) and provisions that roll back important environmental protections. Airlines, for example, lobbied to get policies geared at curbing air travel and reduce emissions delayed or removed in Europe and the US. The oil industry has fought to have plastic bag bans reversed. Naomi Klein calls it 'disaster capitalism', where the political class use the distraction and control measures enabled in catastrophes to create policies that plunder. The fear and uncertainty has already seen racism and radicalisation surface. And it will only increase if we choose a world of division and scarcity, where we fight over insufficient resources and opportunities.

What would it look like if we used the interruption to wake up and save this one wild precious life? To my mind, it would look wild, free, flowing and loving. We'd have to grab all those solutions that already exist and employ them all, all at once. Which would be fun and the very opposite of itchy.

We would need to ride bikes like the Dutch, remove sales tax on electric cars (and ban gas-powered cars by 2025) as they have in Norway, and do fake news resilience training like the Finnish. We could turn to the Nordic 'folk school' tradition (there's a Scandi theme going on here) that fosters a complex inner life, concentrating on moral and relationship skills as well as academic ones, in classrooms.

We would need to plant trees – lots of trees – and other plants to sequester carbon. We'd plant them on roofs, down the side of buildings, in grubby vacant lots, which will in turn cool our cities, clear the air and reduce noise pollution. Smart people are suggesting we bring in a form of national service, as Roosevelt did in 1933, to address youth unemployment and nature conservation. His Civilian Conservation Corps helped rebuild America.

New research shows we can actually save most of that wildlife cruising toward extinction by simply installing more parks and reducing farmland, which we can do by eating less meat and cutting food waste in half and other no-brainer measures, which will feed the world and other such circular goodnesses.

Regenerative farming (mixing perennial crops, sustainable grazing and improved crop rotation), already practised in pockets around the world, can also save us and in a manner that has countless additional and domino-ing benefits. Already wind and solar power–produced energy is cheaper than fossil-fuelled power, once subsidies for the latter are wiped; so we'd have to wipe those subsidies. Similarly, air-source heat pumps that save 30 per cent compared with filling an oil or propane tank already exist.

A report by the International Renewable Energy Agency found renewable energy investment could generate $US100 trillion of global GDP between now and 2050, basically paying for the COVID-19 recovery. And more. Airlines would cut flights where high speed rail services exist, a frequent flyer levy would be applied to the top 3 per cent. who take 70 per cent of flights.

— France has recently done just this.

We could talk wealth taxes, too. In the US alone, the wealthiest 5 per cent of families now hold two-thirds of all household wealth in the country. A mere 5 per cent tax could raise $2 trillion. And while we're at it, we could robustly question what jobs now constitute 'essential services' and shift the income balance. The corona virus got us open to wondering whether a nurse, teacher or meal delivery worker should be paid just as much as a stockbroker. We would defund institutions that fail our humanity.

By the time you read this, you might have learned that defunding the police, for instance, doesn't mean doing away with law enforcement or turning cops out on the street. It's a sophisticated crime prevention policy solution that sees funds that go to the militarisation of police forces and to performing tasks that should be attended to by mental health workers diverted to social services, crime prevention, education and social outreach. It's already worked in Portugal, for instance.

We'd also embrace de-growth economics, a form of economic modelling being pushed by Noam Chomsky, Yanis Varoufakis and Kate Raworth that's not based on more-more-more but simply meets everyone's needs within Earth's biophysical limit. I've become rather obsessed with it. It goes further than sustainable consumption and renewable energy. It sees us work fewer hours in exchange for more home production and leisure (such that we grow veggie gardens,

— I really recommend reading up on it. Kate Raworth's work is particularly inspiring.

and attend to our health, thus reducing all kinds of social costs). It's not about sustainable fashion, but a new aesthetic of 'sufficiency'. Less would see us have to recycle, repair, reuse and join the sharing economy (which builds community). Corporations would have to produce repairable phones, governments would ban 'planned obsolescence' practices, and fashion stores would sell upcycled, pre-loved versions of their ranges (which incentivises making quality garments that last).

Patagonia paved the way a few years back, offering a worn-wear store and free repairs. Walmart, Nike, Nordstrom and Nudie Jeans have made similar moves and a major consumer survey by GlobalData shows that the second-hand clothing market will surpass fast fashion by 2028. This new approach sees wonderfully deviant and cooperative initiatives, like Tesla sharing all its patents with the world to encourage more electric car innovation. This is wild, reconnecting hope on a stick!

Some of these changes would simply be about sticking with stuff we put in place during the shutdown and actually came to rather like, like quitting travelling for meetings, dropping trade shows on the other side of the world, biking (the uptake of which saw Milan commit to installing more bike lanes and bike share schemes) and localisation (the idea of a '15-minute city' where everything you need is a walk away is being pushed in France, for instance). And not allowing governments to roll back the healthcare provisions, cancellations of student-loan debt, free childcare, universal basic income provisions and releasing prisoners on parole, that were put in place around the world.

129 We'd also philosophically live out two radical truths that the virus exposed us to.

First, no one is going to come save us. Not the governments, not the banks, not the neo-liberal markets. This will have to be a social revolution based on a whole lot of us – together – getting fired up, awake, adult and ready. As this sinks in, do you find the notion liberating?

Second radical truth, we are not separate from or above nature. We belong to it. And our salvation mostly comes from rejoining it in its onward flow.

I'm guessing you'd probably agree, making this choice to change and move forward from the itchy disconnected lives we've led, and implementing these new measures doesn't present as hard or unpleasant. It's enlivening, joyous and brimful of love, no?

Me, it makes me beyond excited for the future.

I have been asked repeatedly, 'Do you have hope?' Hell, yes, I do. But this hope I have, it's a radical kind of hope.

It's not optimism. Optimism is as unhelpful as pessimism.

130 Pessimism says, 'We're stuffed, so there's no point fighting.' However, optimism blithely suggests that everything will turn out fine, or that 'some young entrepreneur will solve it'

– Governments worldwide released hundreds of thousands of prisoners. In the US, it became apparent there's no compelling public safety reason to incarcerate 39 per cent of the inmates in state and federal prisons.

(space sunshades!), which also grants a person a hall pass from doing something. To be clear, I am not optimistic.

Unlike pessimism and optimism, hope necessitates action. Rebecca Solnit writes in *Hope in the Dark* that hope is not a matter of estimating the odds. Hope is an 'active state of mind, a recognition that change is nonlinear, unpredictable, and arises from intentional engagement.'

Hope is a magical, suspended state of becoming, between what is and what our souls know to be right. We don't float in hope, we actively swim toward the congruence, tugged by the current of truth.

To hope is our nature.

131 The other interesting thing about hope is that when it is attached to something we love, it's (magically) unstoppable.

I've heard this beautiful question posed before: What if a doctor said your son or your mother had a unique type of cancer and that they could probably try a few different treatment ideas, but there was no guarantee they'd work. All in all, the odds were not great, statistically. What would you do? You wouldn't ask the doctor if you could wait a bit and make your decision when the science was more conclusive, or when we have better optics on whether we can afford it. You'd do whatever it took. Everything.

There was a graffiti poster down the road that I passed each day. 'Daddy, what did you do to fight climate change?' It should elicit the same beautiful, big, courageous answer:

'Everything.'

I mean, we've all heard those stories of what's called 'hysterical strength' where parents lift cars off trapped kids. This kind of crazy shit happens in emergencies.

To love our way to wild miracles is also our nature.

132 It took three years of going all the way down into all the climate science, economic arguments and psychological biases only to come all the way back up with this dead simple line I borrow from Bill McKibben: 'To stop global catastrophe, we must believe in humans again.'

Similarly, when I asked Sister Joan, my new activist nun friend, how we can best rally everyone to join the movement 'back to life', she said, 'Tell them it's the only way to be a full human being again. Show them their real nature.'

In *Man's Search for Meaning*, Viktor Frankl observed that the prisoners who survived Auschwitz were those who turned their focus and hope to living for something beyond themselves, in most cases God or family. Those who based their survival efforts around themselves – their little individualistic 'I' – perished. For me, humanity was the 'something beyond myself' that I was now believing in and living for. And would love so hard nothing would get in my way.

And it became my singular mission – if I'm to be honest in these last few moments together – to ensure that every person, when asked in years to come what they did to fight climate change (or more fundamentally, what did they do to save this one wild and precious life), is able to say, 'I did everything I could.'

That's my honest truth.

It's in our nature to attend to morals and meaning because we are the only animal that is conscious that our time here is finite. The prince of Troy Tithonus lived a life where nothing he did mattered. I mean, if you're not going to die from your choices, you can do whatever you want. Carte blanche. Eventually he became so miserable from this infinite meaninglessness that he petitioned the other gods to make him human so his choices – his life – could matter and be of value. Being human is to do things that matter.

According to — Tennyson's poem.

Plus, it's in our nature to hope, even when – especially when – it feels hopeless, as I know some are feeling now.

Pema Chödrön argues that hopelessness is in fact 'the beginning of the beginning'. It's precisely when we get to that point where we realise there is no external fix and that no one is going to come and save us that we finally draw on our own adult fortitude. 'In the midst of loneliness, in the midst of fear, in the middle of feeling misunderstood and rejected is the heartbeat of all things...'

This idea is probably best summed up in the brilliant headline from a *New York Times* op-ed a while back: 'Stopping Climate Change Is Hopeless. Let's Do It.'

We will also need to do it fast. During the Australian bushfires, residents in threatened areas received text warnings: 'You are in danger and you need to act immediately to survive.' It needs to become the motto for this heroic mission we are on, the rally call for our age.

Will we act immediately? Will we do everything we can, humanity? Will we go further – further than we ever thought we could or would? Because we will survive this if we do.

133 I've played with a few metaphors to make my point. But sports ones often work best. This is my favourite, I think; Dad loved it when I shared it over a Sunday dinner and I know he shares it among his friends and brothers.

It's a bit like in the final minutes of a rugby grand final and the losing side is down three points. (And, by the way, this metaphor is not too far-fetched, either. The Doomsday Clock, developed by the Bulletin of the Atomic Scientists in 1947, ticked over to 100 seconds to midnight in early 2020.) The stands are clearing out, it's looking hopeless.

But suddenly something shifts in the group soul of this about-to-lose team. The standard tactics are tossed aside, and the humans go into what I call kamikaze mode. They throw everything at the situation. The crowd stops. What's going on? They can't believe what they're seeing. They go wild. The whole scene is wild. We're down to the final five seconds, and seemingly out of nowhere and as if by magic, the losing team do everything they can and plant the try or kick the goal. The siren sounds. Hope has favoured the wild.

This kind of sporting miracle happens more often than it logically should. And it's these games that go down in history.

134 When I stand back, in my middle years, in all my yearning aloneness, in my grief, in my endless and aching love of humanity, this is what I know. This darkness we've found ourselves in might just be the very thing that reconnects us to life again. It's taken me to my ultimate edge. I lost friends on this journey – which I had to accept is part of the growth deal. I had to let redundancies drop off. But the fact that these strange times we can't quite believe are here, also demanded that I step into my biggest, most alive self. It's made me look around and love life in a more intimate way. It's made me question what matters and hunt down – in something of a kamikaze fashion – my true north. I had to find my resilience, my grit. I had to come to terms with how appropriate and necessary my rage is. I stopped apologising for my Kali-esque rage, too. And I realised perhaps it had to get this terrifying and lonely before I – we – could connect as deeply and truly as I – we – hope we will.

In Hermann Hesse's *Steppenwolf*, Hermine says to Harry: 'Ah, Harry, we have to stumble through so much dirt and humbug before we reach home. And we have no one to guide us. Our only guide is our homesickness.' It's a crackin' truth.

135 I acknowledge the facts – the statistics are stacked against us. And I pay a solemn nod of respect to the spiritual truth – that death, and species extinction, are a part of life. And yet I am wholly and vibrantly motivated to fight for life in the meantime. Not my life. But Big Life. Our Life, together. That 'meantime' might be a very long time. And so – in the meantime – this way I've walked with you here serves as a wild and precious way to live. Like, really live.

Wrestling with the darkness has left me more committed to this path than I could ever have imagined. And with one last beautiful question that guides me in my most personal moments: 'What is left if we might lose it all?' My answer gets more beautiful by the hour: nature, humanity, and my wildly alive love of it all.

136 I finish with the last lines of environmentalist, entrepreneur, journalist and founder of Project Drawdown Paul Hawken's University of Portland commencement speech from 2009. It's wild.

> *Ralph Waldo Emerson once asked what we would do if the stars only came out once every thousand years. No one would sleep that night, of course. The world would create new religions overnight. We would be ecstatic, delirious, made rapturous by the glory of God. Instead, the stars come out every night and we watch television.*
>
> *This extraordinary time when we are globally aware of each other and the multiple dangers that threaten civilisation has never happened, not in a thousand years, not in ten thousand years. Each of us is as complex and beautiful as all the stars in the universe. We have done great things and we have gone way*

off course in terms of honouring creation...

The generations before you failed. They didn't stay up all night. They got distracted and lost sight of the fact that life is a miracle every moment of your existence. Nature beckons you to be on her side. You couldn't ask for a better boss.

The most unrealistic person in the world is the cynic, not the dreamer. Hope only makes sense when it doesn't make sense to be hopeful. This is your century. Take it and run as if your life depends on it.

you can find more on my website*

1. A full list of science and source endnotes from my book.
2. A resource featuring all hikes in this book, and many more.
3. A Book Club sheet so you can start holding your own *adda* on this topic.

*sarahwilson.com

text acknowledgements

Extract on page 118 taken from Antonio Machado, 'Traveller, there is no path,' as published in *There is No Road*, 2003, trans. Dennis Maloney and Mary Berg © White Pine Press, Buffalo, NY USA.
'Just Beyond Yourself,' by David Whyte, is printed with permission from Many Rivers Press, www.davidwhyte.com © Many Rivers Press, Langley, WA USA.
Extract on page 384 taken from 'Evolution' by Rebecca Elson *(A Responsibility to Awe*, 2018), reprinted here by kind permission of Carcanet Press Limited, Manchester, UK.
Extract on pages 397–398 printed with kind permission of Paul Hawken © 2009.
Grateful acknowledgement is also given to Sister Joan Chittister, Joëlle Gergis, James Hollis, Bill McKibben, Margaret Klein Salamon, Greta Thunberg and David Whyte for granting permission to be quoted in this book.
Thanks is also given to Annika Dean and Martin Rice of Australia's Climate Council for their expertise.
For a full list of resources referenced in this book, please visit **sarahwilson.com**.

SARAH WILSON is the author of the *New York Times* bestsellers *First, We Make the Beast Beautiful: A New Journey Through Anxiety* and *I Quit Sugar*, along with eleven cookbooks that have been published in fifty-two countries.

Previously she was editor of *Cosmopolitan Australia*, host of *MasterChef Australia* and founder of the largest wellness website in Australia, iquitsugar.com. In May 2018, Sarah closed the business and gave all the money to charity. She now builds and enables charity projects that 'engage humans with one another' and campaigns on mental health, consumerism and climate issues.

Sarah lives between London and Paris, is an obsessive hiker and is known for travelling the world for eight years with one bag.